WEiRD
ENGLAND

STERLING

New York / London
www.sterlingpublishing.com

WEiRD ENGLAND

by

MATT LAKE

**Your Travel Guide to England's
Local Legends and Best Kept Secrets**

Mark Sceurman and Mark Moran, Executive Editors

WEIRD ENGLAND

Published by Sterling Publishing Co., Inc.
387 Park Avenue South, New York, NY 10016

© 2007 by Matt Lake

Distributed in Canada by Sterling Publishing
c/o Canadian Manda Group, 165 Dufferin Street,
Toronto, Ontario, Canada M6K 3H6

Distributed in the United Kingdom by GMC Distribution Services,
Castle Place, 166 High Street, Lewes, East Sussex, England BN7 1XU

Distributed in Australia by Capricorn Link (Australia) Pty. Ltd.
P.O. Box 704, Windsor, NSW 2756, Australia

ISBN 13: 978-1-4027-4229-3
ISBN 10: 1-4027-4229-0

Printed in China
All rights reserved

2 4 6 8 10 9 7 5 3 1

For information about custom editions, special sales, premium and
corporate purchases, please contact Sterling Special Sales
Department at 800-805-5489 or specialsales@sterlingpub.com.

Design: Richard J. Berenson
Berenson Design & Books, LLC, New York, NY

Weird England is intended as entertainment
to present a historical record of local legends,
folklore, and sites throughout England.
Many of these legends and stories cannot be
independently confirmed or corroborated,
and the authors and publisher make no
representation as to their factual accuracy.
The reader should be advised that many of the
sites described in *Weird England* are located
on private property and should not be visited,
or you may face prosecution for trespassing.

CONTENTS

Foreword: A Note from the Marks   6

Introduction   8

Local Legends   10

Ancient Mysteries   32

Fabled People and Places   56

Unexplained Phenomena   74

Bizarre Beasts   92

Local Heroes and Villains   112

Peculiar Properties   134

Roadside Oddities   162

Roads Less Travelled   190

This Spectred Isle   204

Tombstone Tourism   224

Abandoned and Underground   246

Index   266

Acknowledgments   270

Picture Credits   271

DEDICATION

To mangle an R.E.M. lyric a little:
This one goes out to the ones
I love. This one goes out to the
ones I've left behind. Fire.

A Note from the Marks

Our weird journey began a long, long time ago in a far-off land called New Jersey — one of those states in America squeezed in between Pennsylvania and New York. Once a year or so we'd compile a homespun newsletter to hand out to our friends called *Weird N.J.* The pamphlet was a collection of odd news clippings, bizarre facts, little-know historical anecdotes and anomalous encounters from our home state.

We had started the publication with the simple theory that every town in the state had at least one good tale to tell. *Weird N.J.* soon become a fully fledged magazine, and we decided to start investigating further these fantastic local legends that people were always telling us about to see if we could find out if there was any factual basis to them. Armed with not much more than a camera and notepad we set off on a mystical journey of discovery. Much to our surprise, we found out that most of what we had initially presumed to be just urban myth turned out to be real, or to at least contain a grain of truth.

After about a dozen years of documenting our bizarre state in our magazine, we were asked to write a book about our adventures, and *Weird N.J.: Your Travel Guide to New Jersey's Local Legends and Best Kept Secrets* was published in 2003. Soon people from all over the United States were writing to us about strange tales in *their* home states, so we went the next logical step and wrote *Weird U.S.*, followed by a whole series of *Weird* state books, such as *Weird Florida* — (talk about <u>weird</u>!)

With the success of our *Weird* state book series, we began to wonder: Could there be a stranger country than the United States?

That question was actually answered many years ago, in a tiny pub on the outskirts of Wivenhoe in south-east England when Mark Sceurman was having a chat with musician, gardener and home-brewer Martin Newell. As Sceurman recalls:

I was very enamoured with how old everything looked around me. But I felt displaced, out of time. I was in a land not like my own. Martin had mentioned that many Americans see their culture as only going back a few hundred years, whereas Europeans view their history as spanning thousands of years. I said, 'This really is a strange land. You English must have many weird stories to tell.'

'More than you'd care to know about,' said Martin.

So when the idea of exploring weirdness outside of the United States was proposed, Sceurman remembered that conversation, and we knew immediately that the kingdom of England was the next stop on our weird journey.

Luckily we had our author at hand. British-born Matt Lake had crossed the pond to

America a number of years ago, and had been hired to edit our *Weird N.J.* book. His work was so good that soon he was making editorial contributions to several of our *Weird* books. We knew that Matt was a kindred spirit in weirdness and that he had developed what we refer to as the 'Weird Eye'.

The Weird Eye is what is needed to search out the sort of stories we look for. It requires one to see the world in a different way, with a renewed sense of wonder. And once you have it, there is no going back — you'll never see things the same way again. All of a sudden you begin to re-examine your own environs, noticing your everyday surroundings as if for the first time. You begin to ask yourself questions such as, 'What the heck is *that* thing all about, anyway?' and

'Doesn't anybody else think that's kind of *weird*?'

Aside from being an intrepid researcher and evocative storyteller, it was obvious that Matt really relishes his Weird work. So we gave Matt the assignment of spending the next year of his life travelling his ancestral home, tracking down all the strange legends, peculiar people and oddball sites that England has to offer. And, not batting on a full wicket himself, Matt was more than happy to rise to the challenge.

So come with us now and let Matt take you on a tour of more bizarre places than you might want to know about, full of cultural quirks, strange sites and oddball characters — some may even be in your own town or village. It is a state of mind we like to call *Weird England*.

— *Mark Sceurman and Mark Moran*

Introduction

Where did you *take* this car?' asked the woman with the clipboard.

I didn't really know how to answer that question. I tried to think of everywhere I'd gone, but all that came to mind was a series of random images. There were pyramids and marble tents in graveyards. There were skulls . . . hundreds of skulls. There were suburban houses with oversized sculptures of marine life sticking out of their roofs. There were hand-carved tunnels under major metropolitan areas. There were abandoned buildings and roads that they say are haunted by headless spectres or legless spectres or whole spectral armies with their extremities still attached. And wasn't there also an inventor who showed me a device he'd built to keep bras warm on winter mornings? Or had I just dreamed that bit?

How could I explain all this to the woman who had rented the car to me? How could I make her understand that I had spent years collecting information about all these bizarre places, and I had rented the car to visit them all?

'England,' I said at last. 'I took this car through England.'

'What, *all* of England?' 'No. Just the bits that matter. Just the weird bits.'

My quest had begun several years earlier, when a manuscript crossed my desk for editing. Its authors were two men from New Jersey who had spent ten years collecting the strangest stories they could find about the peculiar state they lived in. I was impressed. And after the book *Weird N.J.* came out, it seemed as though *everybody* was impressed. Mark Sceurman and Mark Moran had tapped a vein of strangeness that captured the public imagination, and, as they added more American states to their list, they invited me along for the ride. It was a wild ride and continues to get wilder. And the Marks continue to reserve a seat for me.

But somewhere in the back of my mind I was secretly dissatisfied. I knew somewhere a lot weirder than New Jersey. I knew it very well, in fact, because I grew up there. England is steeped in weirdness. It's drenched in it. Every time the weirdness starts to dry out, somebody defies the usual summertime hosepipe ban and douses the place with a fresh sprinkling of it. And it's not just the new weirdness that adds lustre to the Sceptred Isle. There are monuments hundreds and even thousands of years old that just reek of the odd. Even churches, those great bastions

In fact, the Weird Eye comes so naturally to some people that they tend to take eccentricity for granted. But there's a danger involved in that. On a few sad trips, I discovered that, sometimes, the weirdness does wear off. There was once a fantastic pub, the Horse and Jockey, just beyond the main drag in Oxford, which was wallpapered with old newspapers, illuminated by naked lightbulbs, adorned with at least one upright bathtub and generally decorated in the most haphazardly eccentric fashion. Yet, on my last trip to the city of a thousand gargoyles, I walked past it twice before I realised it had been converted into flats. Another one bites the dust.

of respectability are riddled with weirdness — not just in the monstrous gargoyles everyone knows about, but in carvings of female flashers and copulating demons that would curl the blue-rinsed hair of any church-going granny that happened to look up high enough.

All you need to see all this weirdness is the right pair of eyes. Because when you look for the peculiar, you'll find it everywhere. It's what Mark and Mark call the 'Weird Eye' . . . and it's something that I think the British are born with. I found many people along the way who simply had it. Some of them, such as Stuart Campbell, Mark Russell and Sean Hastings, contributed material and photographs for places that I couldn't get to. Some of them pointed the way to sites I'd never even heard of. And some of them actually gave me a lift.

But the good news is that for every fantastically odd place that gets painted beige and sold to yuppies, there are dozens of new peculiar places and people rising up to take its place. England may be succumbing in some parts to biscuit-tin strip-mall architecture, but that just makes the eccentrics try harder to redress the balance. Because, as long as there's an England, there will always be a dedicated band of off-kilter individuals who strive to keep it weird. And there will always be an England.

So come along on a trip through the high spots of England's weirdness, and join the campaign to keep England weird. You'll never look back. Or if you do, you'll see a whole lot more weirdness behind you, struggling to keep up. – *Matt Lake*

Local Legends

The word 'legend' has gained a bad reputation over the past few centuries. When you call a story a legend, or worse, an urban myth, it is dismissed as the product of an overactive imagination. People don't object to imagination when used in films or television shows, but for some reason legends are judged against higher standards. Call us poor journalists, but we don't dismiss a legend just because it contains a few facts we can't verify. Far from it. Legends aren't newspaper articles to be cross-checked with three independent sources before going to press. They are stories told for entertainment, and perhaps a little edification, and they often contain truths that go beyond mere historical accuracy. Compared to the glossier forms of modern entertainment, tales of dark doings and long-dead characters are something of substance, and just as important and interesting as whatever's playing at the local cinema. That's how they got the name legend – at its Latin root, the word means 'something you really must read'.

Local legends are even more significant than classic legends, such as the Lost Kingdom of Atlantis. The local kind may not be as ancient, but they have one distinct advantage: you can pile into a car and zoom off to the places involved. Whether you choose to visit an address in London, a desolate moor or a village far from the madding crowd, you owe it to yourself to give it a try. As we have said, legends may not be historically accurate, but they don't get to be something worth reading about without having some merit.

So, to kick off, we'll begin with a story that travels through ancient Troy, a shoe shop in London, a hillside in Cambridgeshire and a cliff in Cornwall. Oh, and it involves a couple of giants who were mentioned in the Book of Revelation.

We did mention that this was going to be weird, didn't we?

The London Stone

As commuters exit Cannon Street tube station in the City of London, they file past a sports shop. This establishment forms the unlikely focus of ancient cults, waves of foreign invaders, centuries of City government, as well as a natty line in trainers. All these diverse elements meet in a glass-encased lump of limestone embedded in a wall at the junction of Cannon Street and St Swithin's Lane.

This lump of limestone is better known as the London Stone, and was once considered to be the talisman that kept London prosperous. Without it, the city would fail – a surprising idea in itself, because the rock in question is certainly not much to look at.

Many historians believe that its origins date back to the early years of the Roman occupation, the first century AD to be precise, when it acted as a *milliarium aureum*, a gold-painted Roman milestone. Others think it's at least a thousand years older, and this is where the interesting legends begin. One particular myth claims the stone to have originated in the ancient city of Troy. As the story

LONDON STONE
in Cannon Street,
Supposed to be the Milliarium of the Romans, from which they measured distances, to their several Stations throughout Britain.

goes, the exiled Trojan king Brutus carried the ancient relic from the city founded by his great-grandfather Priam, and settled in England under orders given by the hunter goddess Diana. However, on arrival here Brutus was first obliged to quell a race of giants, and only then did he place the stone in London, the city he founded. (Yes, people really did tell stories like these before historians got hold of the past, and we say: Let's bring that era back.) So, before it became known as the London Stone, this chunk of rock was the Stone of Brutus, and the subject of an ancient proverb: 'So long as the stone of Brutus is safe, so long shall London flourish.'

Stories of the stone's original role abound. It may have once been part of the temple to the goddess Diana that stood where London's Guildhall can now be found. Or perhaps it was part of a larger ceremonial stone monument, similar to the stone circle that once stood on the site of St Paul's Cathedral. On the other hand, devotees of earth religions insist that there's an ancient ley line between St Paul's and the Tower of London, and that the

London Stone once stood right on it.

Whatever the stone's original purpose, it was a significant monument for more than a thousand years. Until only a few centuries ago, it sat on the site where authority was granted to the Lord Mayor of London. Unfortunately, in the mid-eighteenth century, it got in the way of a road-widening scheme and was moved thirty-five feet to the wall of St Swithin's Church, where it survived the destruction of the church by the Luftwaffe in 1941. It was then incorporated into the wall of the building that replaced the church – the offices of the Overseas China Banking Corporation. And very soon it will move again, as that building is slated for demolition.

During its long journey through time, the stone has shrunk significantly. When Shakespeare lived in London, it must have still been pretty substantial because in *Henry VI Part II*, Shakespeare recreates the true-life occurrence of rebel Jack Cade whacking the London Stone with a staff and sitting upon it to declare himself Lord of the City. It had become smaller, because court records some fifty years later tell that 'the remayning parte' of the stone was small enough for the spectacle makers' guild to smash their rejects on.

Some attribute the stone's shrinkage to an Elizabethan occultist named Dr John Dee, who chipped samples from many ancient sites for his bizarre alchemical experiments. So, even a vandal of the stone rated it as a significant monument. Sadly, such appreciation of it has dwindled. Commuters pass it by in ignorance, and it's hard to treat anything with great respect when caged behind an iron grille. But at least it's still there, and as long as it's safe behind glass where no passing alchemists can get at it, London will remain safe. We should be grateful for that, at least.

London Altar Stone

When the big Druid revival craze began in the early eighteenth century, people talked about the London Stone as an altar that was used for human sacrifices before the Romans drove the Druids out. Also, William Blake apparently saw visions around the stone that inspired him to write and draw some of his more apocalyptic work. This rock has some strange energy to it. – *SarahW*

Where's the Lady of the Lake?

My grandfather always told me that the London Stone was the very rock from which King Arthur drew Excalibur – the famous Sword in the Stone. If you look closely at it, you can see notches made by the sword, or by the knights who chipped away at the stone to loosen the sword. When Victorian engineers excavated the Cannon Street area during the building of London's mighty sewer system, pre-Roman remains of a possible palace were discovered – no sign of any Round Tables, though. – *Tom Holly*

Gog and Magog

Before England could come into being – according to legend, of course – the exiled King Brutus of Troy had to repel the marauders who were oppressing the good people of this land. This was easier said than done, because the marauders were a race of giants. And not just any giants, but giants mentioned in dire Biblical prophecies. In legends told in London, Cornwall and Cambridgeshire, the coming of these bad guys was foretold by no less an authority than Ezekiel in the Old Testament, as well as by St John of Patmos in his rousing finale to the New Testament, the Book of Revelation.

These fearsome fellows were called Gog and Magog. Biblical scholars through the centuries have come up with many interpretations of just who these obscure invaders were, but in English legend, Gog and Magog are two giants. Except, of course, for the times that they're just one giant called Gogmagog.

As you'd expect from a giant with two names rolled into one, Gogmagog was huge: twelve cubits high; and with a cubit measuring the length of the arm from the elbow to the tip of the middle finger, that's at least four times a normal person's height. Nevertheless, according to the seventeenth-century poet John Milton, Gogmagog was defeated in Totnes and slung into the sea at Plymouth Hoe where:

The giant fell on the rocks below, and his body was broken into fragments by the fall; while the Fretted flood roll'd frothy waves of purple blood.

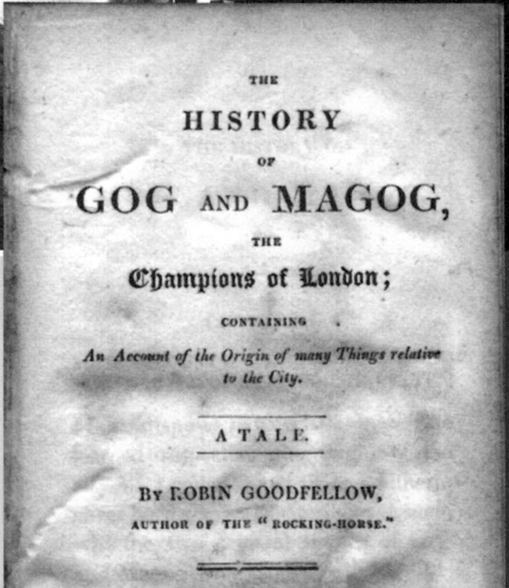

In Milton's time, a huge jawbone and other enormous bones were discovered in Totnes, thus proving to some that a race of giants had once fallen there. The fact that this area is now known as the Jurassic Coast

THE

HISTORY

OF

GOG AND MAGOG,

THE

Champions of London;

CONTAINING

An Account of the Origin of many Things relative to the City.

A TALE.

BY ROBIN GOODFELLOW,

AUTHOR OF THE "ROCKING-HORSE."

LONDON:

PRINTED FOR J. SOUTER, AT THE JUVENILE AND
SCHOOL LIBRARY, 73, ST. PAUL'S CHURCH-YARD;

By J. and C. Adlard, 23, Bartholomew Close.

1819.

gives us more of a clue as to the true origin of all these oversized bones – but that's no excuse for throwing out the legend.

Gog and Magog, the heroes

Oddly, in London the twin giants Gog and Magog are celebrated as heroes, and each year they are trotted out in the Lord Mayor's parade as guardians of the city. We put this down to further proof that London is hardly typical of England – or anywhere else in the world. Bear in mind, however, that Jehovah instructed Ezekiel to 'Set thy face toward Gog, of the land of Magog' – setting face was taken very seriously in the Old Testament.

Although the legend dates from much earlier times, the first reference we could find to London's Gog and Magog tales is a chapbook from 1819. *The History of Gog and Magog*, by Robin Goodfellow, tells of an evil giant named Humbug who kidnaps Princess Londona, but is thwarted by two good giants. Londona goes on to have a son named Cockney, whom Gog and Magog pledge to serve . . . and so on for seventy-nine pages until the story closes with:

And now, heartily wishing all manner of prosperity and renown to the citizens, common council, and aldermen, of the city, in the hope that they will continue to cherish, like Gog and Magog, an invincible animosity against giants and oppressors of every description, nor ever permit any of the Humbug race to domineer again in their Guild-hall, we conclude, as in duty bound, with – GOD SAVE THE PRINCE REGENT.

We'll let this silly take on the apocalyptic monsters slide, in gratitude to the City of London's contribution to the happiness of serious Gog and Magog fans: the two giant statues that stand in the Guildhall. You need to pass through security checks to enter the building, but it's worth it if you're in the area.

Gog Magog Hills

There is a different take on the legend in Cambridgeshire. Here, it is believed that either the twin giants Gog and Magog, or the single Gogmagog, lay down and died of a broken heart near the ancient Iron Age hill-fort of Wandlebury Ring. Their burial mound subsequently became the Gog Magog Hills.

Whatever the legendary origins of the Gog Magog Hills, the place clearly held great significance to people in ages gone by. In the early part of the last century, tales were told of ancient rituals that took place there on the site of a hill figure that had even then long since been buried by centuries of accumulated topsoil. Nobody was really sure of the details, and it wasn't until 1957 that anybody came up with a solid theory about the place – and even then, it was controversial.

The Cambridge archaeologist T.C. Lethbridge excavated the site and published a study that sparked public interest but killed Lethbridge's reputation among his peers. *Gogmagog: The Buried Gods* describes how Lethbridge discovered several Saxon hill figures buried near the ditch at Wandlebury Camp. Using a steel bar for sounding out a packed chalk outline beneath the soil, he discerned the outline of a Celtic warrior defending himself with a round shield against a hail of stones, along with a horse or two and a woman with three breasts. This was indeed a site with hidden depths. Dating the figures at around 200 BC, Lethbridge believed he had discovered a significant religious site – either for sun worship or associated with fertility and warfare.

The academic community considered Lethbridge to have gone off the rails, and cast doubts on his methods and discoveries. From that point on, he retired to Dorset and published increasingly mystical and folklore-based books. But, for at least one person (and his readers), the Gog Magog Hills were of huge historic importance.

Keeping Evil at Bay

Once the threat of attack by giants was a thing of the past, other fears began to take hold of the English imagination. Darker and more mysterious evils lurked in the shadows: there were those with supernatural powers who entered our homes by night, while others rode through the countryside in human form yet sporting antlers. As for the rest, well, they may look harmless, but they portend great disaster.

Wild Hunters

To modern ears, the term 'Wild Hunt' isn't particularly scary; about the most frightening image it conjures up is of a feisty toff in a red jacket bearing down on you because he's convinced you supported the fox-hunting ban. But long before the fox-hunting ban, people lived in terror of a night-time visitation by giant demonic creatures storming through the countryside with black dogs. To get some idea of the terror involved, we advise watching scenes from *The Lord of the Rings: The Fellowship of the Ring* (2001), in which hobbits get chased by ring wraiths, and imagine what it would be like to be one of those hobbits.

That's what the Wild Hunt was like. In medieval times it was closely tied to Norse and German warrior legends, but in certain areas of England it was reported by monks as a factual happening. And it was always a portent of disaster. The only thing to do when the Wild Hunt took place was to take cover and await disaster to befall the one the omen was designed to warn.

In the great Anglo-Saxon history called the 'Peterborough Chronicle', or 'Laud Manuscript', the hunt appears as a bad omen against the new Norman abbot of Peterborough, Henry of Poitou. The chronicle's

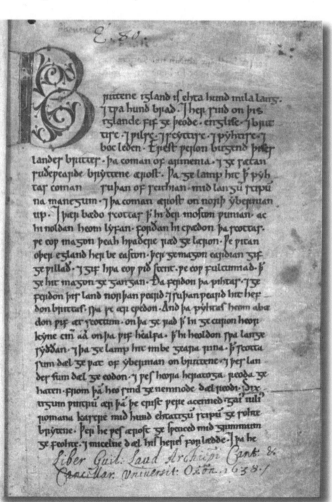

twelfth-century author chided the abbot for setting taxes so high that the poor were forced to steal to feed their families, and further accused the abbot of hanging the thieves he had created – a double sin. Finally, the monkish author chronicled an instance of the Wild Hunt pursuing Abbot Henry. Sure enough, Henry met his Maker sooner rather than later. The Middle English of the original chronicle is heavy going for modern readers, but a loose translation of the hunt that portends the death of Henry describes it thus: 'The hunters were black and vast and horrific, and their hounds were all black and broad-eyed and horrific, and they rode on black horses and black goats.'

Cue *The Lord of the Rings* footage.

Peterborough is not the only place where Wild Hunt legends are told. Dartmoor is home to several such stories, some as recent as the sixteenth century, involving ferocious hell-hounds. There are also legends of spectral hunts at Windsor Great Park. The most celebrated hunter of all is based there, a creature that's not merely a faceless horror, but a creature with his own history: Herne the Hunter.

The Horned One

Any legend that involves a half-man, half-animal creature is almost guaranteed to be terrifying, and even more so if that mythical beast sports horns. It's such a horror that haunts Windsor Great Park in the ghastly form of Herne the Hunter.

Herne shows up during winter at his special oak tree at midnight. He jabs the oak with his great ragged horns and mutilates any cattle grazing nearby. Where Herne comes from is anybody's guess, but several stories have cropped up to explain his origin.

One particular story claims Herne to have been the faithful servant of King Richard II who received a fatal injury when protecting the king from a rampaging wounded stag. As Herne lay dying, a stranger emerged from the forest and offered to save the dying man. The treatment was bizarre but costly: the stranger hacked off the stag's antlers and tied them to Herne's head, miraculously bringing him back from the brink of death. Once he was fully recovered, Herne was feted in Court for his bravery, but little did he know that the stranger had also cursed Herne's skill as a hunter. On discovering the loss of his livelihood, Herne became so distraught that he fled into the forest and hanged himself from an oak tree.

Some say that the Herne legend is based on the story of an old horned god from Gaul named Cernunnos, or that Herne may well be a combination of many legends with a dash of imagination thrown in for good measure. But one thing's for sure: he's not the only horned creature to haunt southern England.

Ooser? You Sir!

The Dorset Ooser is another horned creature with mysterious antecedents. In times past, a huge mask and flamboyant costume took on this weird name and participated in a pagan ritual performed near Dorchester. But quite what the Ooser celebrated or represented is a mystery. He, too, may have been the Gaulish god Cernunnos, or he may have been the bull that featured in the Roman cult of Mithras. The only clue we have to what he looked like is from an early twentieth-century photograph of a moth-eaten carnival mask with huge horns, as the mask itself went missing shortly after the photograph was taken. Nevertheless, from that image, the Dorset County Museum recreated an Ooser and fittingly displayed it near its Thomas Hardy exhibit. (Hardy, after all, did mention the Ooser in *The Return of the Native*).

We'd like to think that the Ooser is another incarnation of Herne the Hunter, but the goofy expression detracts too much from the scary horns. Besides, who could be scared of anything named Ooser?

Witch Marks

Next time you stay in an old hostelry, especially one dating from the nineteenth century or earlier, take a good look around the fireplace. If you're lucky, you'll see a strange pattern of rings scratched into the brick or stone of the hearth; and if you count three rings, you can be sure that people who lived there in past times were in mortal fear of evil spirits. The rings are called witch marks, and they were thought to keep evil at bay.

People used to believe that evil could enter a house through any opening, and a chimney was a perfect access point. To ward the bad spirits off, they would scratch three rings into the hearth every night before bedtime to invoke the Holy Trinity. This would either drive out the evil or prevent it from entering until daylight itself destroyed it. A great example of witch marks can be seen in the two fireplaces at the Fleece Inn in Bretforton, Worcestershire, but there are no doubt dozens more.

Attack of the Killer Rabbit

Unless you really took the killer bunny scene in *Monty Python and the Holy Grail* (1975) to heart, it's hard to work up much of a sweat over the possibility of being hurt by rabbits. However, the good folk of the Isle of Portland, Dorset have a deep-seated suspicion of lagomorphs. Indeed, they regard rabbits with such fear that many old-timers won't even utter the word for fear of disaster.

Before you laugh off this strange superstition, consider what kind of a place Portland is. This limestone peninsula south of Weymouth has a long tradition of quarrying. And what's the biggest fear of anybody who works under hundreds of tonnes of stone? Getting buried under them, of course. Any sign of structural insecurity is enough to send a man packing for the day. And if a burrowing creature should appear in a quarry, you can be sure that the ground is going to be pretty soft somewhere. So, blithely bandying the 'R' word about is like making jokes about bombs at an airport.

The local moratorium on the word rabbit has even had an impact on show business: When Aardman Animation released *Wallace & Gromit: The Curse of the Were-Rabbit* (2005), they printed up special posters for Portland that avoided the dreaded word, using only the phrase 'Something Bunny Is Going On'.

ISLE OF PORTLAND.

[Portland Quarry.]

Hill Figures

What better way to celebrate legends of giants than to make gigantic cartoons of them? At some point in time, some bright sparks had the idea of carving enormous figures into the hillside and then either packing chalk into the outline or carving the image so deep the chalk base beneath the topsoil was revealed. The only trouble with this approach is that in time the topsoil gradually covered the outline once more. To remain intact a carving needs to be re-cut at least every ten years. It follows that there could be hundreds of hill figures a few feet below ground level, their legends buried with them. Fortunately, many still glow white against the green hillsides. And some of them are outstanding in more ways than one.

The Rude Man of Cerne Abbas

Of all the hillside figures, the giant just north of Cerne Abbas in Dorset is the most likely to raise eyebrows. His outline, carved in lines a foot wide and a foot deep, lies between a pagan earthwork called the Trendle and a spring once held sacred to Helith, a goddess of health; and the giant certainly appears to benefit from his location, as he is the very picture of health in one very obvious way.

This character is far more than just a simple chalk outline on a hill; he has a well defined ribcage, two seven-foot-wide circles representing his nipples, and raised eyebrows giving him a rather comical expression of surprise. He's also gesturing to a point on the top of the hill where the sun rises on May Day. However, he's not pointing with his finger. Rather, he's . . . well . . . let's just say this outline has some very specific details – disproportionately large details, perhaps, but very specific. It's small wonder that he's popularly known as the 'Rude Man'.

The giant has spawned many legends, and nobody's really certain who he's supposed to be. Some believe this 180-foot tall figure marks the spot where locals killed a giant for poaching their sheep. Others think this to be a cock-and-bull story, and prefer the idea that he was a heroic figure who carried sacred stones to Avebury and Stonehenge, and then keeled over, exhausted, on the

Dorset hillside to die. He wields a huge knobbly club over his head, which some take to mean he's either a warrior or a god. Then there's his other huge knobbly bit, which strongly seems to indicate he's a fertility icon.

On the other hand perhaps he's Nodens or Nudd, the Celtic god of health and healing, who appears on a number of pre-Roman relics found around Dorset, also naked and carrying a club. Then again, there are those who claim the carving must date from after the Roman invasion because it's clearly the Roman hero Hercules. A travelling academic named William Stukeley, writing in the late eighteenth century, stated that locals called the giant Helis, which he believed to be a corruption of Hercules or of his Greek name Herakles. But Stukeley may have confused the giant with the goddess Helith, whose spring bubbles up near the giant's feet.

Many believe the giant to be a lot more recent than Roman times. Some cite the earliest written reference to the figure as the parish church warden's accounts for 1694, which mention the sum of three shillings set aside for recutting the outline on the hillside. Writing in 1751, the Reverend John Hutchings recounts a local yarn that suggests the figure is a satirical cartoon dating from Henry VIII's dissolution of the monasteries. The local abbot of the time, Thomas Corton, was supposedly prone to at least two of the seven deadly sins, one of which accounts for the club raised above the giant's head in anger, while the

Talking 'Bout My (Organ of) Generation

For three thousand years or more, the hillside and woods around Cerne Abbas have been the focus of notorious May fertility rites. In the late sixteenth century, a writer named Philip Stubbs described these spring bacchanals:

Hundreds of men, women, and children go off to the woods and groves and spend all the night in pastimes . . . I have heard it credibly reported by men of great gravity that, of a hundred maids going to the woods, there have scarcely the third part of them returned home again as they went.

But even a sixty-five per cent debauchment rate doesn't exhaust the fertile magic of the giant. Childless women used to visit him by night to hasten their passage into the family way. Unmarried women would walk round his outline or sleep nestled on his midsection to ensure a quick marriage. Couples wanting to conceive would go about their business under cover of night, lying on whatever part of him seemed to fit the activity best. Even though the National Trust have cordoned off the site with a barbed wire fence, we hear this custom still goes on . . . though nobody's saying whether this is more for the sake of recreation or procreation.

other sin is indicated by the giant's *other* raised club. The fact that the Rude Man's feet point away from the village could also indicate the abbot being driven into exile.

Yet, whether the carving represents a pagan god, a satirical cartoon or just a good night out for thrill-seekers, the Rude Man of Cerne Abbas remains a giant among hill carvings.

Long Man of Wilmington

The giant at Cerne Abbas isn't the biggest boy in the hill-figure world, however. At Windover Hill near Wilmington Priory on the South Downs of Sussex stands a giant 235 feet tall.

Until 150 years ago, the Long Man, as this carving is known, was visible only when the light hit it just right, since its outline was nothing but a shallow grassed-over trench. In the mid-nineteenth century, however, he was reintroduced to society and outlined in yellow brick; unfortunately, some say he lost some crucial details in the process. The Long Man was never as detailed as the Cerne Abbas giant in the reproductive department, but he certainly once had facial details, wore some kind of helmet, and the staffs he held have been described as either a scythe and pitchfork or a club and bow.

As with so many of these figures, the origin and meaning of the Long Man have been lost over time. Many Sussex folk believe he is millennia old, while others think he was a project undertaken by monks from the local priory some time between the Norman invasion

and the fifteenth century. It's even possible that he was created as recently as the eighteenth century, since that's the earliest record we have of his image.

Known occurrences however, include a period incognito – during World War Two, the Long Man's yellow-brick outline was painted green to prevent German bombers using him as a navigation aid – whereas later, in the 1960s, the bricks were removed completely and the outline was redrawn with concrete blocks

One thing is certain, however: he's a target for anyone wanting to get their message across loudly and clearly. When the fox-hunting ban came into force in 2004, pro-hunt activists burned the words 'NO BAN' into the hillside. Anti-war protests and crude painted-on anatomical additions have also appeared. We can hardly approve of these desecrations, so these directions are not for anyone who intends to mess with the Long Man: He's situated south of the village of Wilmington, six miles north-west of Eastbourne. Follow the signs from the A27, a couple of miles after the junction with the A22.

The Scouring of the White Horse

Giant hill figures don't always come in human form, and the one believed by archaeologists to be the oldest of them all (at least, the oldest one that hasn't been completely overgrown and lost to the ages) is an equine figure. The great White Horse lies a mile south of Uffington, about halfway between Swindon and Oxford. Unlike some more cartoonish human hill figures, this 374-foot wide image is an elegant, highly stylised work of art, and until a century ago it was maintained at a big local festival called The Scouring every seven years. English Heritage takes care of those duties now, following a shameful period of neglect early in the twentieth century.

Legend has it that the Uffington White Horse was carved either to commemorate King Alfred's victory over the Danes in 871, or earlier, to celebrate the Anglo-Saxon king Hengest in the fifth century AD. This is all hogwash. The White Horse is much older than that. It has been officially dated back 3,000 years to the late Bronze Age, which throws it open to even more interesting tales of its origin. One theory is that it is a horse goddess named Epona, who was worshipped by Celtic tribes such as the local Belgae. Another idea is that it's a representation of the horse St George rode to the dragon's lair on nearby Dragon Hill (where else?). But the best story of all is that the White Horse is actually the dragon that was slain by St George.

Of course, these aren't the only myths attached to the site. Rumour has it that the horse comes alive at night and canters down to the strangely shaped valley below, appropriately called the Manger. During the old Scouring festival, one of the great entertainments was a cheese-rolling race into this valley – perhaps as a contribution to the horse's diet? We non-country folk know little about the tastes of centuries-old horses, but presumably they enjoy a little rolled cheese for their night-time snack.

The White Horse is accessible from a car park on a minor road off the B4507, opposite the turn-off to the village. Except when he's snacking at the Manger, that is.

Weird Waystations of Worship

Except for some bizarre gargoyles, there's usually nothing particularly weird about your average church. However, if you care to delve into history, you'll find lots of places of worship steeped in strange local folklore. How these weird happenings came about is anybody's guess, but when in doubt, it's always a good idea to blame it on the Devil. And sure enough, scratch deep enough below the surface of any church legend and Old Nick will soon appear.

Twisted Church

Pisa has its leaning tower, Chesterfield has its crooked spire. We know which deviant structure we prefer, and it's the one in Chesterfield. The spire of the Church of St Mary and All Saints leans almost ten feet away from its true centre, in a way that calls to mind the peak of a Mr Whippee ice-cream. Unimaginatively, structural engineers have blamed this on the use of unseasoned wood and a lack of cross-bracing, but we prefer the two local legends.

The first legend involves the Devil (who else?), who was having his hoofs re-shod by a blacksmith in Bolsover. The understandably nervous smith accidentally jammed a huge nail right into the Horned One's ankle, causing Old Nick to leap into the air in agony and swing on the spire to break his fall. The second tale is a saucy gag at the expense of Derbyshire lasses. Legend has it that a young woman on her way to the altar at St Mary and All Saints' was actually a virgin, and the spire turned round in disbelief when it heard the news. Should another woman ever come to the altar in a similar state, so the story goes, the spire will return to its true position.

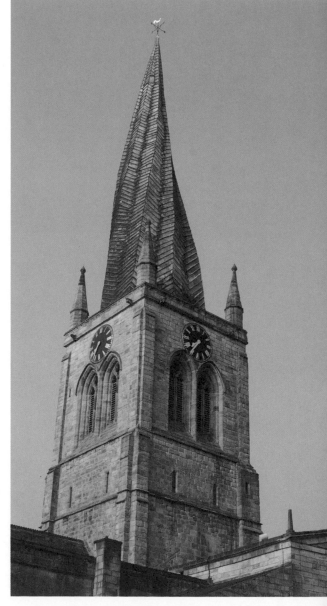

The Devil's Arrows

When he's not trying to destroy churches, the Devil seems to have other targets in his cross-hairs, including Aldborough, Boroughbridge and his own grandmother, who all figure in legends surrounding the Devil's Arrows in North Yorkshire. These three standing stones, visible from the A1 near Boroughbridge, truly put the 'mega' into megalith. Arranged in a north–south line, they are at least twenty feet high, and each sports a strange ridge pattern at its tip, which is probably a result of thousands of years of erosion, yet is very reminiscent of the fletching at the top of an arrow.

Archaeologists are convinced these stones were part of a larger line of up to a dozen stones, dragged from a quarry seven miles away in Knaresborough almost 5,000 years ago. However, over the centuries many other tales have emerged to explain their existence. The most famous of these tells of how the Devil shot arrows from nearby Howe Hill to destroy a town that had annoyed him, but they fell short of the target. The target could easily have been either Boroughbridge or Aldborough, but a bit of doggerel poetry from the early eighteenth century favours the latter. Apparently, before he launched his projectiles, Old Nick shouted, 'Borobrigg keep out o' way, For Aldborough town I will ding down!'

How the stones were formed is also the subject of another legend. As the story goes, the leader of the local Celtic tribe, the Brigantes, was holding a hearing to weigh up the merits of the new-fangled Christian religion, which was winning out over the Druids, when a charismatic stranger came along and swayed the crowd back to paganism with his withering sarcasm. But someone soon drew attention to the ground beneath the stranger's feet, which was melting from the heat of his cloven hoofs. His identity uncovered, the Devil flew into the air, with great streams of molten rock dropping from his hoofs, which now form the stones. Fortunately, the townsfolk's newly found faith saved them from the satanic artillery.

One take on how the grooves came to be at the top of the stones is that the Devil attempted to hang his grandmother off one of the stones, but she struggled so hard that the rope carved deep grooves into it. She broke free, was recaptured, and slung over the next stone, and so on until the Devil ran out of stones, leaving a line of grooved stones in his wake.

It's hard to know which of these legends to favour. But we're told that if you're inclined to interview the principal character in each of them, just walk twelve times round any of the arrows at midnight, in a widdershins (anti-clockwise) direction, and Old Scratch will show up. Despite our usual journalistic thoroughness at Weird Central, we haven't quite mustered the courage to do this ourselves yet. So, until we can interview someone who has, we will just close this subject with the observation 'The Devil was unavailable for comment'.

The Agglestone

On a heath a mile north-east of Studland, on the Isle of Purbeck, stands a 400-ton rock called the Agglestone. This was once a sacred site (its name probably originating from the Anglo-Saxon word *helig* meaning holy), and until quite recently, the stone would rock on its base if you pushed it lightly by hand. However, centuries of people doing this took their toll on its base, which in 1970, crumbled away and the whole stone tipped over onto its side.

This wasn't the first time it had fallen to earth, however, as the rock was reputed to have been thrown all the way from the Isle of Wight by an enraged Devil. Others say Satan was trying to destroy Salisbury Cathedral or Blindon Abbey, or that he was idling away the time by lobbing stones at the Old Harry Rocks on the Dorset coast.

Either way, he seems to be a pretty poor shot, which should come as a relief to us all.

The Devil's Stone

After nightfall every 5 November, when most of the country is setting fire to effigies of Guy Fawkes, the good people of Shebbear in Devon approach the village church armed with crowbars. Before they can commemorate the thwarting of the Gunpowder Plot, they need to thwart a devilish plot to overthrow the village church. Every year, they are honour-bound to turn a big lump of glacial erratic called the Devil's Stone. This rock was supposedly the foundation stone for a church in a village across the river, but when the Devil swatted it away it landed in Shebbear. To protect the village from evil, the stone has to be turned every year.

Nobody we spoke to could explain exactly what the ritual accomplishes, but we're out-of-towners, so we can hardly expect to understand. Nevertheless, we suspect that one particular side effect of the festival plays a part: turning the stone works up a serious thirst, which can be quenched by a few pints at the Devil's Stone Inn afterwards.

Turned to Stone

Not all the rocks in England's local legends started out as devilish projectiles; some of them actually started out as people. Legends of human beings transformed into minerals have been a staple of mythology and folklore since Old Testament days, when Lot's wife was turned into a pillar of salt for looking back towards her home in Sodom, a wicked and cursed city. In England's damp climate a pillar of salt would soon dissolve into a puddle of brine, so when the English dream up a legend, it's usually set in stone.

Long Meg

William Wordsworth cranked out verse about everything in the Lake District, it seems, and the stone circle called Long Meg and her Daughters is no exception. Apparently, 'A weight of awe not easy to be borne' fell upon the Cumbrian verse factory 'When first I saw that family forlorn'. And who can blame him, really? Today, many of the group of standing stones, which can be found near the village of Glassonby, have fallen or are buried; yet, when old William was getting his words' worth out of them, there may have been more than seventy grey granite boulders in that 300-foot diameter circle, with a tall red sandstone monolith called Long Meg taking pride of place to the south-west.

This stone circle is clearly a religious site, especially since the odd stone out marks the point at which the sun would have set in midwinter when the circle was first constructed, about 4,000 years ago. But why stick with archaeological fact when there's a good tale to be told?

As with many stone circles, the dolmens that make up Long Meg and her Daughters were once real people who were frozen in the middle of their worship by an act of black magic. In some versions of the story, the unfortunates were early Christians disturbed by pagans; in others, they were white witches being attacked by a rival coven. Another sad variant to the tale mentions that the service everyone was attending was in fact a wedding. Whichever version of the tale applies to Long Meg, her circle earns all the more pathos because all the stones in the circle were members of the same family.

Bizarrely, the sorcerer responsible for this crime is often said to be the mysterious and spellbinding Michael Scott, a thirteenth-century Scottish mathematician, scientist and alchemist whose fame was so widespread that he's actually mentioned in Dante's 'Inferno' as a man 'who of a verity Of magical illusions knew the game'. Scott also taught the famous Italian mathematician Fibonacci of Pisa. Perhaps the local Cumbrians were suffering from maths anxiety when they cast Scott as villain of the piece, or perhaps some anti-Pictish sentiment was at play. Then again, maybe Scott's fame as an alchemist was so widespread it was inevitable that his name would get dragged into it. Who knows?

But there is hope for Long Meg and her Daughters. They say that if you can count all the rocks in the circle and get the same number twice, it will release them from their spell. We wish you luck trying, however, as there's another spell on the stones that makes it impossible to count them twice and get the same number. It's undeniable that Michael Scott was a tricky wizard, and one clearly good with numbers.

Long Meg Offerings

Some kind of religious observances still go on around Long Meg and her Daughters, but instead of rock worshippers, we seem to be dealing with tree worshippers. On any given day you might find strange bundles, wrapped in cloth, hanging from the branches of trees around the stone circle. It's the kind of thing that leaves you wondering what on earth is going on there? But I doubt your curiosity will be great enough to tempt you to unwrap one of the mysterious bundles. After all, the legend never did state exactly why Long Meg and her Daughters were turned to stone.
– *The Rev Doctor Gil*

Rollright Stones

Back in the days after the Romans had left Britain, several waves of Danish immigrants landed in Northumbria and settled as far south as the Warwickshire–Oxfordshire borders. They weren't always welcomed this far south, if some local legends are to be believed. For example, near the town of Long Compton a huge number of lichen-covered standing stones, known as the Rollright Stones, are all that remain of a Danish king and his invading army.

The king and his troops are part of an oft-repeated tale featuring a witch, an earthquake, an elder tree and some lines of poetry. Approached one night by an old witch, the king was told that he could rule England if he could take seven strides and see Long Compton. Since Long Compton was downhill and he could see it anyway, he thought this was a safe bet. So, the king strode out, but on his seventh step the earth shook and erupted into a mound that blocked his view. The witch chanted:

As Long Compton thou canst not see
King of England thou shalt not be

And the king and his men promptly turned to stone in the woods above the town. They are gathered into three groups that supposedly represent the king, his whispering knights and the common footsoldiers. The witch herself turned into an elder tree. So, if you should encounter anyone who makes you an offer of supreme power, tell them to talk to the elder tree about it – the old witch should still be around somewhere.

Ancient Mysteries

When the past speaks to us, its messages are often written in stone, in a strange language of symbols that nobody understands any more. Bizarre rock formations, rock carvings and stone structures have peppered the English landscape for thousands of years; and there were many more of them before pragmatic country folk mined them for building materials.

What did the standing stones and rock piles and gate-shaped trilithons of rock mean to the people who erected them? What possessed people to make moat-like circular trenches and banks, but leave big roads leading right into the middle? Why would any prehistoric people build an entire artificial hill of chalky dirt? And what's the deal with those strange spirals that Neolithic cultures carved into rocks?

Archaeologists have been taxing themselves for centuries to interpret these signs, but it is true to say that we're not much closer to deciphering a coherent message now than we were in the eighteenth century, when William Stukeley first started criss-crossing England to examine the henges and stone circles that have fascinated us ever since. So, what are we supposed to think when we hike across scrubland to look at mysterious markings or odd groupings of rocks and boulders? Who knows? The message has been obscured by the sands of time; but it's certainly fun to try and dig out a new theory.

Mysteries in the Round

It seems clear to us now that the ancient inhabitants of England had circles on the brain. They littered the place with stone circles and henges for one thing, but their odd obsession extended beyond plain circles to another pattern: the spiral.

To take just one example, Cumbria's large standing stone, Long Meg, is covered with spiral patterns that date from the New Stone Age, five or six thousand years ago. Graffiti, Stone Age or not, isn't a real reflection of the culture, of course, but the spiral appears elsewhere across Britain in much larger feats of civil engineering. In fact, the largest prehistoric structure in Europe, Silbury Hill in Wiltshire, was originally a giant spiral. For centuries, people thought the 300-foot-high chalk mound was a step-based structure of concentric rings. The most recent archaeological digs, however, have revealed that, when it was first built, between 3,000 and 4,000 years ago, people could walk up a spiral path to the top.

So, although we know the spiral pattern was hugely popular, we don't know what it meant to the people who worked with it. What we do know is that after many more centuries, the people of England got a bit more sophisticated with the pattern and turned it into yet another mystery – this time, one you could actually walk on.

Labyrinths in the Lawn

It may sound Greek to most people, but the labyrinth is also a deeply English phenomenon. These twisting circular designs appear across the land under many exotic names – the Walls of Troy and Julian's Bower being two of the more popular ones – but they all refer to the same kind of twisted circular design. A labyrinth is a bit like a maze, but with a single path that leads by a tortuous route to a central point; it is not a puzzle designed to tax your wits, as there's only one possible way you can go through a labyrinth and you can't get lost along the way. And, once you reach the end, slap bang in the centre, there's only one way to go: Back the way you came.

If you can't get lost in them, what are they for? And why do labyrinth patterns appear in such different settings across the country? You can find them carved on a large rock face on the road to Tintagel in Cornwall. They're also worn into the grass of common land near Saffron Walden in Essex, Wing in Rutland and Alkborough in Lincolnshire. More are set in mosaic tile in Ely Cathedral and the church at Itchen Stoke near Winchester. Just what is it about a twisty pattern that we can date from 4,000-year-old ruins on Greek islands that captured the imagination of Britons so long ago?

For many centuries, turf mazes (a labyrinth pattern cut out of the grass) on public land were part of May Day celebrations, and were connected with spring fertility rites. In some cases, we know that maypoles were set up in the middle for maidens to dance round. Rural swains would process through the twisting path, some probably running as fast as they could (perhaps in hot pursuit of a shepherdess or two). When you see young children confronted with a labyrinth these days, it's easy to get the picture – the idea is to tear as fast as possible through the hairpin bends and the last one to the middle's a rotten egg. Although some people think this is a disrespectful use of an old monument, it's a firmly established tradition; in some parts of England, labyrinths go by the name Robin Hood's Race.

However, ask a New Age devotee about labyrinths, and their

answer will inevitably have something to do with Mother Earth and the journey of life. Some will go so far as to say that they are designed to put you in a trance. The expert in earth religions who established Boscastle's Museum of Witchcraft, Cecil Williamson, put it this way: 'Slowly walking, or finger-walking, a labyrinth can induce a trance-like state suitable for the journey into the Other World. With a unicursal (one-way) labyrinth one can't get lost. Start at the bottom and slowly follow the raised path, you will be moving deosil (sunwise) as often as you are moving widdershins (anti-sunwise). Eventually you will arrive, well balanced, at the sacred centre of the symbol and maybe of another world.'

Labyrinths were certainly closely associated with a veil between the worlds in Shakespeare's day: In *A Midsummer Night's Dream*, the queen of the fairies, Titania, comments that 'the quaint mazes in the wanton green for lack of tread are indistinguishable', in a monologue in which she bewails the poor state of affairs in the human world.

So what's the connection between labyrinths and churches? Christians often have different opinions on this. Some say that monks and priests would walk the labyrinth, or prescribe it to their parishioners, as a penance. Others point out that the centre of a labyrinth is shaped like a cross, so it represents a spiritual goal that you should walk towards. There are those who just say that it's easier for them to pray or meditate when they're walking. And the more pragmatic folk treat it simply as a therapeutic stress-busting exercise without any deeper meaning.

Official explanations are few and far between. However, the City of Troy labyrinth near Brandsby in North Yorkshire is an exception. A plaque near the fenced-off lawn labyrinth offers this explanation:

This maze is the one surviving instance in the North Riding of an ancient game. Mazes pass under various names in different parts of England, such as Julian's Bower, Robin Hood's Race, Shepherd's Ring, Walls of Troy or City of Troy. The last mentioned being the name

by which this example has always been known. This is interesting and shows the early association between Yorkshire and Scandinavia where Trojeborg (Troy Town) is the name given to similar mazes. The game and its origin are forgotten.

So there's not much help there either. But explanations aren't really necessary. Anybody who traces their finger along a labyrinth pattern in a book or carved in stone, or walks along one of these lawn mazes (and there have been dozens built in recent years) can come up with their own interpretation, because whatever the original makers intended is a complete mystery, and will most likely remain so forever.

I Walk the (Twisty) Line

Saffron Walden's turf maze in Essex is the largest publicly owned labyrinth in England. The path to the middle is more than 1,600 yards long. It's probably a lot newer than most of the labyrinths in England (the first record of it is as late as 1699), and it's certainly a more sophisticated pattern than the Winchester Mizmaze or Julian's Bower in Lincolnshire. Nevertheless, walking it has a similar effect, in that you spend ages away from the centre, walking round the perimeter, then suddenly find the path is leading you right towards your goal. Then after a quarter-circuit of the central circle, the path leads you off to the outer limits again. If you don't take a patient and philosophical approach to the journey, walking the labyrinth can be downright irritating. If you take it too fast, you can twist your ankle or get dizzy and disoriented. That's why I like it so much. It forces you to pace yourself. You know you're going to get to your destination, so there's no excuse for getting hot under the collar at every turn that takes you away from it. And that's pretty good practice for living. – *MJL*

Cups and Rings

Imagine a tiny scale model of lunar craters with little trenches dug round them, carved into rocks on the moors. What you have in mind now is something that archaeologists call cupmarks or cup-and-ring marks, although the circular depressions are too shallow to be an actual cup or even a cup holder. They can be found dotted around various sites in Northumberland and Cornwall, as well as Scotland and Ireland.

As with any circular symbol, they can be connected with the sun or moon. However, as their placement on stones is much too random to suggest astronomical measurements, perhaps they are something to do with a cult of sun or moon worship; but only perhaps. The most celebrated modern scholar of stone circles, Aubrey Burl, casually mentions these ideas in his book *Rings of Stone* and adds that cupmarks are often associated with burial sites. But that word 'often' means that there are occasions when cupmarks have nothing to do with burial sites, so we're back to square one.

What these circular marks mean is anybody's guess. Care to take a stab at it yourself? Then get on over to Wooler in Northumberland and scope out the visitor centre for hikes that take in these strange markings. Doddington and Rothbury and several other sites within hiking distance have some great examples of this odd and ancient art form. But, of course, no explanations.

Lost at the Cup and Rings

It wouldn't be strictly accurate to say we were lost. One of us knew exactly where we were and where we needed to go. But she was ten and I, her dad, had other ideas. I was the one who was lost, but like most dads, I knew best and I didn't stop to ask directions. Actually, there was nobody to ask, except for a couple of herds of sheep. We were on the high moor outside of Wooler in the far northern bit of Northumberland, so close to Scotland we could catch a whiff of haggis in the air. We were in search of the cup-and-ring marks carved into flat stones scattered across the moor.

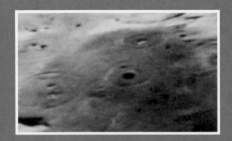

What we really needed was an Ordnance Survey map or handheld SatNav with the precise co-ordinates of the rocks. What we had instead was a sheet of paper with directions written on it. The directions involved following dirt tracks through the heather, taking bearings from hills and woods on the horizon. And moors are notorious for their winding tracks and horizon-obscuring dips.

'We need to head that way,' she said.

'But we must never leave the path,' I added, sagely passing on a little hiking wisdom I had learned from my two weeks in the scouts.

'We already left our trail. It split off back there and we went down the wrong branch.'

We were in a dip that obscured the horizon I had used to take my bearings, and with the grey clouds obscuring the sun, I couldn't even tell in which direction we were going. For all my nuggets of hiking wisdom, I had missed the bit about taking a compass with you. And a map. And, of course, a SatNav. Oh, and it was beginning to rain. However,

I did have a daughter with a sense of direction, so I agreed to back up and take the other trail.

Within two minutes, we were standing by a flat rock pocked with odd carvings. They looked like ripples radiating from the places where raindrops fall onto a pool of standing water. There didn't seem to be any pattern to the way they were clustered. Each mark was geometrically sound in its own way, but didn't seem to relate to any of the marks next to it. Add to this the fact that nobody knows what cup-and-ring marks were made for, and you have a full-fledged mystery on your hands. And out there in the drizzly moors, mysteries have a way of taking on much greater significance. In fact, this site was beginning to creep me out more than a little. So we headed off, the way my daughter thought we should go.

'Y'know, nobody knows what those marks were made for,' I said.

'I do,' my daughter replied.

'Really? What?'

'Navigation,' she said.

This may have been a profound insight. Perhaps cup-and-ring marks are the ancient equivalent of one of those scale models of National Trust sites, and were used by past inhabitants to get their bearings on the moors, showing the henges and round barrow burial sites in the area. But this girlish comment was most likely a dig at my own inability to find the right path. So I followed her lead back to the footpath and to the car. There, on named roads, with an *A to Z* in hand, I was in my element. Out there on the moors, things were a lot more mysterious.

A Plague of Henges

England is littered with henges, many of them four or five thousand years old. Nobody knows why these places were built or what they were used for. In fact, most people don't even know what a real henge is; they only know the word because of Stonehenge, and assume it's another word for stone circle. In fact, it isn't. A henge is a flat area surrounded by a ditch and bank, making a circular or oval stage in the middle. Sadly, thousands of years of English weather and farming and road building have completely concealed many of these ditches, which were once far more common features of the English landscape.

Fortunately, many henges have stone circles attached to them, which makes them easy to spot. They often come in twos, with a stone circle and a henge touching at the circumference to make a figure eight. Long Meg, in Cumbria, once made a figure eight with a large henge that's now completely filled in, but which has been detected by infrared photography. And old records talk of a henge near the oldest stone circle on record, Castlerigg, near Keswick, though it's never been discovered. Mayburgh Henge and King Arthur's Round Table, both at Eamont Bridge near Penrith, are also cases of henges that come in twos. Both are Bronze Age circles and were clearly connected . . . but how? And why?

Modern-day members of the Glastonbury Order of Druids or the Council of British Druid Orders have their own reasons for venerating henges. In fact, when members of the Anglican Church decided to place a stone near Mayburgh Henge to commemorate the turning of the year 2000, a group of thirty pagans showed up in gentle protest at the attempt to Christianise the site. Outnumbered ten to one by church folk, their remonstrance was a model of restraint: They brought ceremonial daggers and swords, for sure, but limited any aggression to mooning the Archbishop.

The construction of Stonehenge was one of the longest building projects in history. Its development spanned 1,400 years . . .

Stonehenge

Stonehenge started life as a circular ditch nearly 5,000 years ago, and has attracted huge amounts of attention ever since. It now sits by the A344 in the middle of the chalk wasteland that is Salisbury Plain, but when Stonehenge was first built, the surrounding region was fairly well populated by the standards of the time. The area is peppered with burial chambers and meeting places for the plains farmers who eked a difficult living out of the chalky soil, and whose ancestors had done the same for a thousand years by the time digging commenced.

The construction of Stonehenge was one of the longest building projects in history. Its development spanned 1,400 years, and went from wooden posts and earthworks, through several waves of stone structures that drew their raw materials from as far away as West Wales. However, even in its early manifestations, Stonehenge was associated with midsummer. One of the few large stones raised at the site in the early days, the Heel Stone, lined up with the point at which the sun rose on Midsummer's Day. Other smaller stones arranged in square formation in the middle of the site also line up with the rising sun at dawn on May Day and Midwinter's Day. Only one other large stone remains from Stonehenge I, and it's fallen to the ground. It's reddish in colour, and we call it the Slaughter Stone because, after a few millennia, any flat stone that's red is bound to attract stories of human sacrifice, while in reality the iron-rich stone is merely rusty. However, the first Stonehenge was mostly not stone at all. It was primarily made of wood, and more than fifty-six post holes surround the site.

The next wave of development, Stonehenge II, came from an invading tribe almost 600 years later. The Beaker Folk seem to have claimed this site as a high-profile

place to show off their wealth and influence, because they imported large bluestones along waterways from the Preseli Mountains in West Wales, and dragged them into the henge with the intention of building two concentric stone circles. They never quite completed the task, though, and after about a hundred years, they just gave up. Either they or the next tribe to take over the area eventually removed the bluestones.

Stonehenge III is the place we see today, more or less. It came about in a further three separate stages, in which stonemasons squared up huge stones and made peg-and-hole joints to hold them in place. They arranged them into five trilithons (the cricket-stumps-and-bails arrangement of three stones that we know so well) in a horseshoe shape. They also buried someone at the open end of the horseshoe. Thirty enormous sarsen stones were dragged over from the Marlborough Downs twenty miles away, erected around the horseshoe and topped off with lintels. Finally, the bluestones that the Beaker Folk had brought were erected inside the circle, some 600 years after they had been imported from Wales.

So that's the history of the actual construction of Stonehenge. However, the important thing is why it was built that way. The confusing layout of stones makes it both easy and hard to figure out. Look at it one way, and the intermingled patterns of stones could be a complicated lunar and solar calendar, with sight lines for sunrises at equinoxes and solstices. From another perspective, it could be a place of death ritual. There are plenty of burial sites spanning thousands of years around the henge. Unfortunately, the earth within the circle itself has been so well dug over it's hard to say whether sacrifices took place there or not. There are plenty of animal bones there, but that's not so unusual. Unfortunately, a couple of centuries ago some enterprising fellow built a fast-food joint bang in the middle to cater to the Regency tourist trade. The cellar he dug underneath his hut spoiled the chances of today's archaeologists undertaking worthwhile digs there.

Its very popularity has actually made Stonehenge one of the least attractive sites for fans of the strange. It's very hard to love a place that's surrounded by a chain-link fence, comes with an admission fee in excess of £5, and is perpetually crowded with sightseers. It's also tough for photographers to get a single shot of the stones that isn't obscured by the backs of people's heads and full of gawping tourists.

Oh, and Stonehenge is also one of the few stone circles in the western world that you can't actually touch. It has suffered so much vandalism at the hands of chisel-wielding souvenir hunters from the eighteenth century onwards that it's now off limits. If you dare venture off the path in the direction of the sarsen stones, English Heritage guards will step up and bustle you away. The only time you can get close enough to touch the stones is at dawn on Midsummer's Day, and it's even more crowded then, with an odd combination of floaty New Age folk and staggering party people.

The real mystery, then, is why anybody would go there when Avebury is only a short drive away.

The Stone Circle that Ate a Village

Some English stone circles must have really good publicity machines. Stonehenge isn't the oldest or the biggest, yet everybody seems to fawn all over it. The less commercial Castlerigg stone circle has gleaned a disproportionate amount of attention, too, because it's the oldest circle in England. Meanwhile, the most staggeringly huge ancient monument in the country is no more than a footnote in the coach-tripping tour schedule.

It's probably Avebury's own fault. Unlike other stone circles, it doesn't have a focal point. It's just too big to have one. Avebury is the Earls Court of stone circles, and

in comparison all the other stone circles in England are more like university ballrooms. Oh, the architecture's nice enough, but they're tiny and crowded and you can't get a decent view of the main attraction. One courtier who wanted to wow Charles II advised him to skip Stonehenge as a mere parish church, and move straight on to the cathedral that is Avebury instead. We echo the sentiment.

Everything about Avebury is huge. The stone avenues that lead to it go on for miles, almost as far away as Silbury Hill and the Kennet long barrow (two huge

construction projects from the same group that built Avebury). Around the outer stone circle is a chalk ditch as wide as a castle moat and a bank that's a quarter of a mile across. Only two arcs of the original outer circle remain, and, peculiarly, many of the stones are clearly concrete fabrications put up in the 1930s in place of stones that had been 'mined' for building materials by the local villagers. And then there are smaller rings inside the main outer wall. When the structure was still intact, an aerial view of it may well have resembled a cartoon head with two big eyes. There may even have been a nose and mouth for all we know; there's no evidence of

that anymore, though. Oh, and there's a village stuck inside the big stone circle too, but that's a much later addition, and it's completely dwarfed by the prehistoric bit.

Weird watchers have seen strange lights at play around the circle at night or twilight, and some say they have seen floating orbs which they associate with ghosts. And anyone who visits the Red Lion Inn in the village (the only pub we know of that's inside a prehistoric monument) will be regaled with so many ghost stories that they'll walk away wondering what on earth Avebury is all about. They won't be alone. You can tell from the sheer scale of the place that this circle and ditch meant something extremely important to the people who built it. It's an enormous work of civil engineering, like a Norman cathedral or a twentieth-century skyscraper. It was clearly built to last (probably in stages, beginning in 4000 BC and ending 1,600 years later) and designed to make an impression. It's done all of those things . . . yet nobody really knows why it exists. Plenty of bones have been found in the ditches, suggesting that death rituals took place there. The shape of several stones suggests to some people that they're male and female symbols, so perhaps fertility rituals took place here, too. But Avebury is too huge a structure to be just about birth and death.

Of course, after a few thousand years have gone by, people tend to lose the plot altogether. Six hundred years ago, the Church declared (a bit arbitrarily, we think) that stone circles were associated with the Devil, so many good Christian folk took it upon themselves to destroy them. The local villagers made some headway into the Avebury circle, as a cursory glance at the village will tell you. Several of the buildings there are built of stone suspiciously like that of the original monument, and until the heir to the Keiller marmalade fortune began a massive reconstruction project in the 1930s, many of the stones lay toppled on the ground.

Under one of these toppled stones lay the body of a man. From the bag of tools found by him, it was clear this fellow had been a medieval barber-surgeon, an itinerant tradesman who cut hair, pulled teeth and performed minor surgery. The idea that he had been trying to topple the stone and got crushed in the attempt was too amusing for hale English folk in the late 1930s to pass up. And the laughs kept on coming: When he was shipped off to London to be examined properly, the Luftwaffe bombed the place where his body was stored. To have been crushed by one heavy falling object may seem like misfortune; to be crushed by a second 600 years later seems more like carelessness. It also seems too good to be true, and sure enough, it isn't. His body turned up decades later, and when it was examined using modern forensic techniques, it turned out the barber-surgeon had actually died of bog-standard plague.

But just so this poor bloke won't have died in vain, heed the warning of the barber-surgeon jokes: When you go to Avebury, touch the stones, hug them, photograph them, recharge your crystals on them if you must, but don't try to push them over. The very least you'll get is a hernia; the worst could be a joke very much at your expense that goes on for centuries.

It's an enormous work of civil engineering, like a
Norman cathedral or a twentieth-century skyscraper.

Mên-an-Tol, the stone with a hole

Cornwall is awash with mysterious sites, but something about the Mên-an-Tol stands out. The words are Cornish for the stone of the hole, although of the three stones standing at the site, only one has a hole in it. There are two upright stones about five feet high and, between them, a single polo-shaped one with a hole wide enough for a full-grown man to crawl through. And that's exactly what people have been doing for hundreds, if not thousands of years.

The site is probably more than 3,000 years old, and a drawing of the site made in 1754 shows that it once had another upright stone making a triangle. In fact, there's some evidence that these stones may have been part of a whole circle. But the focus has always been on the one round stone with a hole. For centuries, it was referred to as the Devil's Eye, probably a result of the tendency of the Christian Church to malign anything to do with old religions. But many do believe the site has strange powers.

Healing is one of its supposed powers. It was a tradition to take children with lung disease or rickets out onto the moor and pass them naked through the hole three times, then drag them across the ground three times towards the east. This must have been quite an ordeal, because the site is quite a hike from the main road, and a mile and a half from the nearest village, Morvah. Adults suffering from rheumatism or spinal pain would, and still do, crawl through the hole nine times anti-clockwise in the hope of gaining relief, though once again, anything must be a relief after crawling through a hole nine times.

Healing is not the only power Mên-an-Tol is supposed to have. A nineteenth-century folklorist claimed that it had the power of divination, and that if you laid two

brass pins in a cross on top of the holed stone, the pins would move in answer to your question. According to others, something to do with the combination of upright stones and holed stones suggests the site may have been associated with fertility, and that crawling through the hole would hasten pregnancy. (Freud was unavailable for comment on why the site needed two or more upright stones.)

So don't be surprised if, after the drive from St Ives or Penzance, a longish walk up the farmyard path, and a hop over the stile, you're greeted by the sight of grown people crawling through a stone with a hole in it. This may look like eccentric behaviour, but it's eccentric behaviour with a very long tradition.

Attack of the Mad Cows

I have heard many stories of people with chronic back pain who gained relief from crawling through the Mên-an-Tol. I was feeling fine on the early summer day when I hiked up there for a solo hike, and decided I'd catch the Mên-an-Tol after visiting a cool standing stone a little farther along the path. This standing stone, the Mên Scryfa, has writing on it, but it's on the far side of the stone, and you have to walk through a cow field to get to it. When I got there, the cows were very curious, and frankly, they scared me a bit. Every last one of them looked up at me as I jumped off the stile and kept on looking. Whenever I made a move, they'd take one step towards me. In the back of my head, I knew that cows are herbivores, but a large group of big animals coming straight at you tends to trump common sense. I had visions of matadors being gored by bulls and people doing the Pamplona Run being thrown up into the air, so when they began to walk towards me en masse, I turned tail. In my hurry, I crossed the stile too quickly, and twisted my ankle. This was a problem: The hike back to the car was a long way, and it really hurt to walk. Not being a hard-core hiker, I didn't have a staff to rest on, so I hobbled. This may sound like temporary madness, but by the time I reached the stile to the Mên-an-Tol, I was weeping from pain and frustration and ready for a miracle. Weirdly enough, that's exactly what I got. I crawled through the hole three times clockwise and when I got up, my ankle didn't hurt so much. By the time I made it back to the car, I could operate the clutch with barely a twinge. Was it a miracle or a coincidence? I don't know. But I tell my story, like the Ancient Mariner, to whoever will listen. – *Coleridge Fan*

Healing on Horseback

In western Cornwall's Kerrier district there's a huge stone with a hole in it right next to a bridle-path that runs through an almost non-existent hamlet called Tolvan Cross. You can just about see the stone from horseback through the thick hedges as you reach the road to Gweek, but if you dismount and try to get a closer look, the stinging nettles will get you. As far as I can tell, this is the Tolvan holed stone, which was a famous healing stone for centuries. It's taller than a full-grown man and has a hole in it small enough for a child or someone really skinny to climb through.

They used to say that if your child was really sick, you could heal her by passing her through the stone nine times clockwise and putting her to bed with a silver coin under her pillow. (Actually, this legend is so old, it originates from the time before clocks were invented, so the practitioners of this cure would have said deosil or sunwise instead.) In fact, like many holed stones in Cornwall, the Tolvan stone is also associated with fairy magic. Here's the odd thing about it, though. It's in somebody's back garden now and it seems really close to the back wall of their house. I hope babies can be passed through it without bumping their heads against the wall. Not much point in healing someone if you give them concussion in the process. – *Drifter*

Interview with a Stone Circle Expert

The thing about mysteries is that *everything's* a mystery to the uninformed. So the *Weird* research team tracked down someone truly informed about England's ancient sites. Lucy Harrison trained as an archaeologist, studied with experts for years, and is now one of the principals of Touchstone Tours, which leads tours of ancient sites around northern England. And yet even to someone who really knows her stuff, these places are still loaded with question marks. That said, in a half-hour chat with her, we did gain some insights worth passing along.

Weird England: Stone circles seem to fascinate everybody, from hikers to modern-day Druids. What's the story with those?

Lucy Harrison: Well, they're *not* Druid sites. That idea started with William Stukeley in the 1700s. He recognised that these circles were pre-Roman and the only thing he knew that was pre-Roman was Druids. That was all *anybody* knew at the time. But the earliest stone circle we know of, Castlerigg, is from thousands of years before the Druids. It may be from as long ago as 3300 BC. It has Bronze Age burial mounds in the centre of it with ash from cremations.

Another possibility is that Castlerigg was built up as a centre for trade. There was a factory in Langdale, a stone's throw away, that churned out stone hand axes centuries before the burials at Castlerigg: These were ritual items, highly polished and not used for anything. In fact, they were useless. So it could have been a place where you bought your ritual axe or had it sanctified.

WE: So stone circles are associated with religious events like Midsummer's Day?

LH: Well, Castlerigg is associated with Beltane and Samhain, basically Mayday and Halloween. Long Meg is a midwinter circle. I think that midwinter was more significant to these people than midsummer. The longest day, the shortest night, that's all very well . . . but what's more important than midwinter? 'Please let the sun come up! Please let it get warmer! We'll do anything, gods! Just make it summer again!' But nowadays people go to all these sites at midsummer.

WE: You hear a lot about stone circles but not so much about piles of stones. Is there anything mysterious about cairns?

LH: Essentially a cairn is a way-marker; but some do have stories associated with them. The cairn at Dunmail Rise at Helvellyn is one of them. Around AD 940, King Dunmail supposedly had a battle with the Saxon King Edmund for the crown of Cumbria: Edmund brought his Saxon troops up from one side; Dunmail brought his Cumbrian Celtic troops up from the other side, and they had a big fight in the middle. Edmund managed to infiltrate Dunmail's troops so that when Dunmail called for his backup, they turned on him. He got killed, but his bodyguards saved his crown, which was the symbol of his authority to rule the area. They ran up the side of the mountain and threw the crown into Grizedale Tarn, then they raised a cairn over Dunmail's body at the top of the pass.

WE: Throwing the symbol of power into the water? That sounds a bit like Excalibur in the Arthurian legends.

LH: They were big on throwing valuables into the water back then! You know where that comes from? Probably from the end of the Bronze Age. Around 1400 BC, the climate changed: There was a period of huge rainfall for 300 years and these massive water cults sprang up, with people saying 'Please, please, please, don't let it rain

anymore.' They've got to appease the water gods and so they throw things into the water. Archaeologists found this all over but particularly in the fenlands. One offering was bronze swords; they cast them in a mould instead of having a blacksmith hammer them out. They used a stone mould, so when it was done, you would take a sword out of the stone.

WE: Drawing a sword from the stone? Where have we heard that before?

LH: A lot of this folklore is probably drawn from verbal accounts. They heard about swords taken from the stone, and thrown into the water, and these details get woven into legends. Think about the story of Long Meg and her acolytes dancing on the Sabbath and being turned to stone. A lot of stone circles – the Merry Maidens in Cornwall is another example – have stories attached that involve women dancing. That was a common thread . . .

WE: Shocking business; clearly needs to be discouraged . . .

LH: Well, a lot of these stories came from the early Christian Church, trying to make these sites out to be involved with devil worship, working people's superstition. The suggestion is that these stories came down from some ritual to do with the sites that involved women dancing among the stones.

WE: So these circles *were* religious sites . . .

LH: They're not necessarily sacred sites; they may just be gathering places, like a local shopping centre. One word that archaeologists use a lot is *ritual*, but ritual is not just going to church on a Sunday. Ritual is also going to the pub on Friday, going to market on a Saturday morning; ritual is what you do for birthdays; what you do for Christmas, funerals, christenings, births, deaths, marriages. Ritual is also about how you vote for your government. Ritual can be social as well as religious. And political. It is about how you judge criminals and what you do with them after the trial.

So it is not just about sacrificing to the gods and listening to the man with the long beard and robes. It's about life events, births, deaths, marriages. It's probably about healing. It's about social interaction. It's about trade, politics and law. All the social hierarchies are involved in it.

Our chat with Lucy may not have lifted the veil on the mystery of standing stones, but it certainly shone a brighter light through it. We're starting to see things a bit more clearly now . . .

Holey Stones!

Big standing stones with holes through them are sometimes called hagstones, but that term is more often used to refer to the pocket-sized holed stones you find in rivers throughout the south of England. Dorset especially seems to yield a lot of these small stones. Most people assume it's a peculiar erosion pattern that wears holes through these stones, but a common folk tale tells a different story. Hagstones are amulets worn to ward off ill health and bad luck, and were often sold to crusaders going off to war and to families with sick people. One classic collection of British folklore, Brand's *Popular Antiquities of Great Britain*, attributes even more supernatural powers to these stones:

A stone with a hole in it hung at the bed's head will prevent the nightmare. It is therefore called a Hag Stone from that disorder which is occasioned by a Hag or Witch sitting on the stomach of the party afflicted. It also prevents witches riding horses, for which purpose it is often tied to a stable key.

They were also used by witches to cast spells, by sailors to prevent leaky hulls and to attract favourable winds, and as wishing stones by people down on their luck.

How the holes in magic hagstones came to be there isn't, of course, explained, but the idea was that once they had brought you the luck you wanted, you should cast them back into the water for others to benefit. Returning soldiers and families that survived bouts of the plague would throw them into the first river they came across. Of course, just to prove how cussed the business of folklore can be, there's a contradictory story: You hold onto your hagstone as long as it continues to bring you good luck, or pass it on to a loved one. A hagstone acquired in any other way (stolen or found) will bring bad luck. And stones found in the water were cast there by the families of people whose hagstones failed to protect them from plague or pestilence. Confused? Join the club. And to be safe, steer clear of hagstones unless they're given to you by a trusted friend.

What Lies Beneath

You just can't knock the workmanship of the hardy farmers and tin traders of Cornwall. When they built a cellar, they built it to last. And when the cellar in question lies beneath the now-ruined Iron Age village of Carn Euny, dates back more than 2,000 years, and is *still* standing, you know it was built to last. The question is why? Why would people who built a solid enough village of stone before the birth of Christ build a sixty-five-foot tunnel beneath it, leading to a domed chamber just beneath ground level? The standard pragmatic answer is that it was for cold storage, which makes some kind of sense, except that there are no shelves or antechambers, and most civilisations built root cellars before they built communal storage. Besides, there's another feature here that doesn't quite add up: it was built in such a way that when the midsummer sun dawns, it shines down the tunnel and lights the place up. It's a puzzler for sure.

In Cornwall, these underground structures are known as *fogous*, just to add to the mystery. The *fogou* beneath Carn Euny is a strange place to clamber through to this day. Carn Euny itself is an isolated and long-deserted ruin of a village located on the hypotenuse of the triangle you get by drawing a line between the delightfully silly village names of Brane, Grumbla and Drift in the western part of Cornwall. The nearest town is much more sensibly named Sancreed.

It's best to visit out of school hours, because tearing around the tunnels without running into school field trips makes all the difference. For one thing, and this can't be overstated, the walls glow in the dark. There's a luminescent moss growing there that gives off a pale green glow that's not quite as bright as a night-light, but which is much better than stumbling around in the dark.

We may never know the purpose of the Carn Euny *fogou*, but then again, in a world that tries to suck the wonder out of everything with simplistic explanations, something with a little mystery makes a welcome change, don't you think?

Birchover Hermit's Cave

Overlooking Derbyshire's Harthill Moor, just up the hill from the vicarage in Birchover, you will find a strange cave in the middle of several gritstone rocks. It's clearly been carved into living quarters, but nobody can say when this happened or who did it. You hear a few hikers rumour that 'the vicar used to go up there to be alone', but this is clearly guesswork based on the few devotional carvings on the wall and an apparent altar on the eastern inside wall. The rocks are so weathered that it's hard to make out the few crosses carved here and there. Of course, there are plenty of newer inscriptions, including graffiti all over the bench carved out of rock outside the cave, but few clues as to the original occupant.

The first written record of the place did not appear until the late nineteenth century, but it seems unlikely that this is the first time it was known. Hermits were a significant fact of life in the last millennium. Up to the thirteenth century, anybody who wanted to live alone was called a hermit, and although they may have been more antisocial than most, not all lived in isolation; in some cases, they performed a significant social function in a community. Hermits often acted as guides for travellers, or set up chapels for quiet contemplation and even acted as unlicensed monks, hearing confessions and offering spiritual advice. Pope Innocent IV brought the age of the free hermits to a close when he determined that they should be properly appointed and adhere to Augustinian rule.

But the Birchover hermit doesn't appear to have been one of these. He's not recorded in any church register or other local document, but perhaps he managed to fly under the Church's radar. The only hint that there was a hermit around these parts in medieval times comes from the accounts of December 1550 of the local big house, Haddon Hall, in which the steward of the Hall gave eight pence 'unto ye Harmytt' for guiding a guest from Bradley to the Hall.

However, nothing in that record ties that particular hermit to this town or this cave. It's all open to conjecture — and to the public, free of charge, assuming you can get your car along the minuscule track from the vicarage without losing one or more wing mirrors to the steep walls of rock on either side.

Whispering Corner

To anyone who doesn't live on the Isle of Purbeck in Dorset, the name Lytchett Matravers sounds strange and exotic. In fact, it's an ordinary but pleasant little village located on minor roads off the A350 and A35. But there's one thing that does make it exotic, and that's the strange phenomenon of the whispering path. On quiet evenings, as you walk along the path to the village church you may hear the muffled sounds of whispered conversations. And even if you stop and listen hard, you still won't be able to make out exactly what's being said.

Quite what causes these hushed conversations has long been a source of debate. Some people suggest it could be ghosts – and point out that the apparition of an old lady was seen inside the church in the spring of 1915. A tenuous link, perhaps, unless the woman was a notorious gossip, and the jury's still out on exactly whose ghost she was anyway. Another favourite explanation for paranormal phenomena in that part of the world is to blame it on faerie folk: It's a place, they say, where the veil is thin between the human world and that of supernatural beings.

As for the real explanation: Who knows? That's why it's in a chapter with the word 'mysteries' in the title.

The Floating Island

It sounded like the kind of story that locals tell in the pub to make fun of tourists, so the first couple of times people told me about a floating island in Derwent Water, we smiled and nodded but refused to believe them. An island that rises above the water every few years in late summer, then sinks beneath the surface to reappear . . . who knows when? How gullible do they think we townies are? But by the third retelling of the story, we felt some research was clearly in order. The little Victorian museum at Keswick confirmed the tale and even displayed a photograph of a woman planting the Union Jack on the land. An 1888 book by G.F. Symons entitled, intuitively enough, *The Floating Island in Derwentwater*, showed a map of where the island had appeared in 1884. In 2005, the mysterious piece of land appeared again.

In July of that year there was an odd-shaped island at the Lodore end that had not been there in the spring. The water level was too high for this to be an underwater hill that is revealed only during droughts. It was a bona fide island covered with reeds and vegetation. But it sat not on the lake bed, but on the lake itself. And it was clearly worth an investigation.

You can't build a bridge to an island that keeps sinking beneath the surface, so your only recourse is to rent a canoe at the Lodore Boat Landing Stage and paddle out. What you land on is the boggiest bit of land in Cumbria (and that's saying something). Covered with the kind of matted green vegetation you see in fish tanks, this island is often barely above water level. Back in July 2005, there was mud and there were stones and sticks on the land, but it had the feeling of being very fragile, almost as if it was just a tangle of weeds. With every step, the land seemed to sink a little, but that may just have been the feeling of feet sinking into the mud.

The place felt ethereal, and over the hundreds of

years that it's been floating and sinking beneath the surface, no doubt many people have come to think of it as truly magical. Of course, by the Victorian era, science had come along and spoiled it all by explaining the phenomenon. The only thing keeping this island afloat is pockets of methane gas trapped underneath it. The gas builds up when vegetation rots, something that happens rapidly during very hot weather, and this accounts for its usual re-appearance in late summer. The island is really just a flap of mud and vegetation that's partly rooted to the lake bed, yet something about its composition allows the gas to accumulate in such volume that it eventually lifts the land to the surface. Over the space of a few weeks, the methane seeps out and dissipates, removing the buoyancy and leaving the land to sink under its own weight back to the bottom of the lake. The longest stint the island has had above water was back in 1831, when it appeared on 10 June and lasted right through to 24 September.

The next time we visited, there was no trace of a floating island at all. But, we did notice one thing: Whenever we spoke about it, the tourists smiled politely and nodded, and clearly didn't believe a word.

The Ley of the Land

Of all the ancient mysteries that criss-cross England, the most modern is the ley line. Leys are what you get when you play join-the-dots with a few ancient monuments (such as Stonehenge, the ancient village of Old Sarum and the hillfort of Clearbury Ring) and get a straight line. Some go further and say that these lines must once have been trade routes. Others go yet further still and say that the lines are actually seats of some strange energy that the ancients were somehow able to tap into. People who use dowsing rods or crystals seem to find they move in significant ways at stone circles and prehistoric mounds such as Avebury, Silbury Hill and Glastonbury. There must be some kind of energy to cause this movement, they reason.

But ley lines may not be quite as mysterious as believers make out. For one thing, they are not part of an ancient tradition. The term ley lines first appeared in print less than a century ago, in a 1925 book *The Old Straight Track* by a Herefordshire businessman and amateur archaeologist, Alfred Watkins. The ideas in his book were foreshadowed by a speech made fifty years earlier by William Henry Black to the British Archaeological Society.

In his book, Watkins spoke persuasively about the alignment of natural and manmade landmarks: 'Imagine a fairy chain stretched from mountain peak to mountain peak, as far as the eye could reach, and paid out until it reached the high places of the earth at a number of ridges, banks and knowls. Then visualise a mound, circular earthwork or clump of trees planted on these high points, and in low points in the valley other mounds ringed around with water to be seen from a distance. Then great standing stones brought to mark the way at intervals, and on a bank leading up to a mountain ridge or down to a ford the track cut deep so as to form a

Some say that these lines must once have been trade routes. Others say that the lines are actually seats of some strange energy that the ancients were somehow able to tap into.

guiding notch on the skyline as you come up . . . All these works exactly on the sighting line.'

Watkins believed these straight tracks were prehistoric trade routes, and were associated with gods of communication from many traditions, including the Greek Hermes, the Roman Mercury, the Norse Woden and the Celtic god Tout or Toutates. That's about as far as Watkins went in his analysis, but after his death several other people went a lot further. The first mention of ley lines as trails of mysterious earth energy appeared in a novel called *The Goat-Foot God* by Dion Fortune. However, an occult-themed novel is not a great place to launch a serious theory about archaeology and geology, especially when the people who adopted the theory used strange instruments such as dowsing rods to track them.

As a result, serious students of archaeology almost universally dismiss ley lines. In his book *Rings of Stone*, the prolific Aubrey Burl remarks that the ley that runs for six miles between Stonehenge and Old Sarum, and extends a further five to the Iron Age hillfort of Clearbury Ring is 'a remarkable alignment'. He adds, however, that as a trade route it's a disaster. 'Within eleven miles, it crossed four rivers, three times unnecessarily, slurped through a mile of primeval swamp, and then waded across another river. As a line it does not exist. Its south end misses Clearbury Ring by a full two hundred metres.'

So among the experts, ley lines have been transformed into battle lines, drawn up between the pro and the con parties. Yet whether you dowse your way along these lines or not, it's pretty hard simply to ignore them.

Some sorry souls live in a world that is increasingly filled with off-the-shelf architecture, recycled entertainment, and soulless chain stores. Even the televised world they look at is populated by prefabricated characters with cut-and-paste dialogue. It's a world slapped together quickly and efficiently and with the single goal of getting things done, so that its designers can move on to the next project.

Thank goodness that the rest of us live in the *real* world, the wide *weird* world with its infinite shades of nuance and variety. The people of this world are well-defined, each a little different from each other, and completely different from what the unimaginative would call societal norms.

Some of England's fabled people are characters as mythic as the Argonauts. The off-the-grid places they inhabit are woven from the same fabric as ancient Troy – but they are woven in a one-of-a-kind English pattern. One thing's for sure: the tales they spawn have a long history, a distinctly English flavour and, if there is any justice in the world, a lengthy future.

Fabled People and Places

Strange Creatures

In Tibetan Buddhist mysticism, there's a peculiar belief that, with enough concentration and meditation, it's possible to conjure a creature out of pure imagination. These entities are called *tulpas*, and usually manifest themselves from deep within the consciousness of a lone traveller. Depending on what's in the mind of that lonely person, a *tulpa* could be either pleasant or unpleasant, friendly or malign. But no matter how it starts out, a *tulpa* has a mind of its own and can change itself into something completely different from its original form. Parents and creative writers know exactly what this is all about.

So what does this have to do with the weirdness of England? Well, it's the most convincing explanation we can drum up for some of the strange creatures that romp through the streets, moors and fens of old Albion. There are other explanations, of course, and you can believe what you want. But, no matter what we think of these tales, they're out of our hands now, and who knows what they will evolve into over the years to come?

Spring-Heeled Jack

If you called on the combined imaginations of the entire staff of Marvel Comics to create a supervillain, threw in a dose of the 1984 horror film *Nightmare on Elm Street* and set the whole thing in England in the early Victorian era, you may well come up with a story about Spring-Heeled Jack.

But you don't need to go to all that effort, because Victorian England has done all the work for you. Depending on which sources you read, Jack was either a high-society prankster who would do anything for a bet, or a fiendish devil-shaped creature that breathed fire, ripped women's clothes apart with steel talons and defied gravity.

The creature who eventually earned the name Spring-Heeled Jack was first seen in 1837 leaping over nine- and ten-foot high walls and running up buildings. He bounced in front of carriages, causing them to crash, then vanished without trace. And he scared young women out of their wits. The reports all describe a very tall man, dressed in a black cape, with bulging eyes that seemed to glow, and a long pointed nose. He carried or wore something sharp and metallic in his hand. And though his attacks were devastatingly scary, they seldom inflicted serious injury.

The attacks began in south London on Barnes Common and Clapham Common, but by October 1837, reports had come in from as far afield as Richmond, Teddington, Twickenham, Uxbridge, Camberwell and Tooting. The attacks left young women with their clothes torn and their bodies sometimes bruised from manhandling, but rarely physically harmed. Nevertheless, as the attacker ran off cackling dementedly, the victims were often scared to the point of psychological damage and from then on subject to fits and acute phobias.

Naturally, these activities created a pervasive atmosphere of fear, so much so that the Lord Mayor of London felt the need to address the situation publicly in January 1838. His statement lay the blame for the attacks squarely on the shoulders of 'a mischievous and foolhardy companion' of a group of rich buffoons, who had dared him to dress up and scare people. Many people believed that the mayor's description was a veiled reference to the riotous young Marquis of Waterford – a misogynistic hell-raiser with no concept of self-control who was well known for taking dares.

Following the mayor's statement, servant girls all the way from Hammersmith to Brixton came forward to speak of similar 'wicked pranks' that had scared some people literally to death. The newspapers began calling the attacker Spring-Heeled Jack, a name that had appeared in Sheffield newspapers thirty years earlier, referring to a hedge-lurking creature also known as the Park Ghost. It's entirely possible that the name was a corruption of the much older word *springald*, meaning youngster. Yet, after 1838, Spring-Heeled Jack meant just one thing: a supernatural attacker capable of leaping over buildings in a single bound.

The attacks came thick and fast, and became more violent; in the early months of 1838, an eighteen-year-old girl named Lucy Scales was blinded by a devil breathing blue fire at her as she walked home from her brother's place in Limehouse, in the East End of London. Two days later, another eighteen-year-old, Jane Alsop, was disturbed in her Lambeth home by a man claiming to be a policeman knocking on her door; he asked for a light and claimed to have trapped Spring-Heeled Jack down a nearby alley. Jane brought out a candle, and saw that the copper was actually Jack himself. He spat a blue and white flame at her and grabbed her hair, but she was dragged to safety by her sisters. More incidents followed, featuring what a witness described as 'an orange-eyed man with metal talons'.

The police never did find the culprit, and the attacks tailed off, but Jack found a new life in penny dreadfuls, the cheap pulp fiction that was a precursor to today's comic books. He featured in two separate series, once as a villain, and then in the 1870s as a flawed hero dressed in a skintight red suit, with a mane, bat wings and horns – in short, a combination of Spiderman and all of the X-Men. After his adventures appeared in print, he would periodically reappear in person all over the country. In 1877, he was seen running over roofs in Norfolk, Lincolnshire, and also at Aldershot army barracks, where he spat fire into a sentry's face and leaped clear over the soldier's colleagues in arms. He was apparently shot at least twice and suffered no ill effects. Even the first Whitechapel murders in the 1880s were attributed to Spring-Heeled Jack, until the newspapers attributed these to a new, more deadly, menace: Jack the Ripper.

Although Spring-Heeled Jack attacks tailed off, you will still catch the occasional mysterious prowler story that sounds familiar. According to some reporting in MysteryMag.com, he resurfaced in the Attercliffe district of Sheffield in the 1970s. Several residents of Westbury Street were attacked in the dead of night by a red-eyed man at least six feet six inches tall, who was later seen leaping great distances to escape capture. Also, a night prowler who sounded suspiciously like Spring-Heeled Jack was chased by police into the nearby yard of Dexel Tyres, from where he simply vanished. That was the last of the Sheffield sightings.

However, we suspect that this particular tale won't end there. As long as there are red-eyed night creatures leaping incredible distances – or people convinced they have seen them – there will always be a Spring-Heeled Jack. And we'll be waiting for him.

Pig Woman

'This Pig-woman do I know'
– *from* Bartholomew Fair *by Ben Jonson*

Of all the bizarre characters of Victorian folklore, the Pig Woman stands apart from the rest. For one thing, we can trace the origins of her tale back over 400 years to a sixteenth-century fair held near London's oldest hospital, St Bartholomew's. The very name Pig Woman is enough to conjure tales of mystery and horror, and it seems that that is exactly what has happened.

There was a rash of pig-woman tales in London in 1814, in which breathless witnesses spoke of seeing a pig's head within a darkened carriage silhouetted by the flickering light of the gas-powered streetlights. Some even claimed to have seen a snout emerge from a carriage window. These stories appeared on the letters page of newspapers about this time, and there was some talk that the woman in question was the daughter of an upper-class family of fashionable Manchester Square in the West End.

Also in London in the early nineteenth century, a number of side-shows at St Bartholomew's Fair would tout the Pig Woman as an attraction, usually a cruel scam involving a shaved bear dressed in women's clothing, doped up to prevent any violent outbursts. Such degrading shows were not unusual in the fairs of the time, which should come as no surprise to anyone who's read the true tale of Joseph Carey Merrick or seen David Lynch's retelling of his life story in the 1980 film *The Elephant Man*.

However, even this was not the first mention in popular culture of a mysterious Pig Woman. The most celebrated goes back to the time of Shakespeare and possibly earlier. Travel opportunities were limited to most people at the time, the only exception being at fair time, when revellers would flock to the festivities at the Priory Church of Bartholomew the Great in Smithfield. This fair was centuries old by Shakespeare's time, and spawned a five-act comedy called *Bartholomew Fair* by the Bard's contemporary, Ben Jonson.

Ursula is one of *Bartholomew Fair*'s villainous characters, and is referred to as the Pig Woman, not only because of her appearance but because of her stall selling roast pork. With the catchy marketing slogan 'Here be the best pigs, and she does roast them as well as ever she did', Ursula's stall openly sold tobacco and liquor, but in private housed a gambling den and brothel. Ursula's character is a cheat who bulks up the tobacco she sells by mixing it with a plentiful herb called Colt's Foot, served short measures of beer and generally bilked her customers. Nevertheless, the roast pork at 'Lady' Ursula's stall was very popular at the market. Not only was it tasty, it was rumoured to have beneficial properties: pregnant women would be encouraged to eat from her stall if they wished to deliver healthy babies, even though Ursula was a shady character whose establishment violated at least two of the Ten Commandments, and probably more. As with Shakespeare's plays, Jonson's comedy drew on widely circulated stories of the time.

It's not hard to see how wilder folk tales might evolve from such ordinary beginnings. A little-travelled class of illiterate country folk, or even insular townspeople on their annual trip to the big fair, would swap cautionary tales about the wicked Pig Woman. Some would mention that they'd seen a play about her, so the stories must be true. Children would overhear adult talk about the wicked goings-on at her stall, but would not understand what it was all about. Over hundreds of years of retelling, the potent mixture of her evocative name and tales of her wickedness could easily transfigure her from a dishonest cook and madam to a disfigured supernatural creature. Yet, as with all good folk tales, it's best to maintain an element of mystery.

Lantern Man

People who live near fens tend to avoid roaming around at night. There are simply too many tales of people wandering off track and being found dead from drowning or asphyxiation the next day. People sometimes blame the demon drink for impairing people's judgment, while on other occasions there has been a strong suspicion that marsh gases make people light-headed and lose consciousness. However in Norfolk, it's not a Will o' the Wisp or flash of methane or too much drink that leads folk to their deaths. In tales told around Thurlton and Horning and other towns on the River Yare, a malign entity known as the Lantern Man is held responsible.

People have been writing about the Lantern Man since the nineteenth century, and have probably been talking about him for much longer. Understandably, he's acquired quite a reputation in that time. He will follow people along paths at night, a flickering light marking his progress. In the days when people travelled on horseback, the Lantern Man would knock you off your horse if he caught up with you. And he follows sound. People with more presence of mind than we'd have under the circumstances have even conducted experiments on this mysterious figure. One person would stay silent while the other stood apart and whistled. The light would move towards the noise. And if you mock the Lantern Man, or especially if you call him Jack o' Lantern, he will follow you home and kill you if he can.

That's what they say happened to an unfortunate boatman from Thurlton in the summer of 1809. Joseph Bexfield plied his trade along the River Yare between Norwich and Yarmouth, and would often tie up for the night halfway between the two towns. On 11 August, his corpse was discovered on the riverbank between Reedham and Breyden; he had been missing for days. On the last night he had been seen alive, he left the White Horse pub in Thurlton Staithe after an evening pint and made his way across the marsh to pick up something from his boat. He dismissed a casual comment from one of his fellows to watch out for the Lantern Man, and that, they claim, sealed his fate.

Whether the Lantern Man is a bogeyman dreamed up to warn people of the dangers of walking through marshes, a variation on a classic folk fiction, or merely boatmen's superstition, we can't say. But whatever he is, we won't be tempting him anytime soon.

The Owlman of Mawnan

Unlike many strange entities, the Owlman seems to have sprung into existence quite recently and is traceable to the researches of only one person – a character known to the world of weird watchers as Tony 'Doc' Shiels. Doc swooped into the Cornish seaside town of Mawnan in 1976 after hearing the bizarre tale of a Lancashire family that had spent their Easter holiday there that year. The Melling family's two daughters, nine- and twelve-years-old, had been so scared by what they saw hovering over Mawnan's church tower, their father Don cut the holiday short and returned to Preston. The girls claimed to have witnessed a huge feathered creature which looked like a man flapping enormous wings to keep himself aloft.

As Shiels continued his investigation, in July 1976 two girls in their early teens approached him with further tales of the beast. Shiels was somewhat sceptical, so he separated them and had them draw the creature and make independent notes about the sighting. The two renditions were similar enough to be from the same source, but in his opinion different enough to prove that there was no hoax involved. The creature the girls described was as big as a man, but resembled an owl with pointed horn-like feathers where its ears should be. They saw it at dusk, and in the twilight its feathers looked grey and its eyes appeared to be glowing. Directly after being spotted, it flew off into the trees, and the girls saw its feet, which had black claws like pincers.

The creature the girls described was as big as a man, but resembled an owl with pointed horn-like feathers where its ears should be.

The sightings continued over the next few years, with Doc Shiels fielding calls from many witnesses once he'd been identified in the media as an expert on the creature. A typical report originated from three foreign students from a local college – also girls in their teens – who told their landlady about something furry and birdlike out by Helford River near Grebe Beach, which lies in the shadow of the old church. The girls' landlady told Shiels about it.

About the only detailed sighting that Doc Shiels did not investigate came from a source interviewed by another researcher, Jonathan Downes. At 9.30 p.m. one evening in 1989, a young couple was walking around the edge of the woods, shining their torches high into the conifers. They saw a winged creature about five feet in height, perched on a branch about fifteen feet off the ground. Two large black claws were visible over the edge of the branch, and it had wings held slightly out. The light startled the creature, which backed away, folding up its legs and wings as it went.

Sightings of the creature continued well into the 1990s, though it's hard to get locals to speak about the subject. If you ever go to that part of Cornwall, the only people talking about the Owlman are tourists who have read about the creature. If the locals know anything, their Cornish reserve means they are unlikely to share it with the rest of us. As a result, some bludgeoning investigators assume that there's no story here, and accuse Doc Shiels of making it all up. They point out that a lot of the Owlman's details match the story of a creature that appeared in West Virginia in the 1960s (later featured in the 2002 film *The Mothman Prophecies*). Does this mean that the whole story is suspect? Maybe, maybe not. We're certainly keeping our files open until somebody reliable captures the thing on film. Owlman Chronicles, anyone?

The Highgate Vampire

Highgate is a few miles north of central London, but since the little village took on an overspill of Great Plague victims in 1665, it has gradually become the dead centre of the city. So it's hardly surprising that it now houses one of the most celebrated Victorian cemeteries in the world.

With such a rich history, it was only a matter of time before Highgate spawned tales of some horror from beyond the grave. And in the late 1960s, the area around Highgate Cemetery saw the first public appearances of the Highgate Vampire.

The vampire tale began with reports of a tall dark figure with hypnotic red eyes walking around Swains Lane and through the cemetery. Once the story had appeared in the newspaper, many people came forward with their own sightings, some going back years. Within months, sightings and reports of mutilated foxes gave rise to hysterical tales of a fiend luring young women out

by night to drink their blood. Reports of satanic rituals in the cemetery provided another possible explanation for the sightings. But the end result was the same: mobs with crudely fashioned stakes patrolled the cemetery looking for a scrap, and vandalism at the old burial ground was at an all-time high.

The sightings tailed off as the hype burgeoned and rival groups of investigators got into verbal battles about what the apparition really was. One group, the British Occult Society, led by a flamboyant raconteur called Sean Manchester, was convinced that this was a traditional blood-sucking creature that could only be stopped by being staked through the heart. (Remember, this was the heyday of Hammer Horror movies, many of which were filmed in Highgate Cemetery.) Another group, albeit with a similar name, the British Psychic and Occult Society, was more interested in gathering evidence than drawing any definite conclusions as to what this thing was.

Nevertheless, both groups agreed that this was an evil entity that needed to be exorcised for the public's safety. So, they performed various rituals to purify the area, including bricking up suspicious crypts using cement mixed with garlic. Of course, messing with anything on sanctified ground is a serious criminal offence, so activities of this kind were bound to attract a strong police presence. They eventually led to the arrest of David Farrant of the British Psychic and Occult Society, even though it was the other group's leader, Manchester, who claimed to have staked the vampire. Manchester made this claim in a self-published book called *The Highgate Vampire*, emphasising that he did this only after it had turned into a giant spider before his eyes. This reeks a little too much of gothic fiction for our taste, but it goes to show how extravagant these tales had become by the mid-1970s.

Interview with a Vampire Hunter

By David Farrant

Towards the end of 1969, the British Psychic and Occult Society arranged an investigation into the Highgate Cemetery affair. It was decided that a continuous nightly vigil would take place at the cemetery, two society members at a time being stationed at the two places where the apparition was said to have appeared; cameras and tape recorders would be set up, because we considered gathering evidence to be of greater importance than any attempt to make direct psychic contact.

Exploration and photographs taken in the cemetery confirmed beyond doubt that satanic masses had been taking place there. Furthermore, it became apparent that these rites had been conducted with great professionalism, some taking place in the maze of catacombs beneath the cemetery. One particular tomb hidden deep within the heart of the cemetery, a small mausoleum which contained no coffins, had been converted into a small temple, and, judging from the inverted pentagram and magical symbols inscribed on the marble floor and walls, it was in regular use. More significant still, the magical signs and symbols used could only be applicable in a rite performed by the highest of adepts in calling forth an entity to the earthly plane.

Just two weeks after the investigation had started, watchers spotted the entity on two separate nights. On the first occasion, it appeared behind two society members on watch; swinging round, they both saw the entity hovering behind them. Abruptly, it disappeared. Two other members saw it through the top gate on Swain's Lane [sic] on their way to keep the nightly vigil. On neither occasion, however, did the entity appear for more than a couple of seconds.

The satanic group using Highgate Cemetery didn't take kindly to having their activities exposed to the public view. The weeks that followed brought a spate of letters to the society threatening 'disastrous consequences'. A typical letter read:

'By your interference with the work of our High Order, you have invoked the wrath of Lord Hadit. By His element and the power of the Seven-Fold Cross, you shall now be destroyed. This is decreed by His Grace, and this wish will be fulfilled through our Order. Be it thus so.'

The letters were signed in blood and adorned with satanic symbols. There was no doubt that the sender or senders of these letters were genuine satanists.

By this stage, public interest in the Highgate Cemetery affair had attracted the interest of Independent Television (ITV). I walked through the cemetery with ITV's film crew and interviewer Sandra Harris, and saw a vandalised coffin lying in the middle of a pathway. Its lid had been ripped off, and the skeleton inside was clearly visible. When the film crew began filming outside the top gate, the cameraman suddenly clutched his throat and passed out. Filming had to be postponed until a replacement took over. Sandra Harris was visibly shaken.

During the interview I took great care to avoid the word vampire, not wishing to fuel speculation that the reputed entity might be a bloodsucker. But when the show aired on Friday, 13 March 1970, hundreds of people besieged the cemetery, including groups of hooligans carrying beer cans and makeshift weapons. *The London Evening News* mistakenly reported that somebody heard 'David Farrant, 24, speak of his plans to stake the vampire through the heart with a wooden cross', which irrevocably branded me as the main instigator of this mass vampire hunt, and a man who quite literally believed in the existence of bloodsucking vampires.

For about twenty years, things remained quiet on the vampire front in Highgate. But in the early 1990s, David Farrant published his account of the big scare in *Beyond the Highgate Vampire*. Several other books followed on both sides of the Atlantic, and in 1997 a group of local historians set up the Highgate Vampire Society to act as a repository of all information about the entity.

With this renewed interest came renewed sightings, even though it is now considerably harder to gain access to the cemetery as it is open only to small groups on guided tours during daylight hours. Whether or not we believe in the supernatural, we must now accept that the tale of the Highgate Vampire is taking off again. Though what exactly this vampire is we may never know.

Letters to the Editor

Early in his investigation, David Farrant wrote a request for information on the Highgate ghost in a letter to *The Hampstead and Highgate Express (Ham and High)*. Here are two of many responses:

My fiancée and I spotted a most unusual form about a year ago. It just seemed to glide across the path. Although we waited a little while, it did not reappear again. I am glad someone else has spotted it; I was convinced it was not my imagination.
– *Miss Audrey Connely (Ham and High, 13 February 1970)*

A figure such as that seen by readers does haunt Highgate Cemetery. I caught sight of it while I was walking around the cemetery. Suddenly, from the corner of my eye, I saw something move and immediately looked around to see a form moving behind some gravestones. My first reaction was that it was somebody mucking about but looking back it seems strange that the thing made no sound and seemed to disappear into nowhere.
– *D. Winbourne (Ham and High, 20 February 1970)*

The Vampire of Kirklees

She laid the blood-irons to Robin Hood's vaine,
Alacke, the more pitye!
And pearct the vaine, and let out the bloode,
That full red was to see.

And first it bled, the thicke, thicke bloode,
And afterwards the thinne,
And well then wist good Robin Hoode,
Treason there was within.

– *Anon,* The Death of Robin Hood, *(1400–1700)*

Most people dimly remember the story of Robin Hood shooting an arrow as he died and asking to be buried where the arrow fell. Fewer people know that this took place in the ground of Kirklees Priory, about a mile east of Brighouse in West Yorkshire. Fewer people still are aware that it was Robin's cousin, the Prioress of Kirklees, who killed him.

Robin went to the prioress for medical care, and she ostensibly opened a vein to bleed him – a common medical practice up to the nineteenth century. But the prioress was in league with Robin's arch-enemy. (Not the Sheriff of Nottingham, silly; this is Yorkshire Robin Hood lore, and the villain of this piece is 'Red' Sir Roger of Doncaster.) The prioress left Robin to bleed to death, and it was probably this gore-fest that gave rise to the legend that the prioress was a vampire. Whatever the actual origin of the story, people say that the grave of Robin Hood is haunted by a female apparition dressed in grey.

All this is hard to investigate. For one thing, the land where Robin's grave stands has been

a woman in medieval clothes moving towards him, making no noise as she floated over the dry leaves and twigs beneath her. Ten years later, the young man made another trip to the site and saw a pale slim woman in an off-white garment, staring with an expression of malevolent rage on her face. In the late 1980s, people visiting the grave found a number of holes the width of fingers in the ground nearby, along with animal corpses that had apparently been bled to death. Another report, which was published in the *Brighouse Echo* just after Halloween in 1995, told of a floating grey woman, 'her black nun's robes flapping eerily while her eyes flashed red and venomous and her teeth bared sharp and white between snarling blood-red lips'.

Some say that various rituals have exorcised the vampire at Kirklees. Others say that the whole thing is a case of an overactive imagination. We can't say one way or another. And we're certainly not going to traipse over Armytage land by night to find out.

the private property of the Armytage family for more than 500 years, and although the family conducts pre-arranged tours of the grave, they are understandably reluctant to have swarms of vampire hunters traipsing around. Also, vampire sites tend to attract the most sensational stories and storytellers, and when you're overwhelmed with tales of distributing garlic and holy water around the grounds, of Wiccan rituals and rites of exorcism, it's hard to get to the root of the matter.

Suffice it to say that all the various tales of Robin Hood agree that he met his end in the grounds of Kirklees Priory in the early thirteenth century. Although the priory itself was destroyed in 1538, during Henry VIII's dissolution of the monasteries, a grave marker in the grounds that dates from the eighteenth century marks Hood's traditional burial site. It is said that, in 1706, Sir Samuel Armytage and his friend, Robert Barr, tried to dig up the grave after a night of drinking. When they got about a yard down something frightened them out of their wits and they ran away.

This is just one of the many tales that surround the site, all of which speak of a deep dread rather than an exciting frisson of spookiness. One autumn in the early 1960s, a teenager from nearby Huddersfield saw

Still Waters Run Deep

Never underestimate the power of water. Pools, springs, waterfalls and wells have been revered for centuries as places with a peculiar magic, hence the strange and almost worldwide custom of making a wish at a well. Yet other legends surround bodies of water. One famous place of legend is the Bottomless Pool – a place that goes to the very core of the earth and contains strange monsters or mermaids, which surface only at certain magical times.

There are dozens, probably hundreds of pools that legend would have us believe are so deep that they are connected to the sea (possibly right on the other side of the world in Botany Bay). From just spending a little time in the Midlands, I heard precisely that story being told of Black Mere near Leek in Staffordshire, and also of Wasson Pool in Handsworth near Birmingham, both places being about as far from the sea as anywhere in England could be.

Beyond these tall tales, there are two particularly noteworthy legends of people getting into deep water around deep water – those of the Peak District's Kinder Scout plateau and Bodmin Moor's Dozmary Pool.

inder Scout

When you combine desolate hiking country with water that seems to defy gravity, you know that strange legends will follow. Kinder Scout is a moorland plateau near Edale village and marks the highest point in Derbyshire. The Kinder river cascades down the gritstone crags beneath the plateau in the delightfully named Kinder Downfall. But when the wind whips up the rock around the Downfall something strange happens. For one thing, the water breaks up into tiny droplets of mist that rise to form a plume that can be seen from miles around. And for another, the waterfall appears to run backwards up to the top of the plateau.

You can't beat mist and apparent defiance of the laws of physics to make a place seem supernatural, so it's no surprise that many strange legends have cropped up about the place. Below Kinder Downfall lies Mermaid Pool, where a creature lurks, although it is seldom seen. Some legends state that if you go to the pool on Easter Day, she will appear and do one of several things: she may grant you a long life, possibly eternal life; she may grant you anything you wish for; or she may drag you beneath the surface, never to be seen or heard of again. People also believe that the pool is either completely bottomless or linked by a tunnel to the ocean, which is why the mermaid is so elusive.

Kinder Scout is also the epicentre of a sort of inland Bermuda Triangle, where planes crash or disappear in mysterious circumstances. According to some reports, including a lengthy analysis by Dr David Clarke and Martin Jeffrey in MysteryMag.com, more than fifty aircraft have gone down in the area since the end of World War Two, and the moors around are littered with aircraft debris. The most celebrated crash took place in July 1954, when two Sabre planes collided and went down nearby on Bleaklow Hill. In June 1993, a Hawker Hunter jet disappeared from radar over the Kinder Scout plateau and smashed into the moors, throwing its pilot from the wreckage into the boggy moor where he presumably sank – his body was never found. There have even been tales of UFOs crashing out there. One thing is for sure – local people often hear planes going down, and they're quite prepared to believe that they are phantom aircraft. Hikers in the area frequently speak of being spooked by the place, though few can explain why.

But you don't have to explain anything in a local legend. Sometimes, it's enough to present the story, then step back to let the details sink in. Brush it off and dismiss it if you wish. But when you're actually hiking in the area, we doubt it will be quite that easy.

Dozmary Pool

South of the town of Bolventor in Cornwall, out in the bleak and legend-laden Bodmin Moor, you can find the deep and creepy Dozmary Pool. It's not too far from the Jamaica Inn of Daphne du Maurier fame, and sits off a narrow potholed road that's signposted from the A30. It looks every bit the classic bottomless pool. The fact that it stands on high ground and is not fed or drained by any stream gave rise to the legend that it was connected directly to the sea. In the sixteenth century, a poem by Richard Carew described the mysterious site this way:

> *Dosmery Pool amid the moores,*
> *On top stands of a hill;*
> *More than a mile about, no streams*
> *It empt, nor any fill*

Like many deep pools, it has legends of water spirits, but in this case it's not just any water spirit. This being Cornwall and steeped in all things Arthurian, local lore has it that this is the lake where the Lady of the Lake hung out. It is supposed to be where she first gave Excalibur to Arthur, and where Arthur on his deathbed instructed Sir Bedivere to sling the sword. According to accounts by Sir Thomas Malory and Alfred Lord Tennyson (and to the film *Excalibur* with Hywel Bennett and Helen Mirren), when Bedivere threw the sword, an arm clad in glittering samite rose out of the water, caught it, and waved it three times before disappearing beneath the surface.

You can't knock a good story such as that. Unfortunately, you can't substantiate it either. For one

thing, some Arthurian buffs insist that Bedivere did the deed near Glastonbury in Somerset, or at Bosherston in Pembrokeshire, or Llyn Llydaw or Llyn Ogwen in Caernarfonshire or Loe Pool in Cornwall. But Dozmary's as good a place as any to stake its claim as the last resting place of Excalibur. As for its bottomless status, well that's easier to debunk. Nobody seemed interested in plumbing the depths of Dozmary, so its legendary bottomless quality was taken for granted. And, since drought doesn't often strike Bodmin Moor, evidence to the contrary has been scant. Nevertheless, on two occasions, in 1859 and 1976, sustained dry weather drained the pool to its dregs – and showed it not to be oceanically deep.

Some folks who are anxious to hold onto the legend at any cost claim that centuries of silt build-up have shallowed out the pond. But that's missing the point of local legends in general. What matters isn't scientific truth, it's the story itself.

Wellspring of Blood

Of all the wells in the world, the one with the most pagan brownie points is probably the Chalice Well in Glastonbury. Not only does it have the peculiar distinction of being within striking distance of Glastonbury Tor, beloved of Arthurian buffs as the probable site of Avalon, its water is so full of iron oxide that it often looks red. You can't see the discolouration clearly from the well head at the top of the slope, but the two springs that originate a little further down have deposited a deep brown stain over the centuries. Because of this distinctive feature, the place has been venerated for thousands of years.

Of course, when the early Church found an old religious site and a liquid that looked like blood, they easily found a way of bringing it under the Christian umbrella. And that's how it became known as the Chalice Well – the site where Joseph of Arimathea hid the Holy Grail. In the era before Dan Brown's *The Da Vinci Code* muddied the waters, the grail was supposed to be the cup that either held the Blood of Christ or the wine he blessed at the Last Supper. So Glastonbury's rusty-coloured water took on a deep significance to the Christian Church even though it has a much older tradition as a sacred place.

Not every place with a legendary past is necessarily a good place. For every holy well in the kingdom, there's a corresponding gate to hell, isle of the dead or town that was built by the Devil. That's what makes England such a great place – its sense of balance and fair play.

Isle of the Dead

In 1995, Bernard Cornwell's *Warlord Chronicles* introduced a chilling idea to lovers of historical fantasy fiction: an island or peninsula where families could send their sick or dangerously violent relatives to live apart from society. A combination of their mental impairments, volatile temperaments and the island's harsh conditions brought a rapid decline in health and premature death to the unlucky inmates. For this reason, the place was called the Isle of the Dead.

The Isle of the Dead is an evocative throwback to European mythology from long before the Christian era. In broad strokes, it roughly equates to Dante's vision of hell or the Ancient Greek underworld: a forsaken place populated by lost souls. There's nothing in written historical tradition that suggests that it was ever a real place, let alone somewhere we could visit today. But when Cornwell located his Isle of the Dead on the Isle of Portland, many people believed that there was more to the story than a case of fantasy fiction.

The believers reason that all societies find a way to deal with their ill and dangerous members, and before more humane treatments for the mentally ill were introduced, the preferred method was segregation. The problem was how to enforce an exile. To avoid the effort of building asylums and prisons, pragmatic older societies would use natural fortresses to keep the inmates from escaping. And what better place than a rough and craggy island or peninsula, protected by cliffs and sea?

There is no real archaeological evidence to support this idea, but that hasn't stopped it from sticking firmly in the public imagination. Whether or not the Isle of the Dead on the Isle of Portland really was an Iron Age prison and mental institution, it's certainly a possibility. And it's not the only place with that reputation: other candidates are St Michael's Mount in Cornwall and Anglesey in North Wales. In fact, about the only island or peninsula that doesn't have such a morbid reputation is Lindisfarne, probably because it's hard to imagine a place that's both a Holy Island and the Isle of the Dead. As for the other sites, you'll sometimes find people using dowsing equipment around the crags, looking for some reading on the energy within the rocks. When we understand what that's all about, we'll get back to you.

> *The Druids claimed that the Isle of the Dead, wherever it may be, was the haunt of Crob Dhu, the dark crippled God; the Christians said it was the Devil's foothold on Earth. But both agreed that men and women sent across its causeway's walls were lost souls – dead while their bodies still lived, and when their bodies did die the demons and evil spirits would be trapped on the isle so that they could never return to haunt the living.*
>
> — The Winter King: A Novel of Arthur, *Bernard Cornwell* (1996)

Unexplained Phenomena

*There are more things in
heaven and earth, Horatio,
than are dreamt of in
your philosophy.*
— Hamlet (Act I, Scene V)

in *a normal world,* the only lights in the night sky are stars,
registered aircraft and meteors. Jellyfish do not fall from the sky.
Neither do frogs or stones. Crops grow straight upwards, and never
flatten themselves into mysterious patterns overnight. And most
important of all, people do not spontaneously burst into flame.

Yes, that's how things are in a normal world. But this is England
we're talking about. We're not dealing with the normal world here.

The Fort of Weirdness

If fans of unexplained phenomena were to pick a patron saint, they would set up shrines to Charles Hoy Fort. In the early years of the twentieth century, this tireless researcher scoured newspapers and scientific journals for reports of strange weather patterns, mysterious lights in the sky, and any other natural event that seemed outside the mainstream. Initially, his writings appeared in scientific and other respected journals, but he noticed that some phenomena were never covered. Indeed, they were quite unscientifically ignored. From then on, Fort took it upon himself to give these second-class citizens of the natural world a thorough examination, always looking for connections and explanations for what he found – but not always managing to find the explanations.

Though he worked mostly in America, his research often brought him to the reading room of the British Museum. His work generated a lot of interest in England and, as a result, several British Fortean societies and a magazine dedicated to the extraordinary, the *Fortean Times,* were set up. His own writing on the subject filled four books — *The Book of the Damned* (1919), *New Lands* (1923), *Lo!* (1931) and *Wild Talents* (1932).

Fort's real genius was in the way he wrote up his findings. Though it never undermines the serious approach he took to his research, there's a lot of wry humour in his tone (a very English approach for a Yank

to take). And it's not at all surprising that he should poke gentle fun at his subject matter. What other tack can you take when you write about jellyfish falling from the sky?

Here's a small sampling of Fortean phenomena from this sceptred isle, drawn from Fort's numerous books. Hold on to your hats, for there's some serious weirdness ahead.

Bath's Jelly Rain

In *The Book of the Damned*, Fort reported multiple showers of jelly that rained down upon the city of Bath. One spring storm in 1871 deposited 'glutinous drops' over the railway station, and twenty-three summers later the city itself was inundated with a storm of jellyfish, each 'about the size of a shilling', or an inch in diameter.

A local vicar examined samples of the earlier spring storm, and saw them metamorphose into some kind of larvae he described as 'minute worms in filmy envelopes'. A similar event happened on 24 June 1911, at Eton in Buckinghamshire. But to Fort, jelly dropping from the sky wasn't the weird thing; it was the fact that the jelly was concentrated in a small area. Whirlwinds could lift heavy objects and drop them easily enough, but collecting thousands of spheres of goo, concentrating them into a single storm and dropping them onto a town, now that was weird. Fort's verdict: 'Such marksmanship is not attributable to whirlwinds.'

It's raining frogs

In *The Book of the Damned,* Fort reported on a summer storm in 1894 that dropped a rain of small frogs on Wigan in Lancashire. Further research reveals that this was not the reason that the mile-long stretch of road between New Market Street and Meadow Street is called Frog Lane; this name was current at least three years earlier. The only other nod history gave to this event came more than forty years later, when George Orwell almost named his landmark work of sociology *The Toad to Wigan Pier.*

Spontaneous shattering

Drawing on a report in *The Times* of September 1841, Fort reported that the windows of the Charton family home in Sutton Lane, Chiswick, were broken repeatedly. The mansion was surrounded by brick walls that prevented anybody from launching a missile from ground level. No nearby buildings afforded a good shot at the windows, and a police guard did not halt the damage. Fort's tongue-in-cheek verdict: 'Poltergeists.'

Sudden darkness

For ten minutes on 15 April 1904, the broad daylight of Wimbledon was obscured by a sudden darkness that made it impossible to venture outside. The report in *Symons' Meteorological Magazine* stated that the shadow came from a smokeless region with no rain or thunder or fog. A similar thing had been reported some decades earlier in London by a Major J. Herschel in *Nature,* when a darkness descended at 10.30 a.m. on 22 January 1882: 'It was obvious that there was no fog to speak of.'

Lights in the sky

In his book *Lo!* Fort reported on some incidents in Peterborough involving strange lights in the sky. On 23 March, at 5.10 a.m., two police constables in different parts of the city saw a light moving across the sky. Four days later, a reporter in the *Peterborough Advertiser* published an interview with one of the policemen, who described the object as 'somewhat oblong and narrow in shape, carrying a powerful light'. There was some talk of a noise like a motor accompanying the event, but that was not corroborated by either of the witnesses. The story had legs for several months, and spread to the *Daily Mail* by mid-May, but by this stage people were dismissing it as a kite with a lantern tied to it. Something similar happened on 15 May in Northampton at 9.00 p.m., but the police discovered that it was the work of a practical joker who had sent up a balloon on fire. Fort's verdict: 'Flying a kite and lanterns at Peterborough at 5.00 a.m., limiting his audience mostly to milkmen, though maybe a joker, could not have been a very practical joker.'

You're in Deep Trouble

Charles Fort may be dead, but Forteana lives on. Take the strange case of the Leicester semi-detached council house that was invaded by slime. Council housing isn't always in the greatest condition, but the worst sink estate couldn't compare with the Boulter family's semi in Leicester after a peculiar goo began to appear in 1989. It slid down the stairs and collected in pools at the bottom. Pretty soon the stuff was oozing into the furniture and staining the clothing of anybody who stayed in the house long enough. It began to blob up in the goldfish tank and choke the fish. And it kept on coming. Scientists at Leicester University examined the material, and found that it was chemically similar to urine, though clearly not from a human, canine, or feline source. Quite what it was remains a mystery.

A Hunka Hunka Burnin'

There's one mystery I'm asked about more than any other: Spontaneous Human Combustion.
Some cases seem to defy explanation, and leave me with a creepy and very unscientific feeling.
If there's anything more to SHC, I simply don't want to know. — Arthur C. Clarke, 1994

Imagine walking into a room and being assaulted by the acrid smell of smoke. You look around, expecting to see charred ruins on all sides, but the room seems to be mostly intact. But wait . . . there in the corner is a square yard of scorch marks. The floorboards have been burned away, and as you move closer to the gaping hole, another smell reaches your nose — something foul that appears to be emanating from a yellow oil around the charred floorboards. You recoil from the smell, but move closer and, as you do, you see something else, something horrific that makes you want to run from the room. At the end of a charred stump you see what's left of a human foot. You have just walked into the site of one of the most dramatic cases of unexplained phenomena — spontaneous human combustion.

SHC is a favourite subject of both the fans and debunkers of unexplained phenomena. It's been hotly debated since the mid-nineteenth century, when Charles Dickens used it as a plot device to get rid of a dodgy character and ignited a firestorm of controversy among thinkers of the day. On one side of the argument there are people who want their scientific mysteries wrapped up neatly before teatime, and on the other there are two camps: people prepared to entertain outlandish explanations, and people consumed by a primal human fear — of being trapped in a deadly fire.

Victims of this phenomenon are often reduced to ashes, with the torso completely missing and only a leg or arm left intact. The site of the fire is usually very contained — most cases spread no more than a few feet from the body, leaving furnishings, paper and other obviously combustible materials unscathed. It looks as if the victims suddenly grew so unbelievably hot that their bodies vaporised, then quickly cooled down again before a real fire could take hold.

Stories like this send a shiver down the spine, and are all the creepier because of the mystery that surrounds them. What might cause a sudden fire to consume just the person in a room, and leave the rest of the place intact? Fortean analysts have come up with some pretty far-out explanations for these peculiar pyrotechnics. Some, for instance, reckon there's a new subatomic particle called a pyrotron that releases sudden bursts of energy within the human body. It's a clever enough hypothesis, but it falls outside traditional scientific thought — and attracts a strong response from sceptical enquirers.

Sceptics point out that many of the victims are infirm or alcoholic and smoke tobacco, a combination of factors that has always been pretty explosive. And the classic 'stop-drop-and-roll' response to burning clothes, while preventing the spread of fire, could cause victims' bodies to burn all the more fiercely. Many victims are overweight, providing a handy supply of fuel for the fire. It's possible, the naysayers claim, for hot ashes to ignite synthetic fibre clothes, or matchbooks in pockets, and cause a very localised fire. Besides, Charles Dickens featured SHC in a work of fiction, and he had learned early on in his career that the public likes supernatural plot twists.

But even experienced firefighters sometimes find the so-called rational explanation inadequate, and some of them are willing to call such incidents the result of spontaneous human combustion. So why shouldn't the rest of us? One of the foremost writers on the SHC phenomenon, Larry E. Arnold, switched from a career in mechanical engineering to exploring the unexplained, and has taken part in numerous radio and television shows in America and Great Britain. His book *Ablaze! The Mysterious Fires of Spontaneous Human Combustion*, is the best documentary source of these incidents, including many of the cases we're looking at here.

We don't feel there's enough evidence to prove or disprove the claim that the victims burst into flames spontaneously. But one thing's for sure: they all met their ends in horrific ways that we can't explain. Their families and friends — and the firefighters who tried to help them — have our support and sympathy.

Girls on Fire

Most cases attributed to spontaneous human combustion happen to adults and often include alcoholic beverages, perhaps because pure alcohol burns so well (though not so well when it's mixed with water inside the human body). That wasn't the case with an event in Sowerby Bridge in Yorkshire in 1899 — or more accurately, two simultaneous events that happened to two sisters. The story was very well known in the early part of the last century, and was revisited in an article in the *Halifax Evening Courier* on 13 March 1985.

The parents of six-year-old Alice Ann Kirby and her younger sister Amy had divorced, and, as part of the settlement, each parent took one child. Alice Ann lived in Wakefield Road with her father at her grandmother's house, and little Amy lived a mile away with her mother in Hargreaves Terrace. Left alone and asleep one morning in January 1899, Alice Ann was discovered in flames by a neighbour, who quickly wrapped her in a rug to staunch the flames.

Over at Hargreaves Terrace the girls' mother was drawing water from the well when she heard screaming. She rushed back to the house to find Amy in flames. Another witness claimed to have seen plumes of flame a yard high shooting from her head. The mother ran towards Wakefield Road to alert her husband, but only got part of the way before she met a neighbour hurrying over to tell her about Alice Ann. Both girls were taken to the Royal Halifax Infirmary where they died within a day of each other.

Sources at the time didn't mention the term spontaneous human combustion, even though it had been bandied about for almost fifty years by then. But given the youthful innocence of the children, that's not too surprising. In the controversy that raged in Victorian times over SHC, victims were often blamed for their own demise because of their reliance on the demon drink. Clearly, they weren't about to take that approach with these children. So they took the route of tragic coincidence instead.

Blazing Bailey

One of the most dramatic English cases of spontaneous human combustion took place in a derelict building in Auckland Street in Lambeth, south London, in 1967. On 13 September of that year, some early-morning walkers noticed a bright light flickering inside a derelict house. Thinking arson, they called the fire brigade, and at 5.24 a.m. Commander John Stacey and his brigade arrived at the scene.

Larry Arnold interviewed Stacey for his book *Ablaze!* and described what the Lambeth Fire Brigade saw when they entered the derelict building: A man curled up at the bottom of the stairs with a blue flame shooting out blowtorch-style from a four-inch split in his stomach. He was clearly in agony, and, like people undergoing operations in the years before anaesthetics, he was trying

to control the pain by biting down on something — in this case, a wooden post at the bottom of the banister. The flame shooting from him was intensely hot and had burned a hole in the floorboards beneath him, but it was contained in a very small area. He was fully clothed, with only a small area of his clothing singed, and the charring of the floorboards barely extended past the hole.

Clearly, though, there was a risk to the building, so the firefighters emptied several fire extinguishers over the man. But the extinguishers seemed to have no effect and the flame kept on shooting out of his abdomen. By the time the fire was finally extinguished, so was the man's life. The victim turned out to be a local alcoholic named Robert Bailey, who had crashed in the abandoned house after a bender. What happened between then and when the fire brigade arrived is anybody's guess. One thing is for sure, though: the gas and electricity in the building had been turned off and there were no signs of a fire or matches anywhere in the building.

At the inquest, coroner Dr Gavin Thurston was going to list the cause of death as 'asphyxia due to inhalation of fire fumes', but after a closer inspection of the events and body, he was less sure. Eventually he listed the death under 'unknown causes', and that's where the case has remained to this day.

Jeannie as a Lamp

Back in the autumn of 1982, three members of the same family were at home in Edmonton in north London. A 61-year-old woman named Jeannie Saffin was sitting in her kitchen with her father, 82-year-old Jack. Her brother-in-law Donald Carroll was elsewhere in the house.

Out of the corner of his eye, Jack caught sight of a flash of light, and when he turned to his daughter, he saw flames all over her upper body. They were at their most intense around her face and hands. Calling for help, Jack tried to get his daughter to the sink, but by the time his son-in-law appeared flames were pouring out of Jeannie's mouth. Both men tried to douse the fire with pans of water as they waited for emergency services to arrive, but still the flames literally roared from Jeannie's body. This terrible roaring sound features prominently in the subsequent inquest report.

The fire lasted only for a few minutes, but it left third-degree burns on Jeannie's face and hands and a small part of her abdomen, where her hands had been resting. Her nylon cardigan had melted a little, but otherwise her clothes seemed relatively unscathed.

She was whisked off to hospital, where she lapsed into a coma and died a week later. The policemen who investigated the fire could find no cause for it, so the explanation for the cause of death was internal burning caused by inhaling flames. Apparently, the family members wanted the coroner to write down 'spontaneous human combustion', but he refused, remaining unmoved by the brother-in-law's harrowing description of the incident: 'The flames were coming from her mouth like a dragon and they were making a roaring noise.' The coroner put it down to death by misadventure, though death by mystery would have been a better description.

The Boy Stood on the Burning Deck

The strange plight of nineteen-year-old Paul Hayes hit the headlines in 1985. On the night of 25 May, he was walking along a street near his home in Stepney Green, in the East End of London, when he felt an intense heat surrounding his torso. The young computer operator felt as though he had been soaked in petrol and set on fire.

Paul's first instinct was to cover his eyes to protect them and run for help, but he fell down and, in his agony, he pulled his knees up and curled into the foetal position. The heat suddenly switched off, and he found himself lying where he had fallen, with burns over most of his upper torso and head.

He staggered to a nearby hospital where he received treatment, but neither the medical profession nor anybody else has been able to explain what caused the sudden fire.

In each of these cases, only one thing is certain: these strange events deserve to be discussed. Whether you fall into the true-believer camp along with Charles Dickens or remain sceptical — it's your call. We'll just report on the cases with as much detail as we can find, and leave the interpretation up to you.

The Green Children of Woolpit

In general, thirteenth-century tales offer slim pickings for entertainment to the modern audience. But there's one exception from the chronicles of William of Newburgh and a fellow cleric, the Abbot of Coggeshall. It features two children discovered near a Suffolk village during the reign of King Stephen.

The event took place a hundred years before the chronicles were written, so it's unclear how many of the details were embellished, but it goes like this: During the harvest, farm workers from the town of Woolpit found a girl and a boy in the fields. They spoke a language nobody around understood, and wore strange clothes in a style nobody recognised. But the most distinctive thing about them was their skin. It was green.

The mystified workers took the children to the local lord of the manor, Richard de Calne. He couldn't understand the children either, but tried to care for them. They refused all food that was offered to them, except for some green vegetables. The boy died soon afterwards, but the girl survived and eventually learned to speak English. Her skin took on a more English complexion too. But her tale raised more questions than it answered: She came from

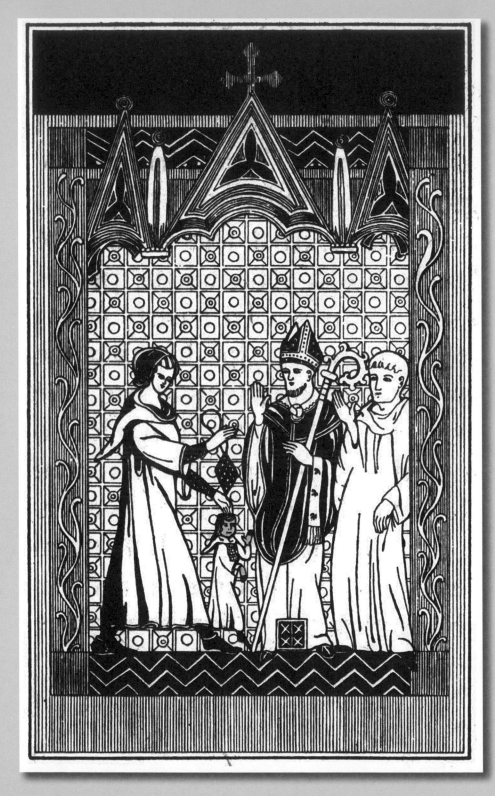

a land where the sun never shone, a place of perpetual twilight she called St Martin's Land. She and her brother were shepherds, and while out in the fields had heard the sound of beautiful music coming from a cave. They abandoned their flock to investigate. They went underground, and emerged into a place of brilliant light, where they curled up in fear and to protect their eyes. It was there that the farm workers discovered them. Nobody could find the tunnel that featured in the girl's story, or any place that resembled this mysterious St Martin's Land. Perhaps she made the whole thing up, or had difficulty expressing details of her past in a language she had only just learned. Whatever the explanation, it's now lost in time. But she could be related to you: she married a man from King's Lynn and lived a long life with him. Nine hundred years later, who knows how many people could claim her as an ancestor?

Farm workers from the town of Woolpit found a girl and a boy in the fields. They spoke a language nobody around understood, and wore strange clothes in a style nobody recognised. But the most distinctive thing about them was their skin. It was green.

Lights! Action!

It seems odd that random flashes of light should so capture the imagination that people in England should give them names. Hurricanes deserve names. Flashing lights don't. And yet they have names . . . many of them. Peg-a-Lantern is one. So is Will the Smith. Not to mention Joan the Wad, the Lantern Man, and Will o'the Wisp. To the erudite, they go by the Latin name *ignis fatuus,* the fool's light. But no matter what name they take, they are moving lights that twinkle and blink out, then seem to reappear a short distance away, as if guiding you off your path. And the fact that they often appear in marshy areas makes this all the more insidious. It's as if they are deliberately trying to lead you into trouble.

Initially, people believed that ghost lights were mischievous or downright evil spirits. Then Sir Isaac Newton came up with another theory: since they appear in marshes, perhaps they are actually plumes of methane coming from decaying organic matter, which spontaneously ignite in the air. It's a nice theory, but it's proved to be a tough one to reproduce in the lab. Another theory is that these lights are caused by something electromagnetic, and this is also hard to pin down. Whatever their cause, ghost lights are very much a reality in many parts of England. And not only in marshland.

In Staffordshire, for example, there are several bogless sites with a history of 'fairy haunts', including the great hiking country of Cauldon Low and the Weaver Hills. Some stone-circle sites are unusually attractive to wandering lights, too. Just over the border in the Derbyshire Peak District, blue lights can sometimes be seen coming from the woods near Harthill Moor and making their way for Robin Hood's Stride by way of the Nine Stones Circle. Castlerigg stone circle in Cumbria is another ancient stone site that experiences low-level flashing lights. All of which prompts the question: Which came first? The stones or the flickering fairy lights?

Incidentally, the laurel for our favourite term for these lights has to go to a Derbyshire expression: the Devil's Bonfires. It's got drama. It's got sound and fury. It's got menace. In fact, it doesn't sound like wisps of light at all.

The Circular Cereal Story

Everybody's seen pictures of amazing geometric patterns in wheat fields, and if they haven't, they can just rent the 2002 movie *Signs* to see plenty of them (along with a lot of other weirdness). Although crop circles appear all over the world, the bulk of them seem to cluster in the chalk land in the old kingdom of Wessex, from Somerset to Sussex. They appear suddenly overnight, or sometimes even in broad daylight. And they consist of grain crops flattened into patterns ranging from simple circles to incredibly complex fractal geometry.

But are crop circles unexplained phenomena? In 1991, Doug Bower and Dave Chorley came clean about their decades-long project of making patterns in crops. Using planks, blueprints and string, they made dozens of crop circles. But Doug and Dave's account doesn't explain the hundreds of other patterns that appear in England and in sixty countries across the world. Or the effect they have on people who step inside them. Many experience nausea and fatigue when standing in the circles. Their hair stands on end and their camera batteries drain. Eyewitnesses see lights or hear buzzing sounds in areas where crop circles appear. Nothing in Doug and Dave's projects could explain that. And besides, crop circles began long before 1987, when they started their work.

One well-known eyewitness account dates back to 1947. While out on the Lincolnshire fens, an 18-year-old labourer named Frederick Smith heard a gentle humming like a swarm of bees which rose to a high-pitched buzz. He passed out, and when he came to he was surrounded by a circle of flattened crops.

Many people believe that a 1678 broadsheet called the 'Mowing Devil of Hertfordshire' is the first document of the phenomenon. A woodcut shows a scythe-wielding demon hacking an oval hole in an oat field near Hemel Hempstead. The legend written next to the picture tells of a quarrel between a farm owner and a hired mower.

Upon the Mower's asking too much, the Farmer swore That the Devil should Mow it rather than He . . . the Crop of Oat . . . next Morning appear'd so neatly mow'd by the Devil or some Infernal Spirit, that no Mortal Man was able to do the like. Also, How the said Oats ly now in the Field, and the Owner has not Power to fetch them away.

It's interesting that the owner of the field was too weak to pick up the oats — this sounds a lot like modern reports of nausea or fatigue when standing in crop circles. When people first see a strange phenomenon, they ascribe it to a supernatural being — fairies, devils, and the like. We now know, for instance, that the dark circles of grass that grandma used to call fairy rings are in fact caused by a root fungus on grass. But the root cause of natural crop circles (as opposed to Doug-and-Dave's) is still a mystery. Whirlwinds, magnetic anomalies from under the earth, electrical storms from the stratosphere — all these have been suggested. The real story? Well, that's still a mystery. But science is working on an answer.

Interview with a Crop Circle Investigator

Many people chronicle and study crop circles. Three researchers who call themselves the BLT Group (John Burke, W.C. Levengood, and Nancy Talbott) have produced peer-reviewed papers for academic journals on the subject. Using field researchers with backgrounds in instrumentation and archaeological research to gather data on site, they analyse the findings. We caught up with one of their researchers, a retired army systems engineer named George Reynolds, and he told us quite a tale of field research in . . . well . . . fields.

Weird England: So what first got you interested in analysing crop circles?

George Reynolds: A friend of mine named John, who was in charge of the handicapped people at a primary school, noticed a big crop circle out there by the hill and told me, 'You've got to see this.'

We pulled up at the top of the hill, right up to the edge of the wheat, walked down the hill and when we got back to the car there it was, eighteen to twenty feet across, right by the car. I said, 'How in the world did we miss that?' and John said, 'We didn't, it wasn't there when we got out.'

I thought we really had something, but I didn't know how to handle it. I knew about the BLT Research group so I called Nancy Talbott, and said I needed some direction. She taught me that you have got to go into the circle and take it apart.

WE: How do you analyse a crop circle properly?

GR: You take crop samples, one foot out, two foot out, four, sixteen, a hundred, in different directions. And you take soil samples. And you send them to a lab for analysis. I take magnetometers to look at the magnetic fields, I take electrostatic meters and radioactivity detectors. You take many, many photographs. I've got a radar detector in my car, and when I got within an eighth of a mile of one crop circle site it started to talk to me: it was going 'Whop whop whop'. The next day, I took the radar detector and hooked it up to a twelve-volt battery

and took it around this place, and everywhere I went the thing was going 'Whop whop whop'.

WE: When Doug Bower and Dave Chorley explained how they made patterns in crops, most people assumed that was it. The whole thing was a hoax or art project.

GR: Crop circles are real, and crop circles are being forged all the time. You do get fakes — I've made my own. There are several ways you can tell a real crop circle from a 'Doug-and-Dave'. When you take it apart, you find that it's not just tramped down in one direction, it's down in three or four different levels, with one layer going east to west, and the one on top of it going north to south. It's not lying down like somebody's tramped it.

When you take a stalk from inside a circle, there's four rings around the stem. We call them nodules. The top ring is bent and it's exploded. Literally blown up. There's three times as much water in the nodule as there is in the stem. Throw it in the microwave for thirty seconds and it'll pop.

WE: What kind of activity could cause that kind of damage to crops?

GR: We don't know. Most people think it's some kind of an energy level that comes down from above.

WE: Couldn't some of the sloppy circles that aren't geometric patterns just be grain growing too high and falling down?

GR: Some farmers laugh at us about the crop circles. They say that as they work the land in their farm equipment, they double-fertilise one little area and it will grow twice

and smaller and smaller, looking like a Mandelbrot series. And they were made in forty minutes in broad daylight.

WE: I've heard tell that people suffering from arthritis get a temporary reprieve inside crop circles, or if they're feeling fine to begin with, they may get headaches and nausea. What could be causing that?

GR: Well, you talk about this physical effect . . . I was down there, all of a sudden from my knee down to my ankle, it went numb, just like I was shot with Novocaine. When Nancy Talbott came along, she knelt down with a camera, and the same thing happened to her. Later that night, every so often Nancy would reach down and touch her leg. She still couldn't feel anything in it.

So I started doing an investigation into magnetic fields. I borrowed a compass that works in the vertical field: the earth's magnetic field is more powerful in the vertical; it comes down at seventy-some degrees. I laid the compass into the crop circle and the compass started to swing like a pendulum. Then it started rotating like a motor. I'd never seen anything like it.

WE: What's it like being in the middle of a crop circle?

GR: There are no insects, no birds, nothing. I had some guy come from the city with his camera, and I told him not to step in the circle — people had trouble with their batteries. He said, 'No, I just charged it last night.' He steps in, and his camera's red light comes on: the battery's dead. So he put the second set in . . . he wouldn't listen to me, he knew everything, he's a smart guy from the city. He stepped inside, and the second battery died on him. That's the kind of thing that happens.

WE: This is a fringe field for a scientist to be working in. Do people outside of the world of crop circles treat you with respect?

GR: I get a lot of lip, but I've learned a lot. You don't argue. If a guy doesn't believe in crop circles, I'll say that's your opinion, I got mine, let's talk about something else.

as much. When the rain falls, that area will get weighed down and collapse. That's their answer to it. So to shut them up, Dr Levengood had me double-fertilise a sample. I got a farmer friend of mine to help. I farmed an area on his land that's twelve-feet wide and 1,200-feet long and fertilised it with the little pellets of nitrogen that farmers use. I laid out two strips. One strip we used the same amount of fertiliser that farmers regularly use. And the other we overfertilised one hundred per cent.

Every two or three days, I'd tramp down circles in both areas. I'd make a ten-foot circle and a two-foot circle, and then I'd alternate them. I noticed certain things happening. After you'd tramped the stuff down, the wheat would try to stand up. And after a couple of days, it would all come up again pointing to the southwest, looking for the sun.

WE: How quickly do the unexplained type of crop circles develop?

GR: There was a pilot flying over Stonehenge taking a bunch of tourists. He shows it to them, and forty minutes or so later he's back again. And this time there's this pattern in a field right next to Stonehenge. You have three arms coming out like this made of circles getting smaller

It's a Bird! It's a Plane! It's . . . a Mystery!

I'm thinking of three little words that people like to say to each other. These words carry a huge weight of expectation, and yet they mean different things to different people. Because of this, they are the source of much excitement, confusion and, sometimes, acute embarrassment. Those words are Unidentified Flying Object. Not since somebody first said 'I love you' have three words caused so much fuss.

Many people associate UFOs with *Close Encounters of the X-Files Kind, The Day the Earth Stood Still* and people in pickup trucks in rural America being whisked off for the kind of medical exams you don't get on the National Health. But there's a centuries-long tradition of strange vessels and lights appearing over Britain, too. A series of thirteenth-century stories tell of a sailing ship floating in the sky that dropped anchor on churches in Gravesend, Bristol and Cloera in Ireland. As occupants of the ship swam down to release the anchor, they were beaten off by the congregation. In some cases, the anchor was left behind and kept in the church or melted down for use in the town. Who knows how that story got started?

Every region in England seems to have its own UFO hotspots. Longdendale between Manchester and Sheffield is one such site. Cannock Chase in Staffordshire is another. In fact almost anywhere else with broads, moors or fells nearby seems to witness a lot of UFO action. But the more information we hear about them, the less certain we are about the whole business. There's a good reason that the first letter in UFO stands for unidentified. We don't know what they are. We're not even sure they actually exist. But that's not going to stop us from listening to people who have seen things they can't explain. And it's certainly not going to stop us from wondering what could be causing them.

A Two-Month Tour

The trouble with most UFO sightings is that they are easy to dismiss. If it's an isolated incident, you can write it off as a hoax, or some kind of natural phenomenon, such as a meteor, ball lightning or reflected light. After World War Two, and especially after the 1970s, science fiction had primed people's imaginations with visions of alien invasion and other mysterious sightings, so the imagination really kicked into play.

That's what makes the sightings of early 1913 so interesting. A strange airship appeared in our air space, and stuck around for more than two months. It was reported on in six British newspapers in cities as widespread as Dover, Liverpool and Hull. The stock theory was that the flying object was a German airship, which makes sense only if you knew nothing about Zeppelins or European geography. A turn-of-the-century Zeppelin could make it from Germany to southern and eastern English port towns easily enough, but Liverpool and Portsmouth? That's pushing it. Besides, the Germans denied any involvement and this was before any inkling of war between Germany and England.

It all began on 6 January, when *The Times* reported some kind of airship heading towards Dover. Eleven days later the scene had shifted to Glamorganshire, where a large flying object 'much larger than the Willows airship' and trailing a dense cloud of smoke appeared to Chief Constable Captain Lindsay. It quickly vanished.

By the end of January, the *London Evening Standard* had compiled a list of towns where the strange craft had been sighted, and it included Dover and Chatham (4 January), Yarmouth (15 January) and finally Liverpool and Aberystwyth (25 January). It seemed to spend a long time in Wales, where most of the detailed reports of its night-time activity came from. During its first month in England, the craft appeared both by day and by night, and at night shone a piercing light that sometimes swung skywards and sometimes illuminated the land far in front of it. It travelled at an estimated twenty to thirty miles an hour.

After 5 February, the sightings suddenly stopped. For more than two weeks, there was no sign of the airship and no whiff of explanation. Then, at around 10.00 p.m.

on 21 February, luminous objects were reported over both Yorkshire and Warwickshire, much farther inland than any of the other sightings. Over the remainder of the month a flurry of sightings took place, stretching from Portsmouth to Hull, and from Ipswich to Hornsea, each time appearing at night and always shining brilliantly.

At the end of February the ship disappeared again, and aside from some inconclusive episodes in April, it was never heard of again. Its identity was never established. The German government denied responsibility vehemently on 26 and 27 February. Some evidence turned up in Yorkshire that a prankster had been sending up fire balloons, but that doesn't account for any of the sightings involving searchlights. The French science periodical *Bulletin de la Société Astronomique de France* stated that the object was obviously Venus, and called the English gullible peasants for thinking any differently.

Perhaps we were gullible back then, but not so gullible that we'd believe a planet would spend a week shining a torch over Wales. So if it wasn't a Zeppelin or a planet, what was this thing? Sadly, from our disadvantage point of a century later, we'll probably never know.

Unidentified Flying Jellyfish

The prize for the smallest UFO on record in England must go to a five-inch object spotted hovering over a hotel balcony in Bournemouth in October 1969. The Mackenzie family was drinking coffee inside when father Alastair saw a blob like a jellyfish glowing and pulsating slightly. After a few moments it moved out to sea, flying at a height of about two feet above the water until it was out of sight.

The Howden Moor Incident

After sunset on Monday 24 March, 1997, people all over England were out of doors looking to the clear night sky for a perfectly legitimate, scientifically sanctioned reason. The comet Hale-Bopp was approaching perihelion, the point at which it passed closest to the sun, and it was visible to the naked eye in the night sky.

On the border of South Yorkshire and the Peak District in Derbyshire, however, people witnessed more than a distant Nike swoop in the sky. From 7.30 p.m. onwards, people out comet-watching saw and heard helicopters, light aircraft and jets flying low around the Howden Moor area. There's nothing unusual so far—there are many airports and military bases in the area—but just after 10.00 p.m. there was a terrific explosion followed by a glowing light on the moors. This had all the hallmarks of a plane crash, and so the South Yorkshire and Derbyshire police mobilised an investigation that would ultimately turn into a search-and-rescue operation involving more than 200 people. They never found any debris or survivors, and no aviation authority reported any lost aircraft.

The newspapers of the time carried only scattered details of the incident, and it wasn't until Martin Jeffrey and Dr David Clarke published an exhaustive study of the incident that the public got to see all the evidence that police investigators saw, and more. Even so, it didn't seem to add up to a coherent story. At 8.30 p.m., motorists on the M62 in West Yorkshire and A61 near Chesterfield saw jets flying quickly in the distance, one of which appeared to dive straight down into the moors. There were no flames or explosions, and no news reports, so they thought nothing more of it. An hour later in Sheffield, a Mosborough resident saw a streak of light heading toward Ridgeway. Meanwhile the car radio of a comet-watcher parked in the Peak District emitted a loud humming noise for several seconds, followed by a noise that sounded like

Another witness . . . saw a large triangular shape in the sky, as wide as a street, with two pink lights on the front of it, and blue lights all round it. It was heading slowly for the moors.

the flapping of bird wings.

Half an hour later, back in the Chesterfield area, two witnesses saw two very different things. A retired RAF officer heard a single-engine plane flying overhead, followed minutes later by two fighter jets screaming past at a very low altitude—so low that they shook the foundations of his house. Another witness, who later appeared in reports under the pseudonym Emma Maidenhead, heard a low humming noise like wet power lines vibrating in the air. She saw a large triangular shape in the sky, as wide as a street, with two pink lights on the front of it, and blue lights all round it. It was heading slowly for the moors.

Fifteen minutes after that, at about 10.10 p.m., the

ground impact. It was more like the sonic boom given off during supersonic flight. With no military craft to account for such speed, people turned to the space debris theory: bolide meteoroids sometimes give off loud noises as they enter the atmosphere. None of this explains the slower-moving light aircraft, however. Two boys with a video camera had videotaped a low-flying light aircraft that night from their Parsons Cross home in north Sheffield. When the police inspected the tape, they determined it was a fixed-wing aircraft with lights on the wing that made it look triangular from a certain angle. However, the time on the tape revealed that the recording took place almost half an hour after the explosion. It may have been a completely different plane. But because it could not be accounted for by any airport and it was clearly not a military aircraft, the police favoured the idea that this was a smuggling flight aiming to drop drugs or weapons at a remote location to be picked up later.

Naturally, UFO chasers believe that it was an extraterrestrial vessel that the MOD tracked on their radar scopes, drove into the ground, and towed away before the police and rescue teams could arrive. Each particular of this theory was denied by the MOD, but then they would, wouldn't they?

So, no single explanation accounts for what happened that night. It seems to be a random series of events. But this part of the country has seen many planes go down over the years. The Dark Peak has been the site of more than fifty crashes since World War Two, with hundreds of lives lost. And some of the more superstitious people in the area attribute the crash to the Phantom Bomber, a ghost-flier that haunts the area.

That's as good an explanation as any. As for us, we just can't account for it. So we'll just file the story under Unexplained and move on.

emergency phone exchange was inundated by phone calls. An aircraft seen screaming across the moors had disappeared over the horizon, followed by a mighty explosion.

When the rescue services failed to turn up any evidence of a crash, the question remained: What had happened? After the Secretary of State for Defence was grilled about the events in the House of Commons, a Ministry spokesperson stated that they had been conducting low-level jet exercises that night, but these had ended at exactly 9.30 p.m., before the explosion and apparent crash-landing. The British Geological Survey determined that the enormous explosion was not consistent with

Bizarre Beasts

For centuries, bizarre tales of impossible animals have been a staple among storytellers.

Most people dismiss them out of hand. For example, everyone laughed when explorers to Africa in the mid-nineteenth century recounted the native's stories of a strange donkey-like creature with the head of an anteater and the stripes of a zebra. And in medieval times people looked sidelong at sailors returning from voyages with the long, straight, ivory horns of unicorns. And when fishermen told tales of sea serpents of impossible size . . . well, they treated it like any big-fish tale.

But in each of these examples, there was a real creature behind the stories. The striped haunches of the okapi were first seen by Westerners at the turn of the twentieth century after forty years of questionable tales. A single-horned Arctic whale called the narwhal gave rise to myths of unicorns. And the sea serpent? Well, since the prehistoric coelacanth showed up in fishing nets in 1938 and proved it wasn't extinct as was once thought, the sea serpent could have been any type of marine life, past or present.

We tend to assume that England's population of wild animals has declined over the centuries. Wolf packs and wild boar once ran wild across the land, although England's never officially had a population of Big Cats in the wild, and snakes are few and far between (and not nearly as scary as the deadly copperheads and black mambas that you find in other countries).

It's no wonder that most people dismiss British wildlife as rather dull and immediately assume that tales of exotic creatures in these parts are either tall tales or pranks. But what if we're wrong? What if there really is a wild beast on Bodmin Moor – or perhaps even a whole pack of them? Are we wrong to roll our eyes when we hear of Yeti in the Border country? Or sea beasts in Falmouth Bay? What if these tales are actually the early heralds to the official announcement of as-yet-undiscovered species . . . the British equivalent of the okapi? Or what if there's something else about these creatures . . . something that's beyond conventional science?

Nobody who's had an encounter with a strange animal, or even a near miss, doubts that they are real. But real what, exactly? Undiscovered native species? Alien species? Ghosts? Just exactly what kind of reality are we talking about?

Fortean Felines

Conventional wisdom has it there are no Big Cats living in the wild in England. If you want to see a cougar, panther, leopard or lynx, you'll have to queue up and pay your admission to a zoo. But there's another school of thought, and it has plenty of eyewitness accounts to support it, which believes there are moorlands crawling with feline giants, who leave behind plenty of mauled carcasses to prove their existence. The victims appear to have been overwhelmed by feline creatures much larger than the domestic species, so people call them 'Alien Big Cats' or ABCs – not as in felines from flying saucers, of course, but as in ones that originate from other countries.

So why, despite the apparent evidence, does conventional wisdom prevail? Because in most cases, all attempts to track down, photograph or gather definitive evidence on ABCs end in failure. A few mutilated prey and some fleeting glimpses from bystanders just won't cut it. Precious few of ABC carcasses have shown up anyway, and most of them can be accounted for as escapees from public or private menageries.

The Beast of Bodmin Moor

Britain is full of terrain suitable for supporting a small population of large predators. The moors around Devon and Cornwall provide enough prey, small and large, wild and domesticated, to sustain a big feral creature. So it's small wonder that some people take reports of a large black cat on Bodmin Moor seriously. Since 1992, dozens of sightings and cases of animal mauling have been reported to the authorities, and the newspapers quickly hit upon a suitably dramatic name for the creature: The Beast of Bodmin. During our hostel-hopping trip around Cornwall, we spoke to several hikers and dog-walkers who had had close encounters with something but never thought to report it to the authorities. So we could easily be dealing with hundreds of sightings over a fifteen-year period. Yet no solid evidence has appeared to support the notion that Big Cats live wild there.

Whenever there's a perceived threat to livestock, the government steps in to investigate. The Ministry of Agriculture, Fisheries and Food (MAFF, now known as DEFRA – Department for Environment, Food and Rural Affairs) had a vested interest in playing down cryptid sightings. And between the months of January and July 1995, MAFF sponsored a study of the area around Bodmin Moor and asked anybody with external evidence to step forward.

Officials studied video footage taken in 1993 and 1994 of what looked like Big Cats, and found that by measuring the suspects against nearby landmarks the cats in question were no larger than domestic moggies. They might have been domestic cats or strays gone wild, but they posed no threat to any wildlife larger than a rabbit. Casts of paw prints were compared to those of a puma and found to be much smaller (except for one, which was clearly a dog's paw). And the dead animals studied had apparently been picked over by several species, including scavengers such as crows, badgers and foxes.

The report concluded:

It was accepted at the start of this investigation that it would never be possible to prove that such an animal, or animals, did not exist, but it was believed that if they did, hard evidence would be forthcoming. . . . No verifiable evidence for the presence of a "big cat" was found. There were only four suspected livestock kills reported in nearly six months, none of which gave any indication of the involvement of anything other than native animals and dogs. There is no significant threat to livestock from a "big cat" on Bodmin Moor.

Nevertheless, the government study did not mean the case was now closed on the Beast. A week after the report was published, a fourteen-year-old boy named Barney Lanyon-Jones picked a large feline skull out of the River Fowey at the southern edge of Bodmin Moor, and gave it to the Natural History Museum for investigation. The museum's assistant keeper of zoology, Dr Ian Bishop, confirmed it was a young male leopard's skull. However, markings on the skull showed it had been skinned using tools and sheared off at the back, which strongly suggested that it came from a leopard-skin rug and had been planted in the river by a prankster. In addition, the skull contained evidence of nesting by an exotic species of insect, which proved that the leopard had died in another country.

Yet the absence of hard evidence (and the existence of a prankster) doesn't necessarily disprove the Beast's existence. In October 1997, experts from Newquay Zoo identified some fresh paw prints to the south of Bodmin as belonging to a puma, and a photograph showing a pregnant puma stalking the moor began circulating. A twenty-second snippet of video showing a black Big Cat apparently on the moor added fuel to the fire. The then MP for North Cornwall, Paul Tyler, began pushing for further investigation, saying that the farmers among his constituents did not take kindly to being dismissed or ridiculed for their concerns.

At the end of the day though, there's still no hard evidence to prove there is a Beast of Bodmin Moor. Yet an absence of evidence also allows for the possibility that there is something out there, and that's quite enough in itself to keep the story going.

Call Him BoB

I'm convinced that the Beast of Bodmin (or BoB, as I prefer to call him) does exist. In fact, because he's been seen for more than twenty years, there would have to be a whole population of BoBs on the prowl. When I was a kid in the boy scouts on a hike, I saw a strange-looking cat, which I looked up in all the nature books and wildlife flashcard collections I could track down. He wasn't the Black panther that most people insist is out there. The closest match I could find was a Lynx caracal, a russet-coloured cat that's smaller than a regular lynx or panther, but is still mighty big and dangerous looking. He also had huge black-tipped ears that made him look all the more fierce. I know that I was that notoriously unreliable source – a child eyewitness – but I know what I saw and I got a shudder of recognition when I saw the caracal in an encyclopedia. – *CryptoBoy*

Dog Escapes Bodmin Cat

I was walking my Springer spaniel around St Kew about five years ago, and he suddenly started to get very interested in something in the woods. It wasn't easy to get a good look at this animal because of the shadows in the woods, but it was a large and black creature shaped like a cat. I called my dog off because I was feeling a bit cautious about this thing. I was right, as it happened. We found a sheep later that was in a terrible state. It wasn't just dead – it had been mauled horribly. I think we must have had a close escape that day. – *Susannah*

Release the Cats!

Nobody should be surprised that sightings of non-native wild animals started to pick up in the late 1970s and 1980s. There was a big fad for exotic cats as pets in the 1960s and 1970s – you could buy them from Harrods, for heaven's sake – and it took the government about ten years to realise that a lot of the buyers didn't have a clue what they were doing. Parliament enacted a law in 1976 called the Dangerous Wild Animals Act that demanded that owners of exotic animals apply for a licence from their local authority, pay a big registration fee, and have local-government officers and vets inspect the premises where the animals were to be kept. With at least nine animal-safety statutes on the books, exotic-animal owners were throwing themselves open to prosecution when inspectors came around, so I bet that lots of owners took the path of least resistance and had the butler drive them out to the moors and set them loose. Out there in the struggle to survive, they could have cross-bred into an entirely new species by now. – *Bill Fields*

Other ABCs

Although the Beast of Bodmin is the most popular Alien Big Cat story in recent years, it's by no means the only one. In fact, there has been a steady stream of them since the 1960s, when people began to spot what they described as a lion on the borders of Surrey and Hampshire. Subsequent reports mentioned Big Cat species almost at random – cheetahs and cougars all featured – but in the media frenzy that followed, the name everyone started using was the Surrey Puma.

The first report came out in 1962 from a water-board worker named Ernest Jellett, who spotted a huge cat stalking a rabbit near Heathy Park Reservoir on the North Downs. Mr Jellett described the animal as flat-faced with large paws and a long, thin tail. Police investigated this report and found a patch of undergrowth flattened by a large animal near where the encounter had taken place. When news broke of the incident, a Mr A. Burningham came forward to describe an encounter he had had on a nearby country lane one August evening three years earlier. He had seen a cat the size of a labrador dog cross the road ahead of him, then crouch in the hedgerow to observe sheep.

Over the next couple of years, Surrey Puma reports filtered through fairly often, containing tales of terrible howling noises and cattle stampeding for reasons unknown. In one report, a bull was found in the woods with scratches and bite marks that a vet declared could not have been caused by any local species he knew of. However, no solid documentary evidence ever surfaced. Certainly, some blurry photographs came to light in 1966, but they were so unclear that it was impossible to tell if they showed any kind of cat, let alone a big exotic one.

The newspapers stopped writing about the Surrey Puma in 1968, when a farmer claimed to have shot and buried it. He never produced evidence of the kill, which is certainly odd, but sightings tailed off thereafter. Until, in the snowfall of December 1970, a family photographed a set of large paw tracks in their back garden, hinting that the story was not entirely finished.

Fast-forward a decade, and the next big ABC story centred on Exmoor. From the late 1970s onward, a combination of livestock deaths and sightings of a six-foot-long cat with a long tail stoked the popular imagination. The creature's pelage was dark – depending on the ambient light, it appeared as either black, dark grey or dark brown – and a motorist who reported a near miss with it described its eyes as dark green. Because the mysterious animal's species was hard to pin down, the newspapers covered themselves by referring to it simply as the Beast of Exmoor. Its banner year was 1983, when up to eighty sheep were found mauled to death, some with large cat tracks near them. Before long, local folklore had it that the creature was a hybrid species, descended from two separate exotic species that had either escaped from unlicensed private collectors or had been released into the wild. The Beast of Exmoor, they said, was part melanistic puma, part leopard.

Whatever it was, MAFF was fed up with it. Local farmers were sustaining huge losses because of its voracious appetites, so in 1988 they called in Royal Marine sharpshooters. The massive operation didn't yield any kills, and fizzled out with reports of a dead foal that looked as though it had been killed by a fox. Perhaps this, MAFF suggested, was the animal responsible for all the sheep deaths? The farmers didn't buy that story; however, over the years, they had come not to expect too much satisfaction from official sources, even though in 1995 MAFF carried out yet another inconclusive study.

Perhaps these strange Big Cat tales will never be explained to everybody's satisfaction. Too many people have too much invested in these stories already. It's hard to placate farmers facing huge losses, and validate the stories of scared or bemused eyewitnesses, and satisfy serious researchers into the fringes of science, and give excitable local storytellers a good yarn to spin.

The Black Cat of Gloucestershire

A few years ago in the Forest of Dean, word around town was that a boy had been attacked and mauled by a wild animal while he was playing in the garden. His father saw it happen and said that the animal looked like a Big Cat, maybe a panther. Whatever it was, one thing's sure: It wasn't native to the Forest of Dean. And it's probably still there. You hear about animal attacks and the discovery of mauled animal carcasses around. Last Christmas, for example, the BBC reported that a man out for a walk before the Queen's Speech found a dead deer near Ruspidge. The kill was recent because the flesh and blood were bright red, and the bones had been stripped bare by some mighty sharp teeth. I'm pretty sure the chap in question made it back to the house before the leftovers from his own meal had cooled. – NotPeggy

Surrey Puma Stalks Old Coulsdon

It all happened a long time ago, but that terrible night in the summer of 1965 remains clear in my mind even to this day. I was eighteen and coming back from a party late at night. My parents' house was surrounded by fields and woods on three sides. I was well accustomed to seeing foxes and other wildlife and not in the least bit frightened of the dark. My route took me through two fields, and the path followed a shallow valley just south of Kenley Aerodrome. Where the two fields met to my right, I heard a noise coming towards me from up in the wood. I stopped still, hoping that I might see some wildlife. The noise approached rapidly and I saw a big cat charging towards me. All in a flash it sped right past me, so close that it brushed my trousers and I could smell the warmth of the animal's breath. I was rooted to the ground in terror as the sound faded away up the hillside. I sprinted home, looking back several times. The next day nobody believed me. My parents were convinced that I had had too much to drink.

I did not dare take the short cut again for several days, even though it meant a really long detour, but finally I plucked up the courage. About halfway across the first field, I saw an animal again. It looked like a big cat on the brow of the hill. As I walked it kept pace with me keeping low in the grass. It appeared to be stalking me. I again sprinted all the way home but this time I did not look back. Soon after this I went to university and I never encountered the Surrey Puma again. – Tim Blewitt

Black Dogs

Black Dogs are the elder statesmen of bizarre beasthood. Tales of British Big Cats date back only a few decades, and although they are baffling, they remain fully within the realms of possibility. By contrast, Black Dog tales date back for centuries, since their first mention in the Anglo-Saxon Chronicle, in which ghastly hellhounds accompanied the ghost riders of the Wild Hunt in 1127. These eerie origins have earned the Black Dog a place among the supernatural beings whose presence threatens something much more frightening than even a severe mauling.

In East Anglia, the dog is best known as Black Shuck. On the Isle of Man, he's the Moddey Dhoo (pronounced Mauther Thoo). In Yorkshire, he's the Barghest and in Staffordshire the Padfoot, to some, he's the Hound of Hell or simply the Hateful Thing. The Black Dog has inspired fictional tales of terror, ranging from Sir Arthur Conan Doyle's *The Hound of the Baskervilles* to J.K. Rowling's character Sirius Black and his Animagus in *Harry Potter and The Prisoner of Azkaban*. There's probably a hint of him in Stephen King's *Cujo* too. It's small wonder that Black Dogs have become one of England's most feared folk creatures. There is also a widespread superstition that seeing one is an omen of death or disaster.

A straunge,
and terrible Wunder wrought very late in the parish Church of Bongay, a Town of no great distance from the citie of Norwich, namely the fourth of this August, in ÿ yeare of our Lord 1577. in a great tempest of violent raine, lightning, and thunder, the like wherof hath béen seldome séene.
With the appearance of an horrible shaped thing, sensibly perceived of the people then and there assembled.
Drawen into a plain method according to the written copye.
by Abraham Fleming.

Black Shuck

Black Shuck is the alpha dog in the whole pack of Black Dog horror stories. He's inspired more terror – and more stories – than any other English animal since he first burst onto the scene in East Anglia four centuries ago. Antiquarians, tour guides and pub bores have been swapping Shuck stories with anyone who'll listen since Shakespeare was a toddler; and he's inspired some professional storytellers too: Sir Arthur Conan Doyle wove him into his Sherlock Holmes mystery *The Hound of the Baskervilles* after hearing the Shuck legend while on holiday in Cromer.

But Shuck was already an old dog by then: He was first written up in 1577 in a broadsheet that describes the events of the dramatic Sunday morning of 4 August, when a terrible storm hit East Anglia. A prolific writer of the time named Abraham Fleming described what happened on that day in the church at Bungay, near Norwich, in a book he entitled *A Straunge and Terrible Wunder wraught very late in the parish of Bungay*. Fleming tells how the congregation 'thought doomsday was already come' when the murderous beast burst into the church. This is his account (with his Old English spelling corrected to make it easier to read):

> This black dog, or the devil in such a likeness . . . passed between two persons, as they were kneeling upon their knees and occupied in prayer . . . wrung the necks of them both at one instant clean backward, insomuch that even at a moment where they kneeled, they strangely died.
>
> . . . the same black dog . . . passing by another man of the congregation in the church, gave him such a gripe on the back, that . . . he was drawn together and shrunk up . . . as the mouth of a purse or bag, drawn together with a string.
>
> . . . On the self same day, in like manner, into the parish church of another town called Blibery, not above seven miles distant [probably Blythburgh, fourteen miles away] . . . the like thing entered . . . and there also, as before, slew two men and a lad, and burned the hand of another person . . .
>
> This mischief thus wrought, he flew with wonderful force to no little fear of the assembly, out of the church in a hideous and hellish likeness.

That was just the beginning of the tales told of Shuck. Four centuries later, two men independently took up the tale where Fleming left off. In 1988, a writer named Christopher Reeve published a leaflet on Black Shuck lore, and a local researcher named Mike Burgess published his exhaustive research, analysis and correspondence online in a site called Shuckland (which is now part of Hidden East Anglia at www.hiddenea. com). Both authors point out that Shuck's name didn't appear in print until a Reverend E.S. Taylor wrote an article for the June 1805 issue of the *Norfolk Chronicle*, and that the name could have originated from a local dialect word for 'shaggy' or from the Old English *sceocca*, meaning 'a devil'.

Whatever his origins, though, Black Shuck has certainly been active. From the listings on the Shuckland website alone, he's shown up more than 200 times in Cambridgeshire, Suffolk, Norfolk and Essex. He's always described as a large dog, but half the time he appears to be unnaturally large. His eyes are often shining, but only in a few cases is there anything unnatural about them (some mention his having only one Cyclops eye, for example). But some supernatural features do creep into the accounts: In quite a few cases, he either vanishes in front of people's eyes, or disappears suddenly and without trace when they are looking the other way. He is sometimes visible only to one person and invisible to others. And once or twice, though he is close enough to be heard, he is seen gliding by without making a sound, and sometimes he leaves a sudden chill in the air. He appears in a smattering of stories and folklore books across the centuries, but seems to show up more frequently in the early twentieth century and in the 1930s – the proximity of his visits to two world wars cementing his reputation as an omen of ill fortune.

In the 1970s, talk of Black Shuck began to enjoy a resurgence, fuelled by letters such as Elsie Harris's to the *Eastern Daily Press* in November 1971. In this she describes an incident from the late nineteenth century when her father was courting her mother in Cromer. The young man was walking back to Overstrand along the main (but unlit) road around midnight, when he noticed a dog following him at heel. A little disturbed by the animal, he tried to give it a whack with his walking stick to chase it off, but the stick went straight through the dog. Elsie Harris described her father as sober and not prone to flights of fancy, so she felt the story had a ring of truth to it, extraordinary though it was. What also had a ring of truth was his reaction to the encounter: He 'took to his heels and ran like hell.'

More stories from the Cromer area began to surface. An old fellow named J.H. Harrison recorded an encounter he and his childhood friend Gooley Craske had near the old railway bridge outside the town. The schoolboys spotted 'a great black animal . . . sort of jumping and gliding quite fast', and legged it out of there, only learning about Black Shuck from their parents after they described the incident to them.

Over the ensuing decades, more tales have crept in – each of them with their own ring of truth. One man out for a stroll spotted a dog in broad daylight along the road in Garvestone, Norfolk, in the late 1970s; he glanced away at another walker, and when he turned back the dog had gone. The animal had been twenty yards ahead, and there was no cover for at least 200 yards in any direction, and yet it had vanished. In another case, a middle-aged couple in a car spotted a huge animal while driving along the A12 near Dedham, Essex, and marvelled at its pony-sized form and large head, even as the temperature in the car, which was being fiercely heated at the time, suddenly dropped. Another couple also experienced a sudden chill when encountering the dog: In the summer of 1970 they were driving at night in Cambridge, near the junction of Arbury Road and Kings Hedges Road, and saw a dog leap clean over their bonnet and hightail it through an allotment. The suddenness of the encounter and the chill that descended on the car made them think of Black Shuck – and conjured up visions of impending doom.

And, be honest about it, if that had happened to you, wouldn't you think the same?

Beach Blanket Shuck

There's a path in Corton, Suffolk, which leads from the cliffs down to the beach; they call it Tramps Alley, and they also tell me that it's a path that a shaggy black dog trots along at night. Whether it's the legendary Black Dog or some other creature, I don't know, but it's there, all right, and it scares the bejabbers out of couples who go down to the beach for a moonlit stroll. – *EADePoe*

Shuck's Death March

Auld Shuck runs through the woods on the Croxton Road, west of Cambridge, and he's an omen of ill fortune. Perhaps he's the ghost form of an old criminal . . . nobody's really sure. But the path he walks leads from the old Caxton gibbet to the crossroads where they buried unrepentant criminals in unsanctified ground. You know that has to mean something. – *Deathwatch901*

Black Dog Tales

By Donna Mucha

He takes the form of a huge black dog, and prowls along dark lanes and lonesome field footpaths, where, although his howling makes the hearer's blood run cold, his footfalls make no sound. You may know him at once, should you see him, by his fiery eye; he has but one, and that, like the Cyclops', is in the middle of his head. But such an encounter might bring you the worst of luck: it is even said that to meet him is to be warned that your death will occur before the end of the year.

> – *W.A. Dutt,* Highways & Byways in East Anglia, 1901.

Some stories of Black Dogs clearly cast them as ghosts or demons that haunt locations with particularly gruesome histories. One such story is from Tring, Hertfordshire, where an old woman was drowned in 1751, under suspicion of being a witch. A chimney sweep partially responsible for her death was hanged and gibbeted. After these deaths, strange things happened at the site. A schoolmaster on his way home one evening saw a flame the size of a man's hat transform into a dog that was 'shaggy, big as a Newfoundland, long ears and tail, eyes of flaming fire, and long teeth'. Frozen to the spot, the schoolmaster watched as the fiendish beast appeared to smile at him, then vanished.

Another tale is set in Peel Castle on the Isle of Man during the reign of Charles II; a Black Dog was frequently seen there, mostly in the Guard Chamber, where he would lie in front of the fire. Though the guards grew accustomed to the Moddey Dhoo (the name the Black Dog is given in that area), one night a guard, who was extremely drunk, decided to goad it. There are two accounts of what occurred then, both with the same result. The first tells of the man that teased the dog becoming instantly speechless and sober, then dying a painful and violent death three days later. A second account of this same incident has it that the guard followed the dog, then, after screaming was heard, the guard reappeared with a look of pure terror on his face. He never spoke again and died soon afterwards.

The moral of these tales seems to be that any attempt to interact with dog apparitions is almost never a good idea. But not all Black Dog tales end tragically. The eclectic Victorian magazine *Notes and Queries* covered an old Devonshire dog tale concerning an elderly weaver from Dean Combe, and the origin of the Pool of the Black Hound there:

After long prosperity he died, and was buried. But the next day he appeared sitting at the loom in his chamber, working diligently as when he was alive. His sons applied to the parson, who went accordingly to the foot of the stairs, and heard the noise of the weaver's shuttle above. 'Knowles!' he said, 'come down; this is no place for thee.' 'I will,' said the weaver, 'as soon as I have worked out my quill' (the quill is the shuttle full of wool). 'Nay,' said the Vicar, 'thou hast been long enough at thy work; come down at once!' So when the spirit came down, the Vicar took a handful of earth from the churchyard and threw it in his face. And in a moment it became a black hound. 'Follow me,' said the Vicar, and it followed him to the gate of the wood. And when they got there, it seemed as if all the trees in the wood were coming together, so great was the wind. Then the Vicar took a nutshell with a hole in it, and led the hound to the pool below the waterfall. 'Take this shell,' he said, 'and when thou shalt have dipped out the pool with it, thou mayest rest, not before.' And at mid-day or at midnight the hound may still be seen at its work. – Notes and Queries, *vol. ii. page 515.*

Whatever form they take, these dogs are infamous around the country. You can always tell a place with a Black Dog story: Keep an eye open for a Black Dog pub or a Dog Lane. Going down the lane at night may be risky, but going into a Black Dog Inn is never a bad idea. You won't have trouble finding one, so drink up. You never know what you might see on the way home.

Almost Human

Common sense tells us that if a species of non-human bipeds lived in the wild in England, many people would have seen them and everybody would know about them. Yet some people claim to have seen a creature in England that is more associated with the Himalaya or North America: the Yeti or Bigfoot. Which raises an obvious question: How could a larger-than-human species survive on the slim pickings available on a fen, chase or moor?

Even people who make a serious study of strange beasts, the cryptozoologists, have a laughable term for such creatures: a BHM, or Big Hairy Monster. They take sightings seriously, but they maintain a quirky sense of humour about it. So what are the rest of us to make of the stories we hear about Yeti-like creatures in the North and the Midlands? And what about the tales of a bizarre dwarf species living in Northumberland? What indeed. Perhaps if we were to take the words of witnesses at face value, we'd have to agree with the puckish analysis that Charles Fort, a collector of strange and anomalous phenomena, dreamed up a century ago: That they fade in and out of this time and dimension through some accident of metaphysics.

The Cannock Chase Bigfoot

From the mid-1990s right through to the present, people have been seeing strange things on the large Staffordshire heathland known as Cannock Chase. From Castle Ring to Cannock Woods, right across to Pye Green and the German war memorial, people have been seeing a large hairy creature, taller than most humans, skulking around. In 2005 alone, there were five reported sightings.

The reports began to come in after motorist Jackie Haughton almost hit a large shambling creature on the Cannock–Rugeley road on the night of 18 February 1995. Jackie slammed on the anchors twenty feet away from this strange pedestrian and had to swerve at the last minute to avoid collision. She saw the creature for only a few seconds before it vanished into the trees, but as anyone who's narrowly avoided an accident knows, a few seconds can seem like a very long time. And what she saw was a tall, hairy creature with 'self-illuminating' eyes.

A more typical sighting happens in wooded areas where the view is less clear, such as the incident after midnight on 24 September 1998, when four people were driving along the A34 behind Cannock Woods. It was a clear night, and the driver and his passengers all saw a tall, man-like creature in a crouch, leaning forward and looking at their car as it approached. They could only estimate his height – a little short of seven feet tall – but one of the group noticed his powerfully built legs, which he estimated as twice the size of his own. According to news reports, a similar seven-foot creature showed up again at Castle Ring in April 2004.

So we're discussing a tall mammalian biped who's been around for a decade or more. It's clearly a hominid – a branch of the zoological tree that includes humans and gorillas and (for *Star Wars* fans) Wookies. For good measure, it also has glowing eyes. In addition to eyewitness accounts, there is secondary evidence: Tree damage that's not consistent with the activities of smaller animals or human vandals.

Naysayers are quick to point out 'perfectly natural' interpretations of what's going on. In recent years, for example, people have noticed the presence of a gang of deer ranging from Rugeley as far south as Walsall. These large creatures could easily account for the tree damage and – if seen from the right angle, at a distance, in the dark, in the woods – could possibly be mistaken for a hairy biped. Of course, deer eyes are not set at seven feet high, and they don't tend to shine at night. But there's another 'natural' explanation for that too: Big Cats in the branches of trees. Cannock has been the location of several Big Cat sightings, and when the pupils of these creatures' eyes dilate to allow fading light to reach their retinas, the light reflecting off the retinas also reflects the blood vessels that coat the back of the eye – resulting in shining red eyes. In darkened woods, a tree trunk and its branches can take on any form that a witness might imagine, especially if that witness is frightened by shining red eyes.

So sceptics and eyewitnesses are at an impasse. Any environment that can support a population of red deer could theoretically support a large hominid, but if there is one out there, he's not leaving a lot of hard evidence behind. There are no carcasses and no reliable photographs either. But, as the area gets built up, the local deer are becoming more and more conspicuous, so reason dictates that if there is a big hairy monster out there, it's just a matter of time before he comes out into the open, too. And we'll be waiting for him.

The Geordie Yeti

Towards the end of 2002, another hairy hominid began to rear its head, this time in Northumberland. Pike fishermen on Bolam Lake began to tell such outlandish stories that investigators converged on the place en masse, sometimes tripping over broadcasting crews from Tyne Tees television station and Radio Four, sometimes meeting members of the Centre for Fortean Zoology (CFZ) or of the Twilight Worlds Paranormal Research Group. And the names they picked for this big hairy monster were all too catchy: the Beast of Bolam, the Geordie Yeti and the Geordie Bigfoot.

The bizarre-beast hunters used an odd mixture of techniques to track down this hairy wild man. They looked at tree saplings snapped as if by a large creature or bent over into odd shelter-like shapes that North American cryptozoologists call Bigfoot teepees. They made sandpits to capture footprints (unsuccessfully, as it turned out). And they even brought out the electromagnetic detectors that ghost hunters use to see if these could shed any light. Many of the investigators found their battery-operated equipment – mobile phones, cameras and so on – lost their charge suspiciously fast in the vicinity. And just to slap some icing on the cake, quite a few of them saw something running through the darkened woods.

Despite all this, not one of them could get a decent picture. And that's too bad, because the stories of what was lurking in that woodland were quite interesting and varied. Among those interviewed by the Centre for Fortean Zoology at the time was a young mother who was in the area three days before. She had felt an intense wave of fear when she saw a huge creature standing motionless in the woods as she crossed the Bolam Lake car park with her son. On several occasions in the previous five years, a group of fishermen had seen the outline of a large man standing in the same woods. During their first encounter, in twilight, they saw something with a human outline but of enormous stature, up to eight feet tall, and with glittering eyes. Their response was natural enough: They ran back to their car and got out of there. Some years later, during a night-fishing expedition, the sounds of a huge animal coming from the nearby undergrowth had disturbed them so greatly that they broke camp early next day. When they were packing up, they found their bait tin had been raided as they slept.

One witness from a Newcastle suburb refused to go back to the lake to show CFZ investigators where he had encountered an enormous man-shaped creature near a hollow tree in Bolam Woods. The experience had unsettled him so much he had resolved not to visit the area again.

The festive gathering of broadcasters and Fortean investigators hanging out at Bolam Lake in late January 2003 had a couple of strange encounters of their own to recount. One person from the Twilight Worlds group reported seeing something in the woods near the car park at around 4.30 p.m., when it was starting to get dark. Half an hour later, the rooks in the woods kicked up a tremendous racket and suddenly fell silent. Someone shouted that they heard something in the woods, and a member of the group suggested everyone turn on their car headlights to full beam to illuminate the trees. Of the eight people present, five people saw something huge in the woods running this way and that to avoid the headlights. The group was too spooked to chase after whatever it was, but when they returned the following week and had one of their group retrace the creature's steps, they realised it must have been larger than an average human and about 130 feet away from the cars.

A little later, a group of schoolchildren admitted to news reporters that they had done a video project with ape suits in the woods the previous summer. But although

the newspapers touted this as a possible explanation for the incidents, their exercise did not coincide with many of the creature sightings. Besides, they claimed their video session had been an exercise to see how easy it would be to fake photographs of a Yeti. But that's where

people are missing the point of this tale: Nobody has come forward with photographic evidence of the Beast of Bolam. Witnesses are seeing something preternaturally large and human-shaped in the woods, but they're not sticking around long enough to take snapshots.

The Duergar of Simonside

If the Geordie Yeti and the Cannock Chase Bigfoot are the Wookies of the British Isles, then the Duergar are its Ewoks – tiny fur-covered creatures no taller than waist-high to an adult human. The legends about these creatures are so old and so steeped in oral history that there's not even a standard way to spell their name – in the few printed stories you can find, you'll see them called Deugar, Duegar and Duergar almost interchangeably. But no matter how the name is spelt, the stories agree that these creatures aren't the cute and resourceful little furballs from *Return of the Jedi;* they're much trickier and more malevolent than that.

The Duergar are indigenous to Simonside, a well-tramped hill that the outdoorsy folk of Northumberland consider a must-hike experience. I have just run out of fingers for counting the number of times I've climbed it, and I've not gone hillwalking for fun in decades – that's some indication of how significant a site Simonside is. Until last year, however, I had no inkling of the Duergar.

For centuries, they have been saying that these creatures carry lights so far off the path that they lure night-time hikers over the precipice or into patches of boggy land and to their deaths. A few well-established folk tales speak of night-time encounters with the irascible little guys, who usually vanish into thin air at some point. There was even a story going around in the nineteenth century that claimed they started up the huge waterwheel at nearby Tosson Mill, an important source of grinding power in years gone by.

It's hard to know what to make of these tales. It doesn't take much delving to realise that their name probably comes from the Scandinavian dwarf race that forged the Ring of the Nibelungs – the Dvergar. The name was no doubt bandied about back when Northumberland was settled by Vikings and other Nordic settlers, and was part of the Danelaw. But why the name should move out of folk stories and become attached to this particular hill remains a mystery. Were there odd sightings of small furry bipeds on Simonside in years gone by? Did they have strange powers to come and go, the way the legendary Black Dogs do? And are they still around?

Those questions, like all questions about England's bizarre beasts, remain unanswered. And the likelihood is strong that they'll remain that way.

Watery Wonders

Most people don't think of England when they think of sea serpents or lake creatures. Instead, they think of the huge monster spotted around Massachusetts Bay in August 1817 that sparked the first wave of interest in American cryptozoology. They think of creatures seen in the wastes of the North Atlantic, or off the coast of the ancient land of Mauretania. And when people talk of lake creatures, the whole world is in the shadow of some animal from a deep loch in Scotland.

Yet England does have its own tradition of sea creatures, rooted both in ancient legend and in modern-day sightings. Who knows how these stories started? Perhaps they are pure fantasy. Perhaps there's a germ of truth to them. Or perhaps, just maybe, they are the truth and nothing but.

Morgawr – the Monster of Falmouth Bay

For more than thirty years, people have been catching glimpses of a sea monster off the south-west coast of England. When the first sightings began in 1975 around Falmouth Bay, reporters and local historians dug up a couple of odd reports from 1875 and 1925, when a strange creature with a long neck was caught in fishermen's nets. Whatever it was, the creature had died some time before and was too decayed for people with only a smattering of exotic marine biology to pinpoint it with any accuracy.

People looking for quick closure to the story dismissed it as a large seal or basking shark. But that pat answer doesn't adequately fit whatever it is people have been seeing in western Cornwall in more recent years.

The sightings of what soon became known as Morgawr, the sea giant, began in September 1975. Two people on the beach and some mackerel fishermen offshore caught sight of 'a hideous hump-backed

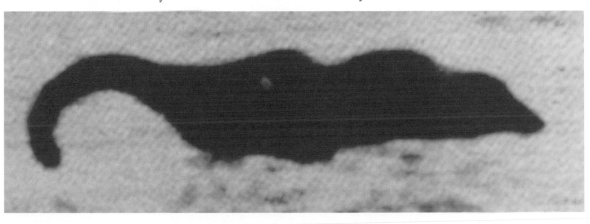

creature with stumpy horns and bristles down the back of its long neck', near Pendennis Point. Over the months that followed, a swimmer off Rosemullion Head had an encounter with a long-necked creature some thirty to forty feet long, and two women from London spotted a creature twenty-five feet in length with a neck the length of a lamp post.

The next detailed description appeared in the *Falmouth Packet* in February 1976, when a witness, who wanted to be known only as Mary F, turned in two photographs taken off Trefusis Point. The silhouette looked like the classic surgeon's photograph of the Loch Ness Monster – something like a cross between a seal and a dinosaur. Mary F described the animal she saw

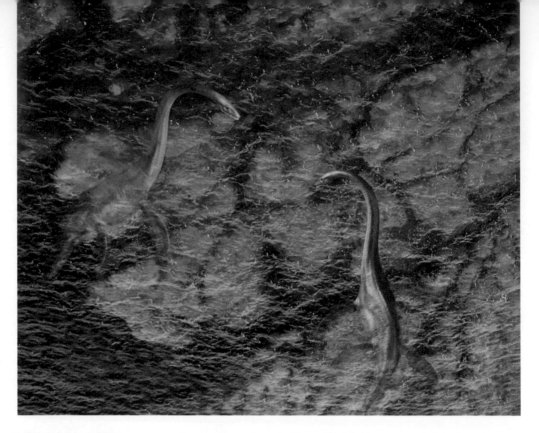

as 'like an elephant waving its trunk, but the trunk was a long neck with a small head on the end like a snake's head . . . the animal frightened me.'

The following spring and summer were littered with sightings that shed a little more light on the creature. Its estimated length varied from fifteen to sixty feet, a wide range that hints at there being more than one of them. (This became more likely when a pair of London bankers on holiday spotted a pair of monsters swimming near the mouth of the Helford River.) Witnesses at a Scilly Isles' sighting that summer described the creature as 'worm-like' and to another man a few weeks later at Gyllyngvase Beach it appeared 'hump-backed' and like a large eel.

Sightings of the creature abated for a while, but in the mid-1980s, Morgawr appeared to the writer Sheila Bird at Porthcurnow. She described him as mottled-grey with a torso twenty feet long and a tail of the same length. It held its head up like a camel, she said, and reminded her of a plesiosaur. Another ten years passed without incident, until an article mentioned an encounter with a creature very much like the one Sheila Bird had described. In 1999, a fisherman and a former employee of the Natural History Museum saw a snake-like creature in the water, and there have been at least two documented sightings this century, in May 2000 and off Black Head in 2002.

But none of these sightings answers the crucial question: Just what is Morgawr? Glomming onto bits of the various descriptions that have come down to us, we could specify it as a member of the sunfish family, which would account for its spiny dorsal fins. It could be a stray barracuda (one was caught off Cornwall in 2002). It could be a shark of some kind. Or a seal (there are plenty of seals in the area). But this doesn't really add up in an area that's densely populated by fishermen, divers and tourists gazing out to sea.

Perhaps some of the more far-out ideas make sense: The surrealist 'Doc' Shiels, who was at the centre of the Owlman sightings in the area in the mid-1970s, followed Morgawr sightings pretty closely, too, and came up with a suitably bizarre way to account for the creature: He called Morgawr a 'parapsychological entity' that exists in many dimensions, is not organic life as we know it, and can change shape and size at will. Nobody ever accused 'Doc' Shiels of being a conventional man of science, but no matter what you may think of his hypothesis, it certainly seems to fit the evidence.

Wild Man of Orford

Not all sea monsters are serpentine. There's a bizarre tale from the late twelfth century that tells of a wild man who lived in the sea off Orford in Suffolk. Unlike most mermaid tales, this creature has never been subject to romantic myths – there's no mention of fish scales or siren-like calls that lure people out to sea. Instead, the earliest written account of this creature, by the chronicler Ralph of Coggeshall, sounds like a straight historical account. It runs (with the Old English spelling adjusted to make it easier to read) like this:

Men fishing in the sea caught in their nets a wild man. He was naked and was like a man in all his members, covered with hair and with a long shaggy beard. He eagerly ate whatever was brought to him but if it was raw he pressed it between his hands until all the juice was expelled. He would not talk, even when tortured and hung up by his feet. Brought into church, he showed no signs of reverence or belief. He sought his bed at sunset and always remained there until sunrise.

He was allowed to go into the sea, strongly guarded with three lines of nets, but he dived under the nets and came up again and again. Eventually he came back of his own free will. But later on he escaped and was never seen again.

Working on the theory that there's no smoke without fire, something unusual clearly showed up at Orford all those hundreds of years ago. This event wasn't being told to make some typical folklore point: It tells of a stranger being caught and refusing to behave like regular folk – and then running away. At the time, Orford wasn't an obscure and isolated coastal town where fanciful stories could thrive. Rather, it was a flourishing fishing port and a centre for importing wine and exporting wool. The question is, then, who or what was the wild man of Orford? Was he a regular outcast from humanity who was just out for a swim when he was caught? Or was he a sea-dwelling hominid? From our vantage point, we'll probably never know. But it's fun to speculate.

Mermaid of Zennor

Once you start entertaining off-the-wall ideas about English sea creatures, it opens the door to all kinds of speculation. Some friends and I wondered if the legendary Mermaid of Zennor might be connected in some way. The parish church at Zennor, near Penzance, has a mermaid carved into it, partly because they used the mermaid as a symbol for Jesus's dual nature (though just how a half-woman half-fish could make people understand Jesus being both God and Man is anybody's guess). The other thing about the mermaid is that there are legends that a real-life sea temptress lived out there and lured young men of the parish out to sea. Could warnings about a dangerous creature in the sea have been more than just a symbol? – *Morgawrna*

Local Heroes and Villains

They weren't English themselves, but the Californian band The Doors might well have been describing the residents of this sceptr'd isle when they performed their song *People are Strange*.

People in England really are strange. Some of them quietly go about their business in a perfectly orderly way, even if their business happens to involve dressing up in leopard-skin trousers and shouting through a megaphone, or declaring themselves ruler of their own tiny kingdom or tap-dancing in the town square.

These are exactly the kind of people who add greatly to England's lustre. Of course, not all are heroes: Some of England's historic characters walked on the darker side, secretly going about a more sinister business. Fortunately, the ratio of local heroes to local villains is just about right: We have plenty of characters to keep us smiling, and just enough villains to make us appreciate the heroes.

Great British Minds

People in England don't think in quite the same way as anybody else in the world. We have our own particular lens that either helps us to see things more clearly than everybody else or distorts our view in a uniquely English way. Things that seem perfectly natural to us strike other nations as peculiar; it's how we get our reputation for a dry sense of humour.

But then there are those English people who even the English think are strange. Some of these are geniuses, some are crackpots and some are both.

DISCREET behaviour is an important part of respectability, and has assisted men and women to be virgins for their weddings, yet some had been to UNIVERSITY and other places of advanced learning, and had sexual friends at that time, and were very passionate, too. Being discreet helps to keep these people —faithful in marriage, as well. See page 4, line 21.

EIGHT

PASSION

PROTEINS

WITH CARE

This booklet would benefit more, if it were read occasionally. And it deserves to be read at all changes of life: marriage, expectancy, menopause, retirement, old age, new situations, etc.

LESS PASSION FROM LESS PROTEIN: LESS FISH MEAT BIRD CHEESE EGG; PEAS BEANS, NUTS and SITTING

EIGHT PASSION PROTEINS WITH CARE

ASK FOR A BOOKLET

10p

Talk About the Passion

In the right city or town and on the right street or square, it's a certainty that you'll find somebody preaching. Most street preachers get pretty manic and try to reach the crowd using the time-honoured method of shouting very loudly, but few become permanent fixtures on their stretch of street (mostly because their voices just won't hold out). That's what made Stanley Green, aka The Protein Man, special. He worked the busiest shopping centre in London – Oxford Street – almost daily for two-and-a-half decades.

In 1968, Stanley Green began parading between Oxford Circus and Tottenham Court Road with a sign extolling the virtues of 'Less Passion from Less Protein'. The sign pointed the finger squarely at the culprits behind passion: 'fish, meat, bird, cheese, egg, peas, beans, nuts and sitting'. The bit about sitting always left people scratching their heads, but it all made sense if you whipped out ten to twelve pence and bought a copy of Stanley's booklet, 'Eight Passion Proteins With Care'.

Stanley self-published this typographer's nightmare by hand at home, and, frankly, it looked like the work of a man who needed a square meal. He switched font size and line spacing at random and set occasional words or parts of words in capital letters for no apparent reason. It was also full of distinctive phrases: Our favourite was his euphemism for the act that resulted from consuming too much protein, 'married-love'. None of this did much to shake Stanley's reputation for being a bit kooky, but if you look beyond the odd presentation, his actual writing makes some kind of sense; and he did seem genuinely interested in the welfare of the people who milled around him.

Stanley's argument was this: Eating too much protein and leading too sedentary a life makes people unhappy. It fuels a desire that can't be satisfied, creates tension between married couples, and creates an unhealthy environment for raising children. It doesn't make single people too cheerful either. Of course, this was not a message that resonated in London in the Swinging Sixties, so he found himself at the receiving end of a fair amount of abuse (he even took to wearing green overalls to protect himself from any spittle that flew his way). But he seemed to shrug off the abuse because it just underscored his belief that these people were unhappy. . . .

Stanley first saw the problems of excess passion during his wartime stint in the Royal Navy, when he was rather shocked at the bawdiness of his fellow sailors. After the war, he took a series of jobs, working at Selfridges, Ealing Borough Council, the Post Office and, finally, as a gardener. By the late 1950s, he had refined his philosophy; so, at the age of fifty-three he took his message to the streets. After six months of part-time proselytizing in Harrow, he took his banner and booklets to Oxford Street to spread the word full time. Until he reached retirement age and got a free bus pass, he used to cycle the fifteen miles to his new place of work each day. And, according to his accounts, he was an extraordinarily successful author, selling 87,000 copies of his book. He also sent copies to five prime ministers (from Edward Heath to John Major), the Prince of Wales, the Archbishop of Canterbury, and a director-general of the BBC. His activities got him arrested twice (once in 1980, then again in 1985) for public obstruction, yet he continued undeterred until his death in 1993.

Somehow, Oxford Street seemed much less fun after that. But when you think back to London in the 1980s, and visits to shops like HMV and the Virgin Megastore, you may recall how miserable many people looked on that busy street as they dodged the press of humanity coming their way. Some blamed the crowds for the grim expressions on people's faces, but at least one man in the crowd placed the blame squarely on the burgers they had feasted on at the newly established McDonald's restaurant.

On Ward. And Upward

Behind the pub in a little village near Grantham (Lincolnshire), there stands a workshop. Inside this stone building is a man earnestly plugging away on his latest invention – a twelve-foot electromechanical carrot that looks like a space rocket from 1930s science fiction. The structure is supposed to provide luxury accommodation for a pet rabbit, complete with a lift. And as you look at this imposing edifice clad in orange fake fur, one question keeps coming to mind: 'What kind of person would invest his time and energy in building that?'

The man in question is John Ward, an eccentric inventor who has been cranking out obscure but well-designed machines and art pieces for more than thirty years. He has designed and built a number of viable electric vehicles, several frivolous musical kitchen appliances, and a torrent of utterly absurd gadgets, such as an electric bra warmer and a hat with a built-in pencil sharpener. In short, he sounded like our kind of bloke, and particularly well worth a visit, plus (and let's not deny the appeal of this little detail) his workshop is behind a pub.

The first impression you get of John Ward is that of an old vinyl LP being played a few revolutions per minute too fast. As he belts out his ideas, he makes leaps from sublime and serious subjects to the frivolous in a matter of seconds, then jumps back again before you've had time to react. After a while, however, you begin to wonder if John Ward is actually playing at normal speed, and that it's you and the rest of the world who are a few revs per minute too slow.

In the three-hour visit we made to John's workshop,

we gave up trying to direct the conversation (and, on occasion, even to understand it), realising that things would start to make a lot more sense if we stopped trying to channel his thought processes. Although he's clearly a bit of a showman, he's clearly got an inventor's brain that works just a little differently from everybody else's.

Take his reaction to a newspaper article he read some years back in which a writer joked that her pet hate was a cold bra. Most of us would probably have laughed once and forgotten about it. John Ward thought for a while, went to his workshop, and came up with a solution. He dismantled a hairdryer, scaled down the heat and air flows, mounted the fan and heating element to two fist-sized perforated plastic balls and, presto!, he had built a viable bra warmer.

John got started on this strange path decades ago when he failed to get industry attention for his bona fide inventions. He had piles of rejections from the motor industry for safety enhancements he had dreamed up. He had a young family and an active mind, and, in his own words, he remained 'a nonentity and professional failure'. But that mind of his kept turning to things he could build. He made an electric car out of bits of a broken washing machine, powered it with a twelve-volt car battery, and let his eight-year-old son drive it to the shops. With a grocery wagon fixed to the back, the little car was actually useful as well as whimsical; and with a snow-plough attachment at the front, it could be used to clear walkways. He built other vehicles along similar lines, including one he called the Woganmobile, in the hope that, like the genial talk show host of the same name, it would soon be everywhere. If any of this sounds like the much reviled Sinclair C5, it's worth remembering that John Ward's electric cars first hit headlines in 1981, two years before Clive Sinclair began developing his electric car and four years before it was launched. Oh, and one more thing: People clamour for John's vehicles.

'Someone wanted to buy a giant electric train that I'd built for the kids to ride on,' he told us, 'I told them it was for the kids, so I wasn't going to sell. And he pulls a big wad of money out and says, "Everyone has their price; what'll it take? You could build me another one just like it." Well, it doesn't work that way. The therapy, if you like, of inventing things is in the act of doing it. Doing the same thing over and over doesn't interest me.'

Which is probably why John gets sidetracked into speaking at corporate events, calling bingo at the local old folks home, being a guest scientist at schools and doing whatever else strikes his fancy. But despite the content of his work and his cultivated mad-scientist persona, he doesn't consider himself out of the ordinary.

'It's a funny culture. I'm a professional failure and a nonentity, but my scrapbook's better than a lot of so-called professionals,' he told us.

'You come across these individuals. This fellow comes along and says "I've got the secret to perpetual motion, I have . . ." and I go "Oh, have you got it with you?" and he says "Ooh, no, I daren't 'cause they'll all want it if I do." And they think I'm bloody crazed. The real crazies are out there, but nobody's bothered to do a head count.'

The Slingshot Hotshot

Before Hew Kennedy came along, people just didn't understand the connection between medieval siege weaponry, dead animals, fire and pianos. Just how dense were people twenty years ago? To our modern eyes, the connection is clear: You build a replica of a fourteenth-century trebuchet, load it up with any projectile, from rocks and pig carcasses to pianos, set fire to the projectile and let it rip.

Of course, it takes a leap of logic from a truly extraordinary mind to make this connection for the first time, and that's exactly the chasm that Hew Kennedy leaped. He had studied old manuscripts that told of a strange device that Edward Longshanks, engineers dreamed up to break the siege of Stirling Castle in 1304. This weapon of mass destruction proved very difficult to track down, but Hew Kennedy is the kind of man who liked a challenge. He found manuscript illustrations of an A-frame with a catapult arm, a slingshot and a counterweight, and he began to build one of his own. The result proved so robust that he was able to sling whole pianos hundreds of feet. Some manuscripts showed trebuchets slinging dead animals in an early form

of biological warfare, so he tried his hand at that, too, declaring that dead pigs were wonderfully aerodynamic. For a crowning achievement, his sixty-five-foot long catapult arm managed to launch an entire car. True, it was only a Hillman Imp, but it was a car nevertheless.

Hew's achievements catapulted his fame beyond his estate in Acton Round, Shropshire, and right across the world. Other trebuchet builders may have performed more daring feats (such as an American enthusiast who launches himself into rivers), but our favourite will always be the man who made pigs fly over English hills.

A modern replica of a medieval trebuchet similar to Hew Kennedy's version.

By and large, the English are very tolerant of their monarchs. The occasional civil war notwithstanding, we seem to accept the rule of kings and queens a lot more readily than most nations do. In fact, we accept our royals so readily that we've let a few extras slip in without any protest. England, you see, contains many kingdoms. Not just the old kingdoms of Wessex, Mercia and so on. We're talking about new and tiny kingdoms called micro-nations, right here on English sovereign soil.

All 3,000 residents of Cuckfield in West Sussex seceded from the United Kingdom in 1965 to gain publicity for local charity events. Somewhat more seriously, the Isle of Dogs in London's Docklands declared itself a republic in 1970 to protest against lack of council funding. They rejoined when public money appeared, but to punish these transgressions, their shores were covered in concrete and turned into a massive shopping and office complex. (Or perhaps that was just the forces of gentrification in the 1990s.)

However, these ersatz states were basically designed along anarchist lines. We prefer those states led by people who proudly call themselves kings and princes. These nouveau nobles may have delusions of grandeur, but they're a lot more fun than most revolutionaries.

We Two Kings of Lundy Are

On two separate occasions people have tried to exercise independence from the United Kingdom by occupying Lundy Island off the north coast of Devon. The first man went by the highly unlikely name of William Hudson Heaven, a sugar plantation heir who bought the place in the 1830s. Heaven pointed out that because Lundy Island was not officially part of any county, the British Empire clearly could not lay claim to it. Therefore, he reasoned, its residents did not owe fealty (or taxes) to the Crown. Yet Heaven retained his right to vote because of his other residence on the mainland. The press enjoyed being able to use the line 'The Kingdom of Heaven', but Heaven never actually claimed sovereignty – the islanders merely called him The Squire.

That wasn't the case with Martin Coles Harman, however, who bought both the island and the contract to administer its postal system in 1924. He was legally allowed to print postage, but Harman stretched the point by declaring that this made Lundy Island an independent dominion within the British Commonwealth. He appointed himself ruler and in 1929 began minting penny- and halfpenny-sized Puffin and Half Puffin coins with his own head on them. This was a tactical error. If the Dominion of Lundy was, as he had stated, 'a self-governing dominion of the British Empire recognising King George as its head', it was bound by the Coinage Act of 1870. This meant that he could be fined for minting currency without the face of the ruling British monarch on it. Sure enough, in 1931, Harman was issued a slap-on-the-wrist fine, and he quietly abdicated. But the island remained in the Harman family until 1968, when it passed to the National Trust.

Roy, Prince of Sealand

The skipper throttled down as we headed for the ladder and then suddenly all hell broke out around us. It was like the water was boiling. We all ducked down. We were being fired at with a machine gun. The skipper lost hold of the steering wheel and the boat spun around. The force of the turn sent us hard into the bulkhead. Ronan shouted "Oh Holy Mary, Mother of God! Let's get the hell out of here!"

The skipper grabbed the wheel. The boat surged away. I got up and looked back. A small figure was shaking his fist and shouting. And then he started throwing gasoline bombs at us. These hit the water bursting into flames. . .

"That guy nearly killed us!" I said. "That's for sure. That man is pretty desperate to hold onto that tower."

Later I learned that Roy Bates created a nation out of that tower and called it Sealand.
– from *The Ship that Rocked the World!* by Tom Lodge

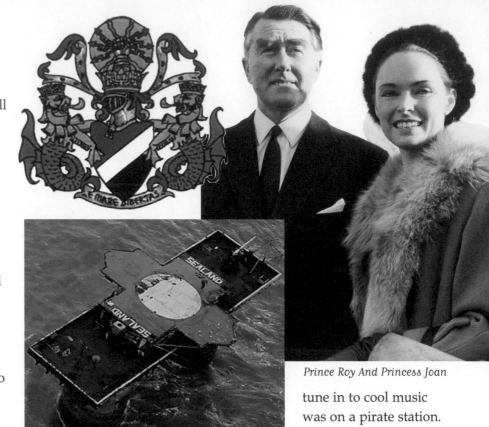

Prince Roy And Princess Joan

Some people are born royal and some have royalty thrust upon them. Others fight for the crown and fight to keep it. Paddy Roy Bates is one of the fighters. He took possession of an island fortress built during World War Two, declared it an independent principality and, in his new role as Prince Roy, fought in court and on the high seas to keep it independent.

Before becoming Prince Roy, Bates was a former army major who owned a pirate-radio station. During the 1960s, pirate-radio stations broadcast music that the BBC wouldn't play from ships anchored outside British coastal waters. Before the BBC caved in and created Radio 1 in 1967, the only place that hip youngsters could tune in to cool music was on a pirate station. The careers of John Peel, Kenny Everett, Tony Blackburn and Dave Lee Travis all started in pirate radio.

Roy Bates' plan for his own station, Radio Essex, included a canny bit of budgeting: Instead of buying or leasing a boat and radio transmitter, he would squat on an abandoned World War Two anti-aircraft fort and use its old US Air Force radio beacon. So, in October 1965, Roy Bates took control of the fort of Knock John Tower in the Thames Estuary and began broadcasting. The plan backfired: The platform was within British coastal waters and within a year he was charged with operating a radio station without a licence and fined. But there was another fort in the Thames Estuary that stood outside British waters: Roughs Tower. Bates set his sights on this.

These were rough times for pirate radio on the high seas. The year before, an offshore entrepreneur named Major

An Audience with Their Majesties
By Sean Hastings

In the summer of 1999, I communicated with Michael Bates, the son of Prince Roy of Sealand, and I flew to England to meet him. In the process of crossing from one terminal entrance to another, I twisted my ankle, falling to the pavement and cutting open my hand. This pratfall was the first impression I made on the members of the Sealand Royal Family.

When I returned from dressing my wounded hand, Prince Michael and Princess Joan were there. The first thing Michael says is 'You don't have to bow down like that. I'm not the Pope.' Michael is a funny guy, but it would have been funnier if I hadn't just injured myself.

This was only my second helicopter ride, so I was torn between the excitement of visiting a micro-nation, fear of flying and wanting to pass out from lack of sleep. Excitement won out when Sealand came into view. It was beautiful. Until I saw it, it could all have been a hoax. Reading about something – even seeing photographs – it's just not the same as laying eyes on it. A tiny bastion of freedom in the middle of a cold sea, I wanted to ask for political asylum and move in that very day.

As we flew over Sealand, I got my first glimpse of Prince Roy. This eighty-year-old man quickly climbed a ladder to the helicopter pad, and jogged over to the centre to remove the mast that prevented unwanted landings. He lowered the mast single-handedly and cleared the way for us to land. I hope I am in as good shape when I am his age. Hell, I hope I even manage to live that long.

The helicopter landed and all disembarked. I shook Roy's hand, and everyone exchanged greetings all around. I made for an old 3.5-inch gun that had defended this fortress from the German Navy in World War Two. There had been guns on either side of the helipad, and on the other side of the deck. Only one artillery piece remained, but it was an excellent symbol of defiance.

My tour of Sealand was a real treat. Each of the columns that hold it aloft is hollow, with seven levels, down to the bottom of the sea. It is the area of a medium-sized building, the only building in the free world. I climbed down to the bottom of each column to make sure they were not full of water. The generator was not running, so all was dark. Michael accompanied me around, and we each carried a flashlight. The ladders were rusted and dirty, and I could only imagine what sort of evil stuff was getting rubbed into the cut on my hand, but I was too excited to care.

When I was done crawling in the columns, I went back up to the main room in the top of Sealand. A huge Sealand flag decorated one wall, and there were bookshelves filled with detective and spy novels. One corner had a TV in it. I had seen a gun rack in another room, and had immediately appreciated that these weapons were a real sign of freedom and independence from Britain, where guns are outlawed and even the cops just carry clubs. But even the TV set was a badge of liberty from Britain, where the government owns the electromagnetic spectrum of smaller frequency than visible light, and charges its citizens for the privilege of receiving such waves. This TV was free!

Oliver Smedley shot and killed Radio City's proprietor Reg Calvert in a dispute over an offshore fort. So when Bates sailed to the Rough Sands sandbar where Roughs Tower was built, he went prepared. The previous week, an employee of Radio Caroline had laid claim to the fort; Bates summarily evicted this squatter, and set about installing some serious defences (allegedly machine guns and petrol bombs) to defend his new digs.

But all these efforts were in vain. A new law designed to kill pirate radio was passed in the summer of 1967; it forbade any British subject from broadcasting into British airspace, either from inside or outside British territory. So Radio Essex never broadcast from Roughs Tower. But the bit about the law applying to British subjects gave Roy an idea. And so was born the sovereign principality of Sealand, which Roy and his wife, Princess Joan, and their son Michael have reigned over ever since. In 1968, a British court agreed that the tower was outside British coastal waters, and therefore outside British jurisdiction. And so Sealand became an honest-to-goodness state.

Prince Roy issued passports, minted commemorative currency, and bestowed titles upon his friends and anybody who was prepared to pay for them. As he spent a fair amount of time on the mainland, he set up a government to operate in his absence, led by a Prime

Minister named Alexander G. Achenbach. Achenbach staged a coup in 1978, holding Prince Michael hostage for a while before releasing him in the Netherlands. Bates simply raised an army, chartered a helicopter and retook the tower.

He arrested the revolutionaries as prisoners of war and repatriated most of them, except for a German lawyer who held a Sealand passport. He held that this man's acts were treasonable, and that he would release him only on payment of a fine of more than £18,000. Germany petitioned the British government for this man's release, but the British cited its own 1968 court decision and denied all responsibility.

And so for more than thirty years, Prince Roy has weathered many storms. Even though a 1987 redrawing of coastal boundaries put the principality within British jurisdiction, the Sealand monarchy goes on. And when Prince Roy retired in 1999, he ceded the government to his son Michael, who was appointed Prince Regent. So far, there has been only one serious legal drawback to Sealand's status: In 1990, an American court refused to recognise Sealand's right to register ships. The Sealand-registered Merchant Vessel *Sarah* had been broadcasting pirate radio just off Long Island in New York, and the Coast Guard swept in to stop it. The connection between micro-nations and pirate radio, it seems, will never end.

And Wye Not?

Because it's already straddling the border between England and Wales, Hay-on-Wye in Herefordshire (and Powys, Wales) has always been an ideal candidate for secession. If it's already sitting on a border, why not just say it's actually *between* the two countries, and declare it a sovereign nation?

That's the question that Richard Booth put to himself, and since he couldn't come up with a good reason not to, he proclaimed that Hay-on-Wye was from that point on a nation dedicated to books, with himself as its king. In a move reminiscent of Caligula, he appointed his horse as Prime Minister.

That happened on 1 April 1978, but Richard Booth was already a well-established local eccentric at that point. He had returned as an adult to his childhood hometown at the dawn of the Swinging Sixties, having earned a degree from Oxford University. He set up shop as a second-hand bookseller in the local fire station, and bought the ruins of the town's castle in 1961 ('You could have bought the whole town for six quid back then,' he claimed). He struggled to establish the place as a book town, importing antiquarian books from all over. 'You buy books from all over the world and your customers come from all over the world,' he reasoned.

This bold rationale, and his strange publicity-seeking claim of kingship, seemed to attract the right kind of attention to this modest little town a long way off the beaten track. With his theatrical crown and his orb made out of an old brass ballcock, he cut a strange figure. Nevertheless, he eventually turned a ramshackle rural community into a bona fide book town with more than three dozen booksellers. In 1988, Hay-on-Wye became the host town of an annual week-long international book festival, which now attracts 70,000 visitors a year.

But King Richard's fortunes turned out to be less great than his kingdom's. When a fire ran through his living quarters in Hay Castle in 1978, he was forced to ramp up the publicity machine to raise money to rebuild. He began to crank out merchandise including flags, autographed pictures, bumper stickers and a series of booklets. Under the byline Wise King Richard of Hay, the collector's items he published included *God Save Us From the Development Board*, *Bring Back Horses* and *Abolish the Wales Tourist Board*.

His disdain of the governments on both sides of his own kingdom came to a head in 2000, when he protested against the abolition of hereditary peers in the House of Lords by investing twenty-one new hereditary peers in the Kingdom of Hay. But even this act of defiance couldn't stop the sneaking admiration of other sovereign nations: King Richard made the 2003 Queen's New Year's Honours list, and in 2004 he became Richard Booth, MBE.

But the shabby King of Hay and Member of the British Empire is less of a feature around town than he used to be. Until recently, he could still be seen restocking the fifty-pence shelves at his castle home, dressed in scuffed shoes and a tweed jacket with buttons hanging loose. But in 2005 he declared his intention of selling up and moving to Germany. His love of books did not, it seem, extend to book people. He would often grumble (or perhaps joke) that the folk the festival brought in were 'A bunch of intellectual snobs talking about themselves.'

But if he truly felt that way, the feeling was clearly not reciprocated. When he announced his intention to sell up and leave, the Member of Parliament for Brecon and Radnorshire, Roger Williams, declared 'His legacy will be that Hay changed from a small market town into a Mecca for second-hand book lovers and this transformed the local economy . . . I for one will be eternally grateful for that.'

Not Destined for the House of Lords

Not every would-be ruler sets his sights on the monarchy. David Sutch took a more modest route to power: He declared himself a lord, dressed up in leopard-skin costumes and a top hat and stood for election – repeatedly. In fact, he stumped at more than forty elections over three decades, and lost his deposit at every one. Perhaps that's unsurprising, given that he was the leading light of The Official Monster Raving Loony Party. Though his successes were modest in terms of votes, he pulled off a major coup: Each time, the announcer of the results had to utter the words 'monster raving loony' with the same gravitas as 'social democrat' and 'conservative'. Few others can make that boast.

In the 1960s, when he was a singer and pirate-radio host, David Sutch changed his name by deed poll to Screaming Lord Sutch, Third Earl of Harrow. At the time, he was staging theatrical rock-horror shows in which he made his entrance in a coffin, handled skulls and daggers, and dressed up as the subject of his most enduring song: Jack the Ripper. Even though he was a terrible singer, he managed to attract some A-list musicians to work with him, including Jimmy Page, Jeff Beck and Keith Moon. In short, his stage show anticipated the kind of thing Alice Cooper would do a decade later, but unlike Cooper, he didn't just sing 'I wanna be elected', he actually went out and tried to make it happen.

Even as an entertainer,

he made nods toward the politics of the day: After the Profumo scandal that brought down the government in the early 1960s, he tried to hire one of the women involved to read from the banned book *Lady Chatterley's Lover* on his pirate-radio show. And he first stood for election in 1963 in the by-election for the Stratford-upon-Avon seat vacated by John Profumo. Under the banner of the National Teenage Party and with the slogan 'Vote for Insanity – you know it makes sense', he scored an impressive (but statistically insignificant) 208 votes, and lost his deposit of £150.

In the General Election of the following year, Sutch stood in Prime Minister Harold Wilson's district. He gained more than 500 votes that time, but still lost his deposit. And so it went on for more than forty elections until the late 1990s. In 1983, he launched The Official Monster Raving Loony Party and stood against Margaret Thatcher in Finchley. Shortly afterwards, the Prime Minister got her own back for the embarrassment he had caused her: She pushed through a measure that more than tripled the deposit that candidates needed to put down to stand for election. But even though Sutch never polled more than a thousand votes and therefore kept losing his deposit, he was not deterred by this indirect tax on his sense of humour.

Sutch's actual policies ranged from the ridiculous to the sublime. The obvious jokes included giving pets the right to vote, demoting Prime Minister

to be open all day and radio stations to be allowed to carry commercials. Not only that, he had the radical suggestion of putting ramps on buses to help the elderly and disabled. So perhaps he wasn't entirely crazy, just ahead of his time.

Sadly for British politics, David Sutch was not a happy man. In 1999, at the age of fifty-eight, he was discovered hanging by a length of multi-coloured skipping rope in the stairwell of his late mother's house. He had long suffered from bouts of depression, and despite being on medicine for a bipolar condition, he had been slipping deeper into depression since his mother's death two years earlier. His last diary entry was bleaker than anyone would have imagined from such a zany entertainer: 'Depression, depression, depression is all too much.'

John Major to John Private, and banning January and February to make winters shorter. There were also elements of more satirical humour: When he declared his age, he quoted a number at least ten years younger than his real age, and finished the sentence with 'plus VAT'. He also questioned why there was only one Monopolies Commission. But surprisingly, some of his policies were later adopted by real politicians and passed into law: In the early 1960s, he suggested that eighteen-year-olds should be allowed to vote. He also wanted pubs

The funeral and gravestone, however, were in much more typical Lord Sutch form. Instead of the classic hymns, the funeral featured Chuck Berry music, and Sutch's gravestone included howlingly bad puns: 'A lord without peer, Sutch is the way it was with him.' Since his death, one of his friends, Alan Hope, has taken on the mantle of the Loony party leadership under the moniker Howling Laud Hope. So Sutch's party goes on. Too bad that Screaming Lord Sutch, the life and soul of the party, quit early.

True Crime –
Pre-Victorian Style

With the publication of pioneering literary works by Edgar Allan Poe and Sir Arthur Conan Doyle, Victorian England became a hotbed of crime writing, both factual and fictional. But *The Murders in the Rue Morgue* and the complete Sherlock Holmes canon have obscured the strange lustre of the true crimes carried out in earlier times. To redress that balance, here's a sample of tales of murder by cauldron and crimes against clothing.

Mr Jarman, Ostrich Killer

Ye Old Ostrich Inn in Colnbrook, Berkshire, is the third oldest pub in England and, according to some accounts, one of the most haunted too. It's midway between Slough and Heathrow Airport, but don't hold that against it. Any place that can screw a plaque on the wall to proclaim that King John slept there en route to the signing of Magna Carta is worth a visit, if only to drink in its ghostly atmosphere.

But the Ostrich has a much darker side to it, one that foreshadowed the grisly work of Sweeney Todd, the fictional demon barber of the Victorian era. The Ostrich's owner, one Mr Jarman, perpetrated crimes against his wealthy customers that the penny-dreadful character of Sweeney Todd would develop two centuries later into his meat-pie industry. Admittedly, there's no cannibalism involved in Jarman's crimes, but there was a fiendish machine designed to separate wealthy clients from their worldly goods. And for publicans in the days before fruit machines, this meant only one thing: A bed on a hinged platform.

Any seventeenth-century traveller unwary enough to look rich and show up alone for the night at Jarman's inn may have been shown to the Blue Room, situated directly above the kitchen. This well-appointed chamber featured a comfortable bed that almost nobody noticed was bolted to the floor. It needed to be. In the middle of the night, Jarman and his wife would go to the kitchen, boil up a huge vat of water (some say ale), and draw the bolts on a trapdoor in the ceiling. The floor of the Blue Room fell down, tipping the contents of the bed into the vat of boiling liquid, instantly killing the occupant.

After a brief trip to the river to dump the corpse, the Jarmans were free to loot his luggage for valuables and sell whatever they could. They did this so often that they got sloppy, and that was their undoing. When they murdered a gentleman named Thomas Cole, they lost his horse and didn't make much effort to find it. It was found nearby and traced back to the inn. It didn't take long to uncover the plot.

Sadly, when we visited the Ostrich nothing of the bolted bedroom remained. In fact, the whole place was closed for renovation and looked as though its famously uneven interior walls were being squared up with Barratt-home precision. From the outside, though, the overhanging first floor looks every bit the medieval building. And the tales those walls could tell would curl the hair of even one of Sweeney Todd's customers.

Admittedly, there's no cannibalism involved in Jarman's crimes, but there is a fiendish machine designed to separate wealthy clients from their worldly goods.

Wanted: For Crimes Against Clothing

Imagine, if you can, walking down a deserted London street in the days when the only lighting came from flickering lamps, and these were so few and far between that even a busy street looked dark and menacing. Now imagine that a stranger walks up to you and aggressively propositions you with a handful of artificial flowers. When you turn him down, he loses his temper, shouts abuse and threats and finally takes out a blade. As you try to run away, he begins slicing the clothes round your legs and waist, slashing straight through layers of dress and petticoat and actually drawing blood. As you make good your escape, he stands shouting abuse before sloping off to his hideout.

What you've just imagined happened to at least thirty women in the space of two years, culminating in a bizarre trial that focused not on the damage done to their bodies, but to their clothes. It is the tale of a menace who stalked women between 1788 and 1790, and who went by the sinister name of the London Monster.

For a couple of years, the Monster's attacks showed up the inadequacies of the standing police force, the Bow Street Runners, and created such a panic that women would wear metal undergarments or even porridge pots beneath their skirts to protect themselves. Eventually, a philanthropic financier named John Julius Angerstein offered a reward of £100 for any information leading to the Monster's capture. Naturally, the lure of a substantial reward brought along many bogus claims, but eventually John

Coleman came along with allegations against a Jermyn Street artisan named Rhynwick Williams for stabbing his fiancée.

Williams made silk flowers for a living, and answered the description made by several of the Monster's victims. The trial posed several problems, however. One was a conflict of interest: Coleman and his betrothed, Anne Porter, were the star witnesses for the prosecution, but they also stood to make a lot of money from a conviction so thir testimony was automatically suspect. Also, the crimes themselves did not fit conveniently under any existing law. The assaults were serious but not deadly, and common assault was a fairly minor crime. Common theft was taken much more seriously so the prosecution took the novel approach of trying Williams under a 1721 statute that classified assault with an intention to tear or deface another person's clothing as a felony.

Fortunately for the prosecution, the testimony of the victim Anne Porter and her husband-to-be, John Coleman, was corroborated by a number of the Monster's other victims, who were able to identify Williams as their assailant. After being convicted of the felony of crimes against dress, Williams was sentenced to the maximum penalty for such crimes, six years in Newgate Gaol. And so ended the slasher's reign of terror. But tales of his attacks fuelled the legends of Spring Heeled Jack in the years that followed, and paved the way for the deadlier and more appalling criminal phenomenon that was Jack the Ripper.

Four-Legged Hero

Not every hero has a chiselled jaw and a noble brow. Some are hairy and panting and smell like old dog. I refer of course to man's best friend and constant canine companion. It should come as no surprise to learn that pets can be every bit the local heroes that humans can. Pets can, at least, be relied upon not to follow up their acts of heroism by marrying reality TV stars or attacking the paparazzi. In the Weird world, every dog, big or small, famous or unknown, has his day.

Slough's Finest

There are many great things to say about Slough. It was the setting of Ricky Gervais's boss-from-hell TV series *The Office*, for one thing. It was also the subject of a classic poem by poet laureate Sir John Betjeman, who opened his ode with the line 'Come friendly bombs and fall on Slough'. But of all the things that are great about the place, none can compare to the memorial the townsfolk erected to the local railway hero Station Jim. They held him in such high esteem that when he died in 1896, they stuffed and mounted him, and put him in a glass case on Platform Five.

Station Jim became Slough's railway mascot when he was brought to the station as a three-month-old puppy, small enough to fit in an overcoat pocket. He learned how to climb the footbridge early in life, and, after about a month, he was sent out to the platforms to earn his keep as the Canine Collector for the Great Western Railway Widows and Orphans Fund. He wore a harness with collection boxes attached, and was trained to bark every time someone put a coin in.

In the days before iPods, portable DVD players and mobile phones, railway platforms were even more tedious than they are now, so Jim became a popular entertainer. He would sit up and beg, stand up on his legs, parade around with a pipe in his mouth and sing along to any music he might hear. He would climb ladders and sit on chairs, and if there were any small children about feeling like a game of leapfrog, he would oblige them.

He would also occasionally stow away on the train. He went to Paddington, Windsor and even as far as Royal Leamington Spa on one occasion. But he was always spotted and recognised because of his distinctive collection-box harness, and he was always seen onto a returning train by the conductor. Except for once, when he bolted from Windsor station and made his way back to Slough on foot.

But Station Jim's real contribution was his charity work. On a really good day, he could clear more than two hundred coins, mostly pennies and halfpennies. Once in a while, a rich and generous fellow might slip a half crown in to the mix, and on one occasion, someone dropped a gold half sovereign into the collection box – a coin with a face value in today's money of fifty pence, but a hefty whack for an ad hoc charitable donation 110 years ago.

Jim was collecting donations at the station on the evening of 19 November 1896 when he suddenly dropped dead. Although he was only a few years old, he had made such an impression that they made a collection to erect a memorial to him. And what better way to remember a hero than to stuff and mount him in a glass case on a railway platform? That's surely worth pausing your portable DVD player to scope out next time you're waiting for a train in Slough.

Brighton Beach Memoir

Strange folk are all around us, but somehow we have a soft spot for the street eccentrics of Brighton. For one thing, there are so many of them! But their numbers are not important – it's the qualities they display: Utterly self-possessed, completely out of kilter with the rest of the world and absolutely unconcerned about it.

One of the more mysterious characters was Happy the Bus Man, who was either a bus conductor or just a big bus fan who waved at buses with a big smile on his face. He was distinctly un-English in his open-smiled way, and would always have a nice word to say to anyone who smiled or waved back. Some people called him Bert, but that might not have been his name.

Another fine example of south-coast eccentricity was Moses, who was quite a fixture on Western Road in the late 1980s and early 1990s. He wore old-testament robes and carried a staff, but just to bring himself into the twentieth century, he carried a television on his back and wore a clock hung round his neck. He wasn't big on road safety, either: He used to walk the line in the middle of the road

The Churchill Square Dancer was a nattily dressed old man who used to play an old tape recorder at a respectfully quiet volume, and tap dance to the tunes. A lot of people never actually realised he was dancing to music, however, because the volume was turned down so low, but that made him look all the more a loveable eccentric.

Boys on Bikes

When most people think about two-wheeled vehicles in Brighton, they think of Mods and Rockers on their scooters and Triumphs. But over the past few summers, I've seen a resurgence of pedal cycles on the seafront that are much more interesting to look at than somebody trying to look like Sting in *Quadrophenia*. For one thing, they seem to be trying to outdo each other in a competition to look the most eccentric.

For example, the Telly Man frequents the West Pier in the evenings with a foot-wide television fixed onto the front of his bike. He's wrapped fairy lights and fake flowers round the framework and seems to delight in the crowd that gathers around his strange vehicle. I've heard people call him Terry, but that may not be his actual name: Some people call him Terry Addict behind his back.

There's another cyclist with electronic entertainment mounted on his bike. He's a bit of a muscle man, and he plays a massive boom box with enormous speakers stuck on his handlebars. Known to many as Mr Boombastic (after the 1990s single), you can hear him coming from way down the beach because he plays his music so loud, and he has a pretty eclectic collection, too: I've heard him play anything from heavy metal shredding to ukulele tunes.

But my favourite is a bloke I like to call Noah, though I've also heard him called Dr Doolittle or the Pirate Zookeeper. He's a white-haired old beach bum with a big earring, tattoos and a parrot perched on his shoulder. But that's not the only animal he carries on his sturdy old grocer's bike. This vehicle is like a two-wheeled ark, with literally dozens of rats, dogs and other creatures either perched in the front basket or stuffed in the cyclist's pockets. The man clearly loves to be surrounded by animals, but I'm not sure that the RSPCA would approve.

You can't knock a good fortune teller. The idea that someone can gaze into the future and tell you what it holds for you is close to irresistible. You just *have* to seek out people like this. But if you do, bear in mind that they don't have to have a crystal ball and sit in a carnival tent to be able to predict the future. Sometimes all they need is to be the spawn of the Devil himself or the reincarnation of a phantom offspring of a nineteenth-century virgin. Don't believe it? Then read on ...

The Prophet's Name is Ursula

Every nation worth its salt needs a famous prophet and soothsayer. Someone who can foretell events so ambiguously that they can't conclusively be proved right or wrong. France had Nostradamus; America had Edgar Cayce; even the Greek island of Patmos had the fellow who wrote the dramatic conclusion to the Bible, the Revelation to St John. For our part, England had Mother Shipton.

Ursula Shipton, a Yorkshire lass, was born in Knaresborough in 1488. She was born in suitably dramatic circumstances: on a dark and stormy night, in a cave right next to the bizarre natural phenomenon still known as the Petrifying Well. Her young mother was an innocent teenage girl tossed out of her community because she had been seduced and fallen pregnant out of wedlock. Oh, and the cad responsible was the Devil himself.

So right away, you know the story is not going to end with Ursula leading a normal life. Sure enough she was born hideously deformed, with a huge crooked nose described in an early biography as 'adorned with many strange pimples of diverse colours as red, blue, and mixed, which like vapours of brimstone gave such a lustre of the night.' She was reviled by her community because of her illegitimate birth and her ugliness, yet she found a niche on the outskirts of society: She began to tell fortunes and

WONDERFUL MAGAZINE.

MOTHER SHIPTON'S *favorite mode of* TRAVELLING.
Pubd by C Johnson.

help out as a village wise woman with herbal remedies and counter-curses to undo dark magic. Eventually, she married a man called Tony Shipton, though they probably had no children (the Mother part of her name was a common enough term of respect for an older woman). She gained quite a following, and after she was widowed she went back to the cave in Knaresborough where she was born. There, she cranked out fortunes and prophecies until her death around 1560.

The first written records of what this hag with a glowing nose foretold appeared in print eighty years after her death. They included such revelations as the fact that Cardinal Wolsey would never visit York. (This was a foregone conclusion, since Cardinal Wolsey had died on his way back to London after cutting short a visit that took him almost as far north as York, more than a century before the book came out). But this tale was only included to establish her as a bona fide soothsayer. More

prophecies followed in collections published in 1684 and then much later in 1862. The really telling verses came in the later volume:

Carriages without horses shall goe,
And accidents fill the world with woe.

Around the world thoughts shall fly
In the twinkling of an eye

Under water men shall walk,
Shall ride, shall sleep and talk

Iron in the water shall float,
As easy as a wooden boat.

To a modern eye, these verses could easily refer to cars, satellite communications or the Internet, deep-sea diving equipment and steel-clad ocean liners. But they could equally easily mean nothing at all. And they could also have been made up by almost anybody between the time of her death and their first appearance in print in the 1862 edition. Nobody's sure of the journalistic integrity of Richard Head (who edited the 1684 collection) or Charles Hindley (who was behind the 1862 edition), but one thing's for sure: Writers who traffic in the tales of soothsaying spawn of Satan may well grant themselves more licence than, say, the news staff of the *Daily Telegraph* (present company excepted, of course).

The Messiah's Name is Mabel the Shiloh

In case you were wondering, the Garden of Eden was in Bedford. In the area enclosed by Castle Street, the Embankment, Newnham Road and Rothsay Road, to be exact. Due to some great advance planning about eighty years ago, several properties in the area were snapped up by a group calling itself the Panacea Society. These days not much goes on around there, but that's probably because we're still waiting for twenty-four bishops from the Church of England to open the Society's box of prophecies and study them for seven days and seven nights in the presence of twenty-four white-gowned virgins. When that finally happens, England will be saved from the twin evils of crime and banditry. Oh, and we'll also discover the news about a messiah called the Shiloh and find out how to prepare for the end of the world.

Confused yet? You will be, because the Panacea Society's beliefs and origins are about as peculiar as any we've encountered. Certainly, they have yet to persuade a quorum of bishops to perform the opening. And that's too bad, because I for one would love to know what's in the box. Or for that matter, how Mabel Barltrop managed to persuade a group of disciples to give up all their worldly goods to join the society.

At first blush, Mabel seems like an unlikely cult leader: She was released from a mental institution shortly after World War One, and began to claim that she was a reincarnation of the Shiloh. This in itself was quite an achievement: The Shiloh was the offspring of a notorious nineteenth-century prophetess named Joanna Southcott, who declared that the Holy Ghost had quickened her and that she would deliver a messiah. Actually, Southcott didn't give birth to anyone, as she was a sixty-four-year-old virgin at the time. But when she died shortly after Christmas 1814, her followers declared that the Shiloh must have been delivered in spirit form, awaiting the end of the world, which Southcott had declared would be at the conveniently distant date of 2004.

The spirit of the Shiloh floated around, waiting, presumably, for Mabel's release from the asylum. And a century later, along she came and started recruiting disciples. With their pooled resources, the Panaceans bought a lot of Bedford property to use as a base for distributing the Panacea, a liquid that would cure all ills because it was made by passing

Mabel Barltrop and children, c. 1907

water through cloth that the prophetess Joanna Southcott had breathed on. Along the way, Mabel produced a box that contained the final prophecies of her (sort-of) mother, which was revered by the Panaceans as a kind of Ark of the Covenant.

And so the story ends, actually. Some people claim that the box was opened in 1927, and contained bric-a-brac including a toy pistol, but no prophecies. Others in the Society claim that that box was a decoy and the real Ark awaits the twenty-four bishops. In the meantime, a few remaining (and ageing) Panaceans still wait in Bedford for the end of the world. Which should have arrived in 2004, plus or minus the standard margin of error for nineteenth-century prophets. Anyone care to revise that estimate?

Peculiar Properties

If you want to find out a thing or two about somebody, there are two sure-fire ways to gain a special insight: Take a good look at where they live, and examine whatever it is they collect. Homes and gardens reflect the inner life of the occupants as well as their outer lives. A manicured lawn, a well-tended house and symmetrically cut hedges are a sure sign that the occupants are either attempting to sell the house or that they have sick minds. *Our* kind of people don't install nice fences and water features; no, they drive a steam train into their front garden. They don't beautify their neighbourhoods by planting privet hedges and a fruit tree; instead, they strap a giant fibreglass fish onto the roof. You may not want to buy such a house, but you won't be able to help yourself from taking a good look at it as you walk by.

And then there are the other kinds of property: The things we collect to fill our houses. Over the years, some of the more interesting private collections have been put on public display in museums – a word that most people forget comes from the word 'muse', and means a place that inspires people. Fortunately for us, a few truly inspiring museums still exist. And by inspiring, we mean they are institutions happy to fill their display cases with shrunken heads, mandrake roots and deformed skeletons – all the while keeping the *really* weird stuff locked away in drawers in a back room.

Sir Francis Drake   Major Yuri Gagarin
the Golden Hind 1577/80   first man in space

Florence Nightingale   Marco Polo
'The Lady with the Lamp'   13th Explorer

Jesse   Boots   Charles Dickens
Boot   Author 1812-70

Charles   RR   Gladys May Aylward
Stewart Rolls   20th Missionary

John Mytton   Frederick Henry   RR
1st eccentric   Royce

George and Richard   Cadbury's   Jemmy Hirst
Cadbury   18th eccentric

Ganxhe Agnes Bojaxhiu   Joseph Cyril
Mother Teresa   Bamford   Excavator

Harold Makepeace   Derek Ball
20th American eccentric   20th Man of God

Jeremiah James Colman   Isaac   S
Colman's Mustard   Singer   SM

Eddie   The Eagle   Bob   'Feed the
Edwards   Geldof   World'

Henry   Ford   Sir Jimmy Saville
Ford

Richard   Lord Cornbury 18th
Branson   govenor who wore
ladies gowns

Lord Baden-Powell   Brian Clough
Founder of Boy Scouts 1908   Football player
and Girl Guides 1910   manager supreme

To most people, doing up a garden involves planting some shrubs, laying a bit of crazy paving and bringing out the deckchairs. Not our kind of gardeners, though. If the landscaping doesn't make you crane your neck so fast you're in danger of getting whiplash, it's not a weird garden. Thankfully, there are plenty of gardens in England that do put you at such a risk.

The Cement Menagerie

If you drive at a sedate pace north from Morpeth or Alnwick in Northumberland for less than an hour, you'll reach Branxton and find the garden of The Fountain House filled with more than 200 concrete statues. They're clearly not the work of a professional sculptor, but who cares? What the art world likes to call *art brut* or outsider art, we're content to call weird, and the Cement Menagerie is weird in the best possible way.

It was the work of a master joiner named John Fairnington and his friends, and it was all for the benefit of John's only child, Edwin. Edwin was disabled, so as a way of keeping him entertained John began to decorate the back garden. The first large piece he installed was a life-sized panda made of cement on a wire frame filled with rubble to keep it stable. Shortly afterwards came camels and horses and a fountain garden with little mermaids and large dolphins and alligators. As a retired man, John had plenty of time to expand his repertoire to include life-sized human statues. There's a dashing Lawrence of Arabia astride a camel, a cigar-toting Winston Churchill flashing a V-sign, a Virgin Mary, and a hilariously cartoonish bespectacled man. John was so prolific in his statue-making

that when Edwin died in the early 1970s, a decade before his father, the plot was crammed with seventy-five large statues and twice that number of smaller ones.

You can still walk around the Fairningtons' back garden with the current owner's blessing, as long as there's an 'Open' sign on the driveway. We'd advise you to take advantage of this opportunity – it's a rewarding experience. The garden's a peaceful place with lots of unexpected touches (and a marvellous collection of flowering plants that really sets off the art). Like all good gardens, it looks interesting from pretty much every angle, and whether you focus on the whole collection or one single statue, it's a visual feast.

But here's a little tip from someone who has spent hours wandering around the place: For a special treat, take a close look at the eyes and mouths of the statues. The pupils and irises of the eyes are usually made of old marbles, which can be either interesting or disturbing depending on the colour of the marbles. And the teeth are often real teeth or dentures. The wild boar sculpture has real pig's teeth and tusks, which are getting a bit ropy after all these decades. And you haven't lived until you've seen Lawrence of Arabia flashing a pair of the National Health's best faux gnashers.

Last Post

There is a lawn on the Isle of Wight with a bright red post-box on it. It's on the road between Newport and Ryde, but unlike most pillar-boxes, it's tucked away in someone's back garden, where the public can't get to it. Oh, and to make it all the more distinctive, it's standing next to 170 other post-boxes. This is quite possibly the largest concentration of red enamel paint anywhere on the planet, and it's a strange and wonderful sight to behold.

Although this is a private collection in the grounds of a house wittily dubbed 'Last Post', the owners, Arthur and Kim Reeder, were genial enough to invite us over, feed us sandwiches and lend us a couple of pairs of wellies in which to make our way across the muddy field to the boxes.

There are rows and rows of GPO (General Post Office) boxes, with different royal initials and different crowns on the front, ranging from slender ones ('ones you can cuddle' by Arthur's rule of thumb), to double-sized ones and vast conjoined-twin pillar-boxes that weigh close to a tonne. There are several examples of the slightly tapered and much-reviled 'roofless' 1978 model. And there were dozens of box-shaped boxes too. And they all came in a surprising variety of colours. When we commented on that, Arthur dropped the bombshell: British post-boxes were not always red.

'Until the 1870s, they were all dark green. But in the gaslit streets, people kept walkin' into them. They couldn't see 'em, see? So they painted 'em brighter. Now, there're still green ones – these grass-green ones are for the Republic of Ireland; those letters stand for *Puist agus Telegrafa*, their post office. Blue is Guernsey's corporate colour, so their post-boxes are all that colour. This green one here is National Trust green, and came from the very northernmost tip of Scotland.' Fair enough, but what about the one with the black-and-white horizontal stripes round the base and mustard-coloured top? What was that all about?

'This one here is in wartime livery,' he told us. 'During the Blitz, a directive was sent around for street furniture – which means lamp posts and bollards – to be highlighted to prevent people having collisions with them during the blackout. The basic idea was bands six inches thick up the item to a height of about three feet. Some cases, they even painted tree trunks.

'Now, the directive was not meant to apply to post-boxes, so all areas did it differently. Some painted just the base white, some painted white stripes, so you had red and white hoops, black and white . . . some would even paint a band round the mouthpiece. It was done a little bit ad hoc.

'The military was petrified that the Germans would

drop gas bombs on us so they came up with the idea of painting a reactive paint onto objects. I can't recall all the compounds, but when mustard gas came into contact with the top of this post-box, it would turn cherry red.'

He paused just long enough for an idea to occur to us before he delivered his punchline:

'You do wonder – how would anyone know the difference?'

And then he was off to show us his collection of post-bags from across the world – all of them gifts from people who had heard about his pillar-box collection. He sorted through ones from various postal companies – France's *La Poste*, Germany's *Deutsche Post*, Singapore Post – while searching for the pièce de résistance, an impressive tent-sized bag from New Zealand Post.

Barely pausing to draw breath, he moved on to compare crowns from the front of two post-boxes. He told us that two were produced the same year, but looked different. One had 'E II R' on it, the other didn't. There was another difference: The crowns.

'Right – here comes the history lesson. Our present Queen, E II R, is Queen Elizabeth the Second of England, Wales, Northern Ireland, the Channel Islands, Guernsey . . . everywhere but Scotland. She's Queen Elizabeth I in Scotland. So, in deference to the Scots, there is a St Andrew's crown on this box.'

And so it went on, for close to three hours. And we didn't even notice how the time had passed. It was as if we had just fast-forwarded through the afternoon. That's why Arthur's collection makes sense. To an enthusiast and raconteur like him, these things aren't just massive iron containers; they're chunks of social history with some great stories behind them. But most of all, they're a strong contender for the crown in the 'Most Distinctive Lawn Furniture' stakes. And given the competition, that's saying something.

Edward Prynn's 'Fauxhenge'

A stone's throw from Treyarnon and Padstow on the north Cornish coast is the tiny village of St Merryn. It's a pleasant little place, but no more so than dozens of little Cornish towns we've visited. However, down the road that runs by the church is a house with something that you won't see anywhere else in Cornwall, or in the rest of England for that matter. We're talking about the little bungalow of retired quarryman Edward Prynn, which is dwarfed by the contents of his garden. Basically, Ed has filled in every spare square foot of his plot with Neolithic-style monuments. In Ed Prynn's garden, there are stone circles, standing-stone arrangements and a holed stone that looks just like the ancient healing stone Mên-an-Tol from a little farther west. There's even a tripod arrangement with an eighteen-tonne capstone on top that slants slightly worryingly towards that house; Ed wittily calls this the Angel's Runway.

This is clearly a labour of love, and the sad thing is that Ed can barely see it. Until the late 1960s, he worked as a digger driver in a local quarry. An accident partially blinded him in his right eye, and then, when he was just thirty-two, a piece of steel pierced his left eye and completely blinded it. After his world went dark, he went through a divorce and slowly began building a little house for himself on a plot of land he owned at Tresallyn

Cross. Ten years before the house itself was finished, he turned his attention to assembling a collection of standing stones.

As a small child, Ed had experienced a moving religious experience at one of Cornwall's sacred-stone sites, and in his enforced early retirement, he began developing a faith system that incorporated conventional chapel-going Christianity with older druidical customs. He is now an archdruid and wears flowing robes, teaches dowsing and performs ceremonies that are the subject of much conjecture in the village. Although he's absolutely sincere about all of this, you still get the impression that he's got more of a sense of humour about such things than you'd expect from a religious man.

At any rate, in the early 1980s, while he was still living with his parents, and with only

the shell of a house to call his own, he enlisted some of his old quarrying buddies to drop a big stone next to the work-in-progress he called his bungalow. After the Rocking Stone was in place, he decided he wanted a truly massive stone, and the quarry manager obliged in 1983 by delivering a seventy-five-tonne, thirty-six-foot long megalith which the boys at the quarry called 'The Peacemaker'.

Unfortunately, it split while it was being installed, so the lads broke it up into pieces and made a stone circle, which Ed entitled the Seven Sisters. He named each of the seven stones in the circle after an important woman in his life, with the tallest (Marion) standing fourteen feet out of the ground. Jackie, Marjorie, Monica, Aunty Hilda and Music Maker fan out on either side, but he's not telling anybody the name of the seventh stone. There are some things a gentleman never talks about, apparently. But the stone in the middle of the circle is still called the Peacemaker.

There are two holed stones on site. One of them is supposed to have healing powers if you crawl through it, and the other is a wedding stone at which Ed himself conducts marriage ceremonies. He explains that in times past, people would marry for a year and a day and renew their vows if it still seemed like a good idea. Today, Ed Prynn will marry you for any length of time the two of you feel is appropriate, and provide you with a certificate, too.

There are also two six-foot chunks of quartzite in Ed's henge garden that did not come from local quarries.

They came from Mount Pleasant in the Falkland Islands, and travelled 8,000 miles to St Merryn to be installed at Ed's place in 1985.

Most people would probably be content with a stonehenge in their garden, but after Ed finished building his house in the 1990s, he started to cover the outside walls with slate tiles engraved by Glynis Kent, a friend of his. Each one includes the name of a hero or friend, illustrated with a cartoon or logo or other graphic element. The names on the front of the house cover philanthropists and eccentrics, ranging from the founders of companies he admires (including Coca-Cola, Boots, and Cadbury) to famous eccentrics, such as Joshua Norton who declared himself Emperor of the United States in 1859, and historical figures ranging from Joan of Arc to Margaret Thatcher. The names on the side of the house are personal friends, and are colour-coded to reflect the level of help they have provided him: Names in red have helped him a little, those in blue and purple have helped him a lot, names in gold have helped so much he will never be able to repay them.

And still the man wasn't finished! Underneath the bungalow is an underground temple modelled on a Bronze Age fogou (an underground structure), which Ed calls the Womb of Mother Earth. In the middle of this seldom-seen chamber is a piece of Italian marble called the Drekly Stone. It turns out the name is a play on words: Touch the stone and make a wish when you're fully clothed and you'll get your wish eventually. Touch it naked, and you'll get your wish directly (drekly . . . directly . . . geddit?). All of which leads us back to the suspicion that Ed's got a sense of humour about all this.

Ilton's Druid's Temple

Next time you're driving along the Ilton to Masham road in North Yorkshire, here's a diversion worth pursuing. Turn off towards the Swinton Park Estate, park at the end of the road and hike for five minutes along the trail and soon you'll come to what looks like a miniature Stonehenge.

The circle of dolmens, menhirs, trilithons, altars and quoits looks like a bona fide prehistoric site of worship. But it's actually the result of a whimsical job-creation scheme from the 1820s. The local squire, William Danby, set the local unemployed to work for a shilling a day constructing what he called a Druid's Temple. When it was complete, he set aside funds for a professional hermit to live there. Any soul who could survive seven years out there would be guaranteed an income for life, and anybody who successfully applied to live there would be given food for the duration of his stay. Given the fact that the site is bleak and freezing during the winter and fly-infested and far from running water during the summer, it's more than surprising that one candidate made it over halfway to winning his annuity: Old local histories mention that someone lived there for four and a half years before calling it quits.

Forbidden Corner

At first blush, the story behind the Forbidden Corner sounds like something from a bygone age: The honorary British Consul to Ecuador builds a pleasure garden on his family's Yorkshire estate to entertain his family and friends, and later opens it to the public. The result is a four-acre puzzle that takes two or more hours of dedicated brainwork to solve – and as long as you like to meander through. The garden is a collection of mazes, statues and paths that lead seemingly nowhere, all linked by a sheet of cryptic short poems that provide the clues that eventually lead to an underground grotto.

This reeks of the kind of architectural folly that was popular in the eighteenth century, and the unbridled self-indulgence of the idle rich in the 1920s. But the Forbidden Corner is deceptive in that way (and in a whole lot of other ways, too).

The Forbidden Corner is actually the brainchild of entrepreneur and diplomat Colin Armstrong, who put the whole thing together in the early 1990s. Having ploughed some of the profits of his various businesses into the Tupgill Park Estate near Leyburn, Armstrong hired architect Malcolm Tempest to design a pleasure garden for the site. By the end of the decade, Armstrong decided to let the public in on the joke. It caught on fast, and now gets some 100,000 visitors a year. In fact, it's so popular that visitors must book in advance so that the place doesn't get too crowded.

At various turns, the Forbidden Corner looks like the highly coiffed garden of an English stately home crossed with a version of Disneyland designed by surrealists. Linger too long in one spot and you may find yourself squirted by a statue inspired by the Manneken Pis in Brussels.

Take the wrong path through the hedges and you'll reach a door that won't open or a turnstile that revolves the wrong way, and will have to turn back. Look for meaning in all the symbols you see and you'll be thwarted: There are simply too many random limbs sticking out of walls and hands gesturing out of hedges for every little detail to be of help in solving the clues. And if you drank too much coffee before you entered, don't expect to find a public convenience quickly. There are facilities on site, sure enough, but this is a place without maps and uniformed guides, so relief may be a long way off.

Clearly, there is a goal in sight

(other than finding the gents, of course), and that's to locate the underground grotto. You could probably enjoy your visit without walking along the River Styx and into this not-exactly-scary vision of the Underworld, nevertheless it's a fitting climax to the visit. It's also a prison you can escape from only by using your brain. But by the time you get there, you'll be used to living off your wits. There are so many tantalising twists and turns and teasing glimpses of places you can't actually get to along the way, that when you're stuck underground in a revolving circular room full of doors that lead, again, seemingly nowhere, you'll be surprised that you will actually be able to find your way out. Eventually. Perhaps . . .

Our favourite little touch, though, is the

heraldic-looking symbol that appears on weather vanes and murals, not just in the Forbidden Corner, but also on the fronts of cottages throughout the Tupgill Estate. It's a leg shedding drops of blood, held aloft by an armour-clad arm. Nobody at the Forbidden Corner was able to confirm what this meant, but after a long free-associative discussion, we have come to the conclusion that it's a visual pun that Colin Armstrong included as a private joke. And we narrowed it down to two possible puns: The arm's clearly strong, because it successfully yanked off a leg … so does it mean that Armstrong is just pulling your leg? Or is it that the place cost him an arm and a leg to build? We don't know and it's just yet another imponderable from a garden that's full of them.

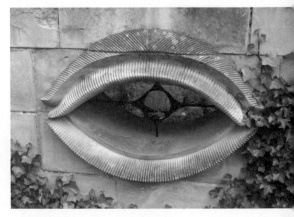

Most people are used to only a few choices of roof covering. You've got tiles, slate, thatch and that's about it, really. Or perhaps you'd prefer something more along the lines of fibreglass marine life?

Land shark!

Most tourists visit Oxford to see the obvious high points: The Bodleian Library, the pub where C.S. Lewis and J.R.R. Tolkien used to go, or the city's many gleaming spires. Not me though, I went there to see the house with a shark sticking out of its roof.

Disappointingly, when I asked someone at Oxford's tourist information centre, 'Do you know anything about the fellow who stuck a shark through his roof?' I got the reply 'Oh, he's not there anymore.'

Luckily for me, he was talking about the homeowner, not the shark. You can still see the shark from the bus that goes through Headington, and you can also see that the house it occupies hasn't been looked after for a while. The roof into which the shark is diving has begun to crumble, and the information label has long since vacated its spot on the front gate. As a result, passers-by are, sadly, no longer informed that the piece was designed by John Buckley and erected in August 1986, and that it was installed as a protest about nuclear proliferation.

Local cinema-owner Bill Heine decided to make a very different statement from the one everyone else was making at the time (that is, joining the CND, wearing *Atomkraft? Nein Danke!* badges, and sitting in fields outside American air bases). On the forty-first anniversary of the bombing of Nagasaki, Heine hired a crane to lift a twenty-five-foot, four-hundredweight fibreglass sculpture through a hole in his roof. When the press clamoured for an explanation, Heine declared:

'The shark was to express someone feeling totally impotent and ripping a hole in their roof out of a sense of impotence and anger and desperation . . . It is saying something about CND, nuclear power, Chernobyl and Nagasaki.'

Predictably, the shark caused a huge uproar. Almost immediately, Oxford City Council inspected the premises to ensure the item posed no threat to public safety, and when the investigation proved the sculpture was quite secure, they tried to force its removal on the grounds that it was a development made without planning permission. Bill Heine was having none of it. For five years, he held the council at bay, and finally he appealed to the Secretary of State for the Environment, Michael Heseltine. In 1992, Heseltine's inspector Peter Macdonald issued a statement:

It is not in dispute that the shark is not in harmony with its surroundings, but then it is not intended to be in harmony with them . . . As a 'work of art' the sculpture ('Untitled 1986') would be 'read' quite differently in, say, an art gallery or on another site. An incongruous object can become accepted as a landmark after a time, becoming well known, even well loved in the process. Something of this sort seems to have happened, for many people, to the so-called 'Oxford shark'. The Council is understandably concerned about precedent here. The first concern is simple: proliferation with sharks (and Heaven knows what else) crashing through roofs all over the City. This fear is exaggerated. In the five years since the shark was erected, no other examples have occurred. Only very recently has there been a proposal for twin baby sharks in the Iffley Road. But any system of control must make some small place for the dynamic, the unexpected, the downright quirky. I therefore recommend that the Headington shark be allowed to remain.

And remain it has. Bill Heine has moved on to host a phone-in show on Radio Oxford, but his protest is still sticking out boldly on New High Street in Headington. Sadly, though, the house it's sticking out of is a bit of a mess. The roof seems to have collapsed a bit, and the attic space is clearly now a pigeon sanctuary. The front garden is overgrown with thorny vines and the windows are filthy. If this giant sculpture was ever intended to impress, it could certainly use a better plinth. But perhaps the environmental message behind the sculpture is expanding a bit. The tangle of undergrowth obviously absorbs more greenhouse gases than a well-manicured lawn would. And on the hot summer day we visited, the ripe blackberries growing wild in the yard were delicious. So, we say more power to Mr Heine . . . as long as it's not nuclear power.

John Gladden's Fishy Roof

Strangely enough, Bill Heine is not the only person with marine life installed on his roof. Croydon businessman John Gladden does too, but he never was a man to adopt a low profile. To attract attention to his business, he parked a bright yellow tank nearby. When the police began sticking parking tickets on his tank because it was too big for the parking space, Gladden did what most people who believe they're in the right do: He ignored them. When the number of tickets passed a hundred and the police started to apply some pressure for him to do something about it, he sprang into action: He had two ten-foot fibreglass pigs made, installed them on the tank and parked it in the forecourt of the police station.

It's hardly likely that such a bloke would have a normal-looking house. Sure enough, the Gladden residence features a fifteen-foot statue of a swordfish on the roof, and as a testament to his run-ins with the police, there's an American-style patrol car parked in his driveway with a life-sized fibreglass policeman mounted on its roof, bending over ready to receive a spanking from a massively oversized hand.

Beam Me Up

It's a scene of pure movie magic: The security officer from the first season of *Star Trek: The Next Generation* beams down to twenty-first-century Leicestershire, where she meets a chatty ex-DJ from Leeds and ends up back at his flat, only to discover that it contains a transporter pad in the bedroom, an infinity mirror in the ceiling and a voice-activated dimmer switch that speaks back in the dulcet tones of the *Enterprise's* computer.

The best thing about this episode is that it all happened in real life. It was captured on film in the Star Trek documentary *Trekkies 2*, in which Denise Crosby (who TNG fans will remember as Tasha Yar) spanned the globe at sub-warp speeds to see what Star Trek fans get up to. And to our way of thinking, one of the best examples is Tony Alleyne, whose mission has been to boldly redecorate his flat in Hinckley in the style of a Federation starship.

Alleyne's eye for detail and authenticity impressed Crosby in the documentary, but somehow failed to impress some of the other women in his life. In fact, he began the project after his wife left him, as a way to keep out of his own personal black hole of depression. He candidly admits that for a couple of years after his marriage broke up, he lost his way, until a friend lent him a manual with blueprints for the equipment used in *Star Trek: The Next Generation*. He decided to build a transporter coil as a kind of therapeutic exercise (adding 'as you do' in such an offhanded way that it really seems as though he believes it's the kind of thing that would occur to anybody). It took him a couple of years to finish

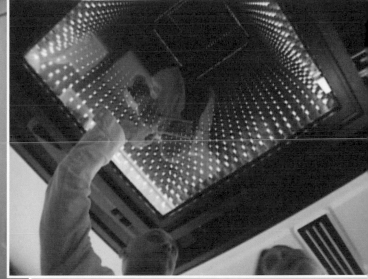

you want to go through space, that's what it feels like', no doubt doesn't help things much either.

Perhaps that's why on the several occasions Tony has put the flat up for sale, none of the bids came close to his asking price. He insists that he wasn't actually expecting to sell the house for £2 million (the asking price on eBay) – he set the asking price that high because he wanted to show off pictures of the interior to the widest possible audience without being in danger of losing his home. And what better way is there to show off his business Twenty-fourth Century Interior Design?

But all the background details aside, Tony's flat is a thing of wonder. There can't be many homes in Leicestershire, or anywhere else in the world, that feature a voice-activated lighting system with a built-in dimmer, a transporter console with sound effects and, best of all, a doorbell that plays a recording of Patrick Stewart's voice announcing 'Welcome to the twenty-fourth century'. And if you can't boast that, what kind of a science-fiction fan are you?

the console, but he liked the result so much that he kept on going with other futuristic projects, until his entire apartment was like a Federation starship.

Despite its visual appeal, this is clearly not an easy place to live in. There's no washing machine or cooker, because they took up too much room, and the refrigerator's been replaced by a warp coil. Tony sleeps on the floor. The reading material in the Smallest Room consists of memorial plaques that list the names of Federation members who were killed or missing in action. And the place feels a bit claustrophobic because all the windows are obscured behind thick black perspex. (Possibly the view of Hinckley just wasn't Gene Roddenbury enough for the décor.) Not even the infinity mirror he installed in the ceiling can shake the closed-in feeling, and Tony freely admits that it doesn't appeal to a lot of women. The fact that he justifies it by saying, 'If

Playing the Numbers

Studying maths has never been a particular favourite among school students, but it clearly made an impact on some architects and homeowners in years gone by. How else can you account for the geometric eccentricities of some of the country's older houses? We picked three peculiar older properties at random and, as it turns out, three is a significant number for one of them in particular . . .

Three's a Crowd

Sir Thomas Tresham spent the greater part of two decades of the sixteenth century staring at the four walls of a prison cell for practising Catholicism in defiance of Queen Elizabeth I's law forbidding the celebration of mass, and his incarceration clearly got to him. By the end of his imprisonment, his cell was covered with cryptic scribbles that none of his gaolers could understand. But this was only the beginning of Tresham's eccentricity. After his release, he set his strange codes in stone on buildings on his Northamptonshire estate, and these codes still cause people to scratch their heads in bewilderment to this day.

For instance, Tresham built a lodge in the middle of the estate's rabbit farm, a mile outside Rushton, which is now managed by English Heritage. However, this is certainly not the kind of simple dwelling most warreners would have lived in. Tresham constructed a three-storey triangular building with three gables on each of its three sides, three windows on each side, three ornamental panels on each face, each containing three triangles or wheatsheaves set in a trefoil (a three-lobed leaf). There's a Latin inscription on one of the walls,

testimonium dant, which means 'three bear witness'; and the faces of the building contain many numbers, including '3309', '15' and '93', each of which is divisible by three. When you add together the individual digits in these numbers, they too are divisible by three.

It would be fair to say that Tresham had developed something of a fixation on a number somewhere between two and four. The standard text-book reason for this has something to do with his faith in the Holy Trinity – a faith so deep that it cost him almost twenty years of freedom. Beyond this devotion, however, some of the numbers may have personal significance to Tresham: He was released from captivity in 1593, for example, which could account for the '15' and '93' on two of the walls. Yet, other examples are more of a mystery. Elizabethans and Jacobeans were very fond of symbolism in their paintings and architecture, but even by their standards this was a bit over the top. The rule of threes in this building runs very deep indeed, where even the individual walls are based on multiples of three – each measures thirty-three feet. In fact, it comes as something of a surprise to stumble upon something that's not derived from three, but there is one example: A heptagon containing a smaller heptagon surrounded by seven eyes. Although, if you add the faces of the shapes to the number of eyes, you still come up with a multiple of three. You just can't escape it . . . which is presumably what Tresham was thinking during all those years he spent in prison.

Deal or no Deal?

You can trust a gambling man to celebrate a big win in style. But few do so in as grand a style as George Ley, a schoolmaster and member of Combe Martin town council, did during the late seventeenth century. Ley won a fortune at cards and decided that he would commemorate the fact by building a house. In the expansive style of the high roller, he decided the house would reflect his love of card-playing. The property, now a pub and bed-and-breakfast on the north coast of Devon called the Pack o' Cards, is one of the strangest looking buildings around.

Ley bought a plot of land exactly fifty-two feet by fifty-two feet (to reflect the number of cards in a deck), and built a four-storey building on it (one storey for each suit). On each storey, there were thirteen rooms (the number of cards in a suit). And there were fifty-two stairs and even fifty-two panes of glass in the windows, well, until a couple of years later when King William III's government imposed a tax on windows and Ley bricked up some of his to save a few quid.

To top off the card theme, George Ley insisted that the house resemble a house of cards 'such as a child might make'; and sure enough, the Pack o' Cards does look as though the architectural model was made by somebody with a dealer's deck and a steady hand. As an occasional patron, I can state that the crib is much more comfortable than you'd expect of a building more than 300 years old. In fact, it's quite a deal.

The Round House

Don't be fooled by the name of Exmouth's most famous weird building. It may be called A La Ronde, a French term meaning round, but it's actually a sixteen-sided building. Each of the rooms in it radiates out from a central octagonal atrium and is shaped like a slice of pizza with a big bite taken out of it. It was originally designed for, or perhaps by, two spinster cousins, Mary and Jane Parminter, in the late eighteenth century, and was passed down to unmarried women in the family for the best part of a century. It was only when the family ran out of spinsters that it went briefly to a male relative, who installed an attic, a dumb-waiter and a huge collection of seashells on the upper-storey walls. The unusual design was intended to provide the women with plenty of light by which to do their needlepoint and other spinsterly activities. However, during our most recent visit in the hottest July on record, we discovered another benefit of having sixteen outside walls: Except for the room getting the most direct sunlight, the place was comfortably cool. In fact, thinking about it, it's strange that we don't have more hexadecagonal buildings in this energy-efficient age. Or, on reflection, perhaps it isn't – those pizza-slice rooms could get uncomfortable after a while.

Museums Without the Mustiness

Some of the most interesting museums in the world started out as private collections that people stored in cupboards that they would open up and show to their guests. These pieces of furniture were called cabinets of curiosity, and they possessed an aura of excitement, mystery and entertainment that remained popular into the Victorian era and the age of the public museum. Somewhere along the way, however, something went desperately wrong. Museums became respectable, and somehow got the reputation for being boring. Thank goodness there are some places that retain the spirit of the original collectors.

Oxford's Cabinet of Curiosity

If the Pitt Rivers collection in Oxford did not exist, nobody now living would have the imagination or the inclination to create it. It takes a peculiar mixture of brains, resources and sheer perversity to establish a museum that cheerfully places shrunken heads, boats, totem poles, musical instruments, bottled witches and eighty-year-old hot cross buns in the same room. It also takes a particularly Victorian love of collecting and a Byzantine sense of order. I would even go so far as to say that it takes someone whose name itself is a curious mixture of regular names and apparently random nouns. In short, it takes someone like Lieutenant-General Augustus Henry Lane Fox Pitt Rivers. And there's nobody around like him anymore.

Officially, the Pitt Rivers Museum is an anthropological collection attached to Oxford University's Museum of Natural History. Actually, it's a collection of the weirdest artefacts the world has to offer. And instead of doing what many museums do, which is to slap all the artefacts from Bronze Age Europe in one section and all the pieces from nineteenth-century India in another, the Pitt Rivers chooses

to arrange things by type instead. This means that in the section devoted to musical instruments, you can see how cultures all over the world traditionally make their xylophones. In the fire-starting section, you'll see a Kenya Kamba fire drill sitting next to some nineteenth-century English matchboxes and a pouch made from goat testicles that the Lhota Nagas of India use to keep their tinder dry. And in the burial customs section, you'll see just how many cultures used to shrink the heads of their dead enemies, or paint their skulls and strap horns to them, or thread thongs of reeds or leather through their nose holes and eye sockets – disturbingly, there are a lot more of these than you might expect.

It's these common threads between cultures that make the Pitt Rivers Museum such an interesting venue. Yes, the shock value of the more bizarre items brings the crowds in, but what keeps them coming back is the fact that all of humanity is represented here. There's no better example of this than in a contemporary battle shield from Papua New Guinea that bears an image of the cartoon character 'The Phantom'. Heroes are heroes, and

if 'The Ghost Who Walks' was good enough for newspaper readers in 1930s America and 1970s England, he's good enough for Wahgi warriors in the twenty-first century.

Another attraction of the Pitt Rivers Museum is the absence of flashy lights and self-consciously modern décor. In fact, they keep the place so dark that the attendants carry small torches and often hand them out to visiting groups. The stated reason for the pall of twilight that hangs over the room is that the curators don't want harsh light to fade the pigment on exhibits in the body ornamentation section; a better reason is that shrunken heads look much creepier in the half-light.

And just as you think you've exhausted everything the museum has to offer, an attendant will slip over to the exhibition case you're examining, notice that you're looking at silver good-luck charms from Italy, and whip open a drawer you hadn't even noticed to show you somebody's lucky potato or the dried tip of a human tongue that a resident of Tunbridge Wells used as a charm in the 1890s. Or perhaps he'll draw your attention to the dried eelskin or sheep organs that were carried around in Carlisle to ward off rheumatism, or a stoppered bottle that's supposed to contain the trapped body and soul of a witch, or peace pipes and hookahs and cola-bottle bongs, or anything else that strikes your fancy. And in this place, that could be pretty much anything.

CHARM for WARTS.
OXFORDSHIRE.

Go out alone & find a large black slug. Secretly rub the under side on the warts & impale the slug on a thorn. As the slug dies the warts will go.

Smooth Operators

To lovers of the macabre, London Bridge tube station is a veritable Mecca. People stumble out of the warrens of the London Underground into the streets of Southwark in their droves and stand in long queues to visit the London Dungeon. However, enough ink's been spilt on the London Dungeon experience already. Suffice it to say, if animatronic models of plague victims vomiting into buckets are your thing, you'll love the London Dungeon. But if you then hop straight back on the Tube, you'll miss out on an experience with a genuine history of sickness and suffering that's much less slick (and therefore much better).

No other museum visit quite stacks up to the experience of (almost) getting your leg amputated in front of a live audience – without anaesthetic or pre-operative sterilisation. Somehow, I'd signed up for just such an experience, and I was pretty much enjoying the show until a twelve-inch sacrificial dagger called a Liston knife came out, followed by an ebony-handled bone saw.

This all took place in the Old Operating Theatre at St Thomas's Church. To call this great little place a historic building and medical museum would be accurate, but missing the point completely. True, it's the attic of a Norman church and Florence Nightingale is said to have worked there, but it's

> *Behold at Southwark an ancient spital, built of old to entertain the poor.*
> (Peter de Rupibus, Bishop of Winchester)

now a place that cheerfully mixes strange art projects and performances with genuine medical artefacts. It also enthusiastically espouses all of England's medical history, including the bits about leeches, screaming and trading with grave robbers. In short, it's our kind of place.

The operating theatre is a sky-lit circular room you get to by climbing a precipitous spiral staircase. The operating table is surrounded by viewing platforms which once sat up to 150 apprentice surgeons, who would watch the unfortunate patients being held down on the table and cut up in the interests of saving their lives. Predictably, nobody much wanted surgery in earlier times. Anaesthetics weren't introduced until the mid-nineteenth century and neither were sterile operating conditions. If the pain and the risk of post-operative infection didn't put you off, the bloodstains

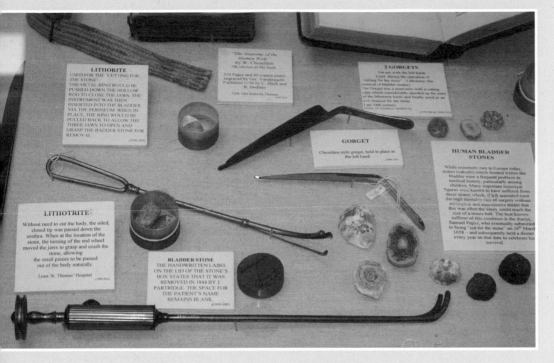

snipping jagged bits with a bone nipper. I zoned out completely during the description of what post-operative infections looked like. About the only thing that didn't really worry me was the description of leeches, which were used to suck out infection along with the blood. I figured they were getting what they deserved. However, I did feel a bit faint on being shown photographs of a leeching demonstration that my 'doctor' and a colleague had done the previous year; her leech was enormous by the time it dropped off her arm.

Of course, the Old Operating Theatre does actually slip something educational into the mix. Some of the surgical tools on display don't necessarily make you wince, though frankly the eye does tend to gravitate towards the instruments used to remove bladder stones or drill holes in the skull.

The medicine display manages to escape being macabre while remaining very curious. There are sheaves of dry plants everywhere, since St Thomas's attic was also used to prepare herbs for medicine. Most of these medicines seem to tap into the same vein that herbalists embrace today, but there are a couple of preparations that seem too horrific for words. As I left the museum (on two legs, thank you very much), I gave silent thanks that I was never prescribed a dose of snail water; this multi-purpose remedy was particularly favoured by St Thomas's eighteenth-century physician Dr Richard Mead and its recipe includes six gallons of garden snails, three gallons of earthworms, various herbs and eight gallons each of wine and spring water. I'll take the wine and spring water, barman; you can hold onto the worms and snails.

and screaming from the patient before you surely would. Yet if you broke your leg and gangrene began creeping in, hacking the limb off was your only chance of survival. A 50 per cent chance, certainly, but a chance nonetheless.

In the church garret where the operations took place all those years ago, you can now witness live talks and demonstrations of the techniques they used to use. Hence my stint on the table, nervously eying the Liston knife and bone saw, and trying to ignore the evocative narrative from the woman in the blood-stained apron.

'It may seem odd to build an operating theatre in the attic of a church, but it meant they could have a skylight to let in a lot of natural light. Of course, it was built with a double floor, two layers of floor packed with sawdust to soak up the blood and prevent it dripping through the ceiling of the church, which you can imagine would be a little bit disturbing for the people below.'

I knew she wasn't actually going to remove my leg, but that didn't stop me from wincing when she talked about circular cutting motions, peeling skin back and

Roadside Oddities

When people say, 'It's the journey that counts, not the destination', they sum up what travelling across England is all about. Even though petrol has been taxed into the stratosphere, and the country is littered with speed cameras, and many of the roads are so narrow you have to back up whenever you see a car heading your way, the English seem to be in love with road travel. And whenever large numbers of people are mobile, there will always be someone at the roadside providing entertainment of some sort.

Sometimes such attractions are there to lure money out of the unwary motorist, other times they are there simply to inspire wonder. And sometimes they are there for no good reason at all, created by people who don't seem to realise just how strange their works look.

Whether you're looking for unusual roadside attractions, fun days out or things that make you scratch your head and say, 'What on earth was that?', Albion has what you're looking for. Pull over up ahead – there's an oddity coming up right now!

In their time, no doubt, Nelson's Column and the statue of Peter Pan in Kensington Gardens probably struck people as strange looking. But a lot of weirdness has passed under the bridge since then, and if you want to make heads turn now, you've got to work at it. Of course, some artists put people right off by trying a little too hard; those of us with typical British reserve tend to look the other way when confronted by such show-offs. But then there are the works of wit, humour and just plain peculiarity that keep us staring – even if we happen to be driving at the time. It's these pieces that are worth celebrating, starting with a trifecta of statues along the unlikely setting of the northbound lane of the M5 in Somerset.

Willow Man

If you're going to pick a place for a really big roadside oddity, the best starting point is to find a really big road. And that's exactly what South West Arts and Sainsbury's did when they commissioned a statue from willow sculptor Serena de la Hey. They picked the biggest road that runs through Somerset – the M5 – and asked Ms de la Hey to construct a forty-foot statue beside it. In cooperation with the local authority, they located a field beside the motorway near Bridgwater, brought in tonnes of local willow branches, and set de la Hey to work. After three weeks of construction, the Willow Man was unveiled in September 2000, and, except for a five-month break in 2001, he has stood there ever since.

The *Willow Man* is a big-haunched individual with thin tapering arms and something of a pin head, striding purposefully south towards Taunton, facing the traffic on the northbound side of the road. Of course, this means that anyone who's driving south along the M5 gets mooned at for at least a mile before they pass him, but that's just the luck of the draw. From whichever side you spot the *Willow Man*, he cuts an impressive figure; the cable-like branches of willow woven over his steel skeleton cause his surface to resemble the muscle diagrams in *Gray's Anatomy*. And his sheer size and strangeness have made him something of a local mascot. Some people even call him The Angel of the South, in reference to Antony Gormley's gargantuan metal sculpture in Gateshead called the *Angel of the North*.

However, not everybody liked the *Willow Man*. In fact, eight months after he was unveiled, in the dead of night, someone braved the foot-and-mouth infested field in which he stood and set him alight. By morning, all that was left of him was his steel skeleton and a pile of ash. This is the fate that routinely awaits some of de la Hey's smaller willow sculptures at the Glastonbury Music Festival, where the 'burning man' is something of a crowd-pleaser each year. But this individual act was clearly arson, and a crime for which the culprit has yet to be brought to justice.

Yet, even as a skeleton, the *Willow Man* still met his public obligations: Two months after the fire, he kicked off a national charity drive called Wrong Trousers Day, in which everyone was supposed to wear outrageous trousers to raise awareness and funds for children's hospitals. The *Willow Man*'s trousers were baggy Fraser tartan slacks made by a balloon company, and were pulled up over the skeleton using a thirty-foot cherry picker. By

October 2001, Serena de la Hey had rewoven willow branches round his skeleton, making him respectable once more.

So, the *Willow Man* remains by the side of the road. But he may not be there forever. For one thing, he seems to attract a lot of birds who, although they seem unable to nest in his branches, are certainly willing to try and pull bits off him to take elsewhere. And when the statue was originally constructed, the authorities granted planning permission for only ten years. We're now more than halfway through that term. Who knows what may become of him in 2010?

M5 Dinosaur

As if we needed more proof that the northbound stretch of the M5 near Bridgwater is an extremely popular spot for weird roadside statuary, here's another example. This charmingly loopy dinosaur bares his teeth at passing traffic a few miles south of the *Willow Man*. What does it mean? It's art, and doesn't need to mean

anything. Except, perhaps, that it's a good idea to get into the slow lane a few miles north of Taunton and stay there for half an hour. There's plenty along the way to keep your passengers entertained.

Humphrey the Camel

The Willow Man may be the biggest example of roadside strangeness along the M5 around Bridgwater, but it wasn't the first. That accolade goes to a fibreglass camel named Humphrey who had been standing in a field by the motorway for almost twenty years by the time the *Willow Man* appeared.

Humphrey is a much more humble structure, but he's got a lot of personality. He began life in the 1980s as a fixture on a carnival float as part of a charity effort to raise money by Bridgwater's Young Farmers Club. After the event he spent several years migrating between the gardens of various members of the carnival club: Whenever a member of the club got married, he'd appear in the front garden after the honeymoon and stay there for a few weeks. When the last members got married, he took up semi-permanent residence in their field, peering over the hedge at the motorway traffic near Junction 24.

And there he has engendered a strange affection in the public. Occasionally he disappears to do charity gigs for fire stations or carnivals, and every time this happens the local BBC station receives worried calls enquiring after Humphrey. People send hats and sunglasses for him to wear when the seasons change. And a local carpenter built a baby camel named Boo to keep him company. Boo has taken up residence on a platform by Humphrey's side, which has given rise to all kinds of stories. Some say he's Humphrey's son and wonder where the mother is; others say he's a relative from Sidmouth; others just wonder where all this is leading.

Whatever the story behind Humphrey and Boo, it's clear that people keep a weather eye open for them both. They stand as a testament to the English love of crazy roadside statuary. Because when you think about it, what could be stranger than commuters looking for tales about what is, basically, a twenty-five-year-old bit of leftover decoration stuck in a field for a gag?

A Bigger Digger

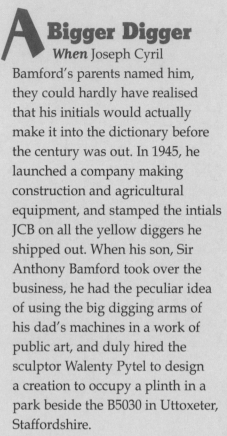

When Joseph Cyril Bamford's parents named him, they could hardly have realised that his initials would actually make it into the dictionary before the century was out. In 1945, he launched a company making construction and agricultural equipment, and stamped the intials JCB on all the yellow diggers he shipped out. When his son, Sir Anthony Bamford took over the business, he had the peculiar idea of using the big digging arms of his dad's machines in a work of public art, and duly hired the sculptor Walenty Pytel to design a creation to occupy a plinth in a park beside the B5030 in Uttoxeter, Staffordshire.

Pytel designed a monstrous green metal statue that extends several articulated JCB bucket arms in different directions across the field. The project was so immense that it took three JCB divisions to carry it out: the Experimental Department, Research Drawing Office and Works Engineers worked together to design a four-stage construction plan in which each successive stage was bolted to the one below.

It's hard to judge the scale of the thing as you drive past it, as you do if you happen to be on your way to Alton Towers. But if you park up and go into the field where it stands, you can see that even the concrete plinth is taller than most people – and the statue itself dwarfs the plinth. Up close, this *Terminator*-style nightmare is actually quite

frightening, and lives up to the sculptor's goal to make an abstract work that suggests something immense and powerful.

The effect is spoiled a bit by its name, *The Fosser* (which comes from the Latin for 'digger'), but most people don't know its name anyway. All they know is that it's opposite the JCB plant, and that when you see it, Alton Towers isn't far off. With all due respect to Staffordshire's premier theme park, we think that this statue makes a much more interesting destination.

Concrete-Cow Town

The mark of a good roadside attraction is that you associate it strongly with the place you saw it. This is what happened to Milton Keynes in the late 1970s, when a Canadian-born artist, during a residency with the Milton Keynes Development Corporation, created a little herd of life-sized cow sculptures out of fibreglass and recycled materials.

The herd was later moved into a field in Bancroft Park just off the H3 road, and has stood there ever since. To some, they reflect MK's quirky humour. To commentators looking for a cheap laugh, they are artificial animals that are ideally suited to a highly stylised and almost surreal town. Whereas to the ultra-dismissive, they're just plain stupid.

Naturally, we fall into the first camp. Any town in the

middle of real cow country that imports artists to make artificial cows is our kind of place. Especially since one of them looks suspiciously like a tapir. But we wonder sometimes whether we're in a minority.

Liz Leyh created the faux Friesians with the help of a few other artists and children from local schools. From the very start they have attracted much attention, not all good, from the general public, and care and protection of the herd have at times been an onerous task. The broadcast media looking for cheap laughs would often make caustic comments about the sculptures and, by association, about Milton Keynes in general. And some have come to regard the cows with disrespect. Sometimes, this disrespect takes the form of outright vandalism, which is expensive and time-consuming to fix, as well as being mean-spirited. Sometimes, the problem is theft. The herd's smallest calf, nicknamed Millie Moo, was taken away under cover of night a year or so after she was put in the field, and had to be replaced. A decade later, someone held her replacement to ransom – and although nobody's saying whether a ransom was paid, she somehow reappeared some time later.

Some of the responses to the installation have been a little wittier. Periodically, people repaint the herd in pyjamas or zebra stripes. After someone referred to the public art project in terms of bull droppings, a few brown concrete pats appeared to the rear of some of the herd. And, on one famous occasion, a papier-mâché bull was fixed on the back of one member of the herd.

Despite the occasional unauthorised modification, the cows continue to flourish. In fact, they have even been copied and installed at the home end of the local football stadium, locally known as The Cowshed. And you know that a roadside oddity has done its job if it becomes the mascot of your home team.

Periodically, people repaint the herd in pyjamas or zebra stripes.

The Jurassic Paddock of Milton Keynes

The concrete cows aren't Milton Keynes' only folk-art animal statues. South of the town centre in the area known as Peartree Bridge, stands a green triceratops staring at the woods. He's a strange presence for a number of reasons. For one thing, he has his back to the access road, so to get a good view of him you need to clamber uphill from the bus-stop on the main road through bushy undergrowth. (You could brave his paddock, perhaps, but it's private property, and he shares it with two enormous horses, who looked a bit protective when we visited.) And the other strange thing about him is . . . well . . . he's a bright green triceratops in a paddock in Milton Keynes. What more do you want?

He was built in 1979 by folk artist and local character Bill Billings, a man given to entering local parades in an 'upside down' suit with fake legs sticking up from his shoulders which obscured his head and made him look like a giant walking on his hands. It was fairly inevitable Billings would take on a monumental project at some point, and when he did, it caused a bit of a stir all round, especially in the local planning offices.

Bill had not gained planning permission to build a substantial structure on his land, and there was a rumour circulating that it could be taken down at any minute by council workers. It's hard to say at this point how serious that threat was, but photographs of Bill lying down in the belly of the beast to prevent any such action did the rounds of the local media. Eventually, of course, the issue blew over. Almost thirty years on, the triceratops still stands, though he has been obscured by decades of growth from Milton Keynes' trademark shrubbery. But he's well worth a quick trudge through the bushes – or a hike from the Grand Union Canal at Peartree Bridge if you're less adventurous. Just keep an eye open for his equine paddock mates – they appear to be his bodyguards.

Reiver's Curse Stone

Most public memorials celebrate local or national heroes. There's hardly a small town in the nation that doesn't have a poignant bronze plaque listing the names of those who gave their lives in the Great War, innocently believing it would be the last great conflict mankind would ever face. That's what makes the Millennium Subway in Carlisle such an oddity. The subway leads to Carlisle Castle, and etched onto the subway floor are the names of many northern families – the Armstrongs, Taylors, Youngs, Trumbles, Hetheringtons, and dozens of others – but not in commemoration of their service to the country. The reason behind this listing can be found at the castle end of the subway, where a huge polished boulder has carved upon it an inscription in Middle English that systematically and thoroughly curses every man-jack of them.

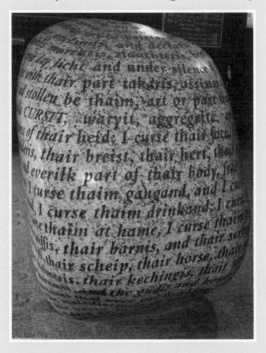

If you can negotiate your way through the strange old border spelling of this curse, you'll read that the heads and all the hairs on them, the mouths, noses and tongues, the hearts, stomachs, and arms, every part of the body, before and behind, within and without, of all the families listed are consigned in perpetuity to the deep pit of hell with Lucifer and his minions.

Predictably, a few of the locals weren't overly pleased with this monument. But it stands as a reminder of the terrible crimes that took place on the borderlands between Scotland and England, which stoked national hatred for centuries and possibly has residual effects to this day. In days gone by there was a systematic scheme of raiding and pillaging across the border known as reiving. The reiver families would hang around while their neighbours' cattle were being fattened up, then when they were at their peak, nip over and steal them, and burn crops and houses while they were at it, killing anybody who got in their way. As with all border feuds, each side blamed the other for starting it, but that all became academic after a few centuries when neither side showed any signs of letting up.

In the end, it took a massive public relations campaign to put a stop to the reivers. This began with the powerful curse you can read on the Cursing Stone in the Millennium Subway. It was composed in 1525 by Gavin Dunbar, the Archbishop of Glasgow, and issued from the pulpit. Before long, the curse was taken up in English and Scottish churches all along the borderlands and repeated until it became clear to the majority of the population that the border problem wasn't because the English or the Scottish were rotten, it was just that these seventy families didn't know how to play good neighbours.

This may be small comfort to anybody (including me) who happens to see his mother's family name among the accursed, but nobody ever said that history was going to be pretty. And it's much better to have your history uncensored, even if you have to endure a sixteenth-century curse or two on your way to visit another heritage site.

Stop or Go?

Of course, some public artworks are just plain silly. The concrete and glass merchants who transformed the run-down Isle of Dogs in London's Docklands into the gentrified Canary Wharf decided it would be fun to put dozens of traffic lights onto one pole in the middle of a roundabout. Driving through London is stressful enough, even for seasoned drivers, without adding contradictory traffic signals into the mix. And there's an even stranger side to the Traffic Light Tree: Roundabouts utterly flummox foreign visitors, who can just about handle driving on the left, but are all too often inclined to steer right at roundabouts and travel round them anti-clockwise, yet the tree was designed by a French artist, Pierre Vivant. Which raises one obvious question: *Quoi?*

Some places are strange from the very beginning; some have strangeness thrust upon them; and others just get stranger as time goes by. But no matter how they got that way, it's the places that get the most visitors that acquire the most far-reaching reputation for strangeness. And in England, the most visited places are undoubtedly pubs.

The Crooked House

There's only one pub I've ever visited where I had to clutch the bar in order to stay upright enough to order the *first* beer of the day. That place is The Crooked House in Himley, near the Black Country town of Dudley. For more than a century, one end of this old farmhouse has been sinking into the ground. Its left side is a good four feet lower than the right, setting it at an angle of 15 degrees, and the doorway, floors, windows and shelves inside are a confusing mixture of angles that makes it very difficult to orient yourself.

The result is that it makes even the soberest individuals feel drunk, which is a disadvantage for a place that's in the business of selling alcoholic beverages. When you feel that dizzy and disoriented when you first walk in, it's astounding that they can make a profit selling you intoxicating substances.

The Crooked House has been operating as an inn since the late eighteenth century, under the names of The Glynne Arms and The Siden House. It was over-mining for coal by local landowner Sir Stephen Glynne that led to the property's current state of structural unsoundness. But practical Staffordshire folk don't pull down a perfectly good inn just because it tilts a bit. From the late nineteenth century onwards, the pub has been an attraction in its own right. On our first daylight trip to the place, it was hard not to laugh out loud as we

rounded the corner and saw the building. There's not a right angle to be seen in the doorway, and the window sills and frames seem to bend in the middle in an attempt to stand up straight.

Inside, the first thing you see is a grandfather clock leaning towards the bar. People get a kick out of resting empty bottles or marbles on the bar and window sills and floor to see which way they will roll. But the process of carrying a couple of full glasses to your table is hair-raising. The only way you can stay upright is by staring at the line of the fluid in the glass, but that doesn't help you figure out where your feet should go. We certainly don't advise carrying a tray of drinks in such a place: That would be asking for accidents.

The best thing about the place is that nobody behind the bar will say, 'You've had enough', if they see you miss your footing. In fact, sure-footedness is a bad sign: You know it's time to leave The Crooked House when the walls and floor seem perfectly normal.

If you want to make something permanent, you set it in stone. Throughout the world, this has applied to commandments, laws and the faces of heroes. In the Weird world, it applies equally to handbags, teeth, teddy bears and codes. On trips across the more mysterious parts of England, we have uncovered a variety of monuments in stone that leave you scratching your head. Whether it's something to do with a fifteenth-century witch or an eighteenth-century member of the Knights Templar, if it's weird, it's bound to be written in stone somewhere.

That's What We Call Bridge Work!

In most parts of the world, hearing the words dentures and bridge in the same sentence could only mean one thing: There's a prosthodontist or one of his patients in the room. In that respect, Pateley Bridge in Nidderdale is not like most parts of the world. On the outskirts of town there is a work of civil engineering with a little something extra built in, and it's known locally as the False Teeth Bridge. At the end of an extremely narrow road, over a small creek, there's a road bridge with dentures set in the concrete.

It's not easy to get to the bridge or see the teeth, which makes you wonder exactly what they're doing there in the first place. Locals who are prepared to talk about it are unanimous in their explanation, if a little fuzzy on the details. They slipped out of the pocket or mouth of the fellow who was mixing or laying the concrete, and had stuck fast by the time he was ready to do anything about it.

But that's really only half of the story. When they repaired and resurfaced the bridge, the original set of teeth was buried. There was a huge uproar, so the builders deliberately slipped in, not one plate, but a top and bottom set to make up for it.

The Petrifying Well

For at least 600 years, people of the North Riding of Yorkshire have regarded a waterfall in Knaresborough with some suspicion. At the end of a beautiful stretch of valley bisected by the River Nidd, there's a spring that tumbles over a rocky outcrop in a pleasant little grotto. But this is no ordinary outcrop: It has an odd sweeping shape that looks like nothing else in nature, and it has another curious feature: Anything you hang under the torrent of water will turn to stone. It may take a few weeks or months, but even something as light or fluffy as a teddy bear or a hat will grow hard and heavy. It's small wonder the place became associated with the fifteenth-century local witch and prophet, Mother Shipton, or that it has been a tourist attraction for nearly 400 years. The real wonder, of course, is how it does what it does.

In a more superstitious age, the obvious answer involved some kind of magic, and when you stare at the items strung up under the falls or on display in the nearby museum and gift shop, it's hard to shake that impression. All the petrified pieces are pale with rough edges, and if you can sneak a quick touch, they are all rock hard and heavy. Even when you know the secret, it's still easy to imagine they got a glance from Medusa or one of her Gorgon sisters somewhere along the way.

The management of Mother Shipton's Estate constantly hangs new items in

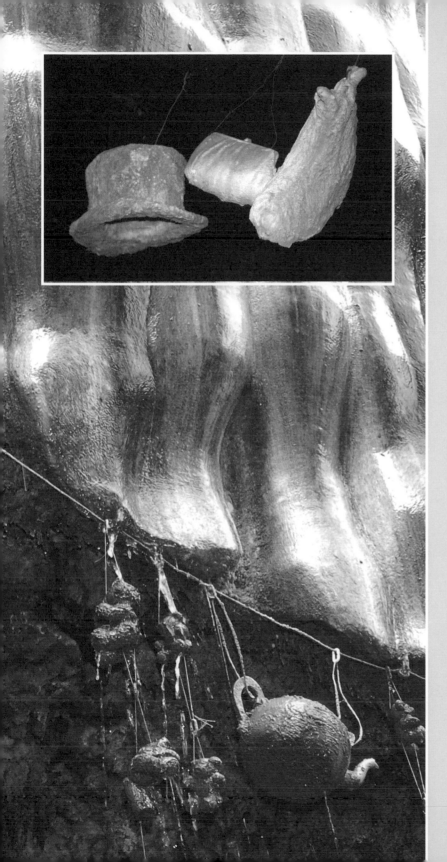

the streaming water – teddy bears seem to be the favourite item, but we've seen bonnets, pith helmets, broomsticks, shoes, socks and even toy lobsters. In the museum and gift shop, you can see more historic examples, including Agatha Christie's handbag, an old rotary telephone, Queen Anne's shoes, a Victorian parasol and one of John Wayne's cowboy hats.

The real story behind the petrifying falls is to be found rattling around in kettles across Yorkshire. The water there is generally pretty hard with minerals that tend to form scaly deposits. It's a constant source of concern for tea drinkers across the county, and makes it hard to get a decent lather from your soap or washing liquid. The spring in Knaresborough is so heavily saturated in minerals that they come out of solution much more readily. It takes less than six weeks to coat the fur of a small teddy bear with a thick layer of minerals, effectively making it look and feel like stone. A larger item may take a few months, but the results are the same.

Some items left under the falls have even become part of the landscape: Two of the curves on the rock face at the top of the falls are actually hats left by visitors from the Victorian era: One is a top hat, the other is a lady's bonnet. Over the decades, the distinct shapes have smoothed out into curves, and will eventually register as little more than bumps. Knowing that makes you wonder just what else might be underneath some of the other curves of that peculiar rock face.

You have to pay quite a hefty sum to park up and walk down to the Petrifying Well at Mother Shipton's Estate, so you should really make a day of it and take in some of the more conventional entertainments in the area. But frankly, they're not as mind-boggling as the petrified parasol in the Mother Shipton Museum.

The Da Vinci Shepherd's Code

Two hundred and fifty years ago, the ancestors of the earls of Lichfield developed the mansion and grounds of Shugborough Hall in Staffordshire. The hall itself is interesting in a National Trust kind of way, but the ornaments in the gardens are the real draw. One in particular has a nasty habit of sticking in your mind for days: It lies between two decorated columns and an arch and contains a code that's baffled ten generations of visitors. Even Bletchley Park cryptographers can't figure out what it means, and they cracked the Nazi Enigma code.

Beneath the pleasant pastoral scene rendered in marble in the middle of the monument lie ten letters. The first and last ones, a 'D' and a 'M', are set slightly below the rest, and are generally thought to stand for the classic Latin tomb inscription *diis manibus*, which consigned the deceased to the gods of the Underworld. The ones in the middle, 'O.U.O.S.V.A.V.V.', are still a mystery. Some clues point to the Knights Templar, which in the post-*Da Vinci Code* era makes many people wonder whether it has something to do with the Holy Grail.

The scene for which these letters serve as a caption shows a shepherd pointing out an inscription on a tomb to two women. The inscription reads *Et In Arcadia Ego* ('I am also in Arcadia'). In itself, this isn't much to write home about, but it turns out that the scene is a mirror image of *Les Bergers d'Arcadie,* a painting by the seventeenth-century artist Nicolas Poussin, who was known to have links with the Priory of Sion. The Priory of Sion is deeply embroiled in Grail legend, so when Michael Baigent, Richard Leigh and Henry Lincoln wrote *Holy Blood, Holy Grail* in 1982, they leaped upon the Shugborough monument as a clue in the quest for the Holy Grail. Years later came Dan Brown's *The Da Vinci Code* and, at that point, the gloves were off. The Shepherd's Monument became the focus of all kinds of bizarre theories and rumours.

Some thought it was significant that this picture is the mirror image of Poussin's painting – but couldn't imagine what the significance was. The fact that the tomb looks like a topless pyramid hinted at Masonic or Rosicrucian symbolism. The presence of two women in the Shugborough monument, as opposed to the single one in Poussin's painting, clearly meant something . . . but what? And what are all those mysterious letters about?

In 1987, Margaret, Countess of Lichfield wrote a letter to a researcher explaining her theory that her ancestor (either Thomas Anson or his brother George) erected the monument as a love token to his wife. When the wife was showing the monument off to a visitor, she suddenly remembered a line of poetry about a shepherdess named Alicia that she had learned as a child, 'Out your own sweet vale, Alicia/Vanish vanity twixt Deity and Man'. The initial letters of that snatch of poetry track with the letters on the Shepherd's Monument, because, like today's mobile phone text freaks, eighteenth-century lovers used the letter 'U' to stand in for 'you' and 'your'.

In 2004, Richard Kemp, the manager of the Shugborough estate, issued a challenge to two cryptographers who were stationed at Bletchley Park during World War Two to crack the code, and they came up with a variety of explanations. One of them believed that the middle letters stood for the Latin phrase *Optimae Uxoris Optimae Sororis Viduus Amantissimus Vovit Virtutibus* (which roughly speaking translates as 'Best of wives, best of sisters, a most loving widower dedicates [this] to your virtues'). Perhaps this is a memorial, then, from one of the eighteenth-century Anson brothers to his dead wife.

The other cryptographer claimed it was a secret message connected to the Priory of Sion, and translated it as the strange phrase 'Jesus H Defy', which by tortured logic could be encouraging people to reject the notion of Jesus as a deity – a big thing among the Knights Templar, apparently.

Other theorists believe it to be a Masonic or Kabbalistic code indicating the location of the Temple of Solomon or the Tomb of the Patriarchs in Hebron. However, these theorists have never actually shared the locations.

Whichever theory you prefer, the code remains a bona fide mystery. Sober-headed puzzle fans and budding cryptanalysts can swing by the memorial any time during Shugborough's opening hours to ponder the mystery. Just be aware that the National Trust recently began charging for entrance to the grounds, not just to the Hall.

Gargoyles and Grotesques

People have the wrong idea about churches. Waves of Puritanism in Shakespeare's time and in the Victorian era stripped these places of the earthy good fun that is an essential part of the English national character. Churches embrace many more aspects of the human condition than just piety, and in some cases, this shows in the buildings themselves. Look at any old church and you'll see cartoonish carvings, such as the more benign pictures shown here from Exeter Cathedral, and more than a few images of horror.

Gargoyles (the decorative waterspouts on churches) and corbels (the carvings under church roofs) are not symbols from the Gospels or the Old Testament, and have little or no religious background. Many are more akin to the imaginative workings of the pre-literate precursors of Stephen King or Dean Koontz, people steeped in visions of horror. Horses with truncated faces, demons and animals eating people, and even creatures engaged in distinctly carnal activity adorn plenty of Norman churches.

So what are these carvings all about? Some say that they were designed to trick any passing demons into moving right along and away from the church: 'No need to stop and haunt this place, it's already possessed', or 'This is what we do to demons round here: Turn them to stone and hang them out to dry'. Others say that the monstrosities were a way of scaring parishioners into line: 'There are demons outside the church; you're only safe on the inside'. Or perhaps they symbolised something to an illiterate peasant society that we in the literate world just don't understand anymore. Some believe that the characters pulling their mouths open are supposed to indicate the gates of Hell. To us, they look more like six-year-olds pulling faces.

One thing these grotesques don't try to do is tell a story. It's very rare in an English church to find frescos of a demon poking one of the damned into hellfire. That's more prevalent over the English Channel, such as in the Cathedral of St Etienne in Bourges. French sculptors seemed to take their gargoyles much more seriously than

our ancient chisellers did. By comparison, our gargoyles seem rather puckish.

Grotesques went out of style after the Norman period, with a couple of revivals along the way before they hit the big time again during the Victorian era. But often when the Victorians revived an idea, they didn't do enough research to get it completely right. For example, the gargoyles on Tower Bridge, which were slapped on towards the completion of the project in the early 1890s, are bog-standard heraldic dragons. Oh, they're well made, but they lack personality.

For personality, you need to fast-forward to the latter part of the twentieth century, when St Peter's Church in Dorchester was renovated. The doorway to that church now portrays the vicar who served the church at the time of the renovation, right down to his thick-framed Ronnie Barker-style glasses. He's not likely to scare off any passing demons, but he'll raise a smile on the face of anyone who looks left as they enter the church.

Sheela-na-gigs
Of all the church carvings
you're ever likely to see, there are none more earthy and, frankly, embarrassing than Sheela-na-gigs. Sheelas celebrate the distinctly un-churchlike practice of female exhibitionism. They show women, usually hags, lifting their skirts and showing their all. Sometimes, their tongues loll out of their mouths or their eyes bug out in exaggerated lust. This is not an isolated tradition: Researcher John Harding has tracked down sheelas all over the country, and believes they were even more prevalent before offended parishioners had them removed.

Harding's website, www.sheelanagig.org, lists more than six dozen surviving sheelas on buildings dating from the Norman invasion onwards. These are spread out across the country, with clusters of parish churches in Shropshire (including Tugford, Church Stretton and Holdgate), and scattered examples across the country from Northumberland through Derbyshire and Oxfordshire, to as far south as Binstead on the Isle of Wight. In each case, the sheelas brazenly display their own inner sanctum to anyone passing by.

Quite what this display has to do with any Christian tradition is anybody's guess. The most popular theory is that they are throwbacks to the Old Religion, included on churches for the same reasons that Celtic scrollwork appears on churches: Because the people liked seeing them and the craftsmen were good at cranking them out. Some people believe that Sheela-na-gigs may be incarnations of an old pagan goddess, possibly of fertility.

Another possibility is that they were designed as a kind of aversion therapy to disgust lusty swains and keep their minds off their favourite deadly sin. If this truly is the case, then it doesn't seem to have worked. Many of the sheelas (especially the one above the priest's door at All Saints' Church in Buckland, Buckinghamshire) appear to have suffered from localised erosion, which indicates that the statues were once habitually given what the politically correct might call 'inappropriate attention'. This leads us back to the interpretation that the Sheela-na-gig was a symbol of fertility or good fortune. Perhaps the idea was to touch them for good luck, like a Buddha's belly or a mezuzah.

Our favourite interpretation, though, is that the Sheela-na-gig was an old Celtic heroine-deity who appeared to future kings in the guise of a hideous and lecherous old woman. Think of a pantomime dame, take away the jokes and the songs, and you've got the idea. If the prince succumbed to the dubious charms of this creature, she would then reveal herself as a beautiful goddess and grant good fortune to the kingdom during his reign. If his seductress turned out not to be a Sheela-na-gig, well, he had just made a licentious old hag very happy.

While this sounds a lot like a marketing campaign put about by the Old Hag's Guild, it apparently took root in the popular consciousness, because churches all over the country have these carvings on them, usually on the exterior round doors and windows. From our post-Victorian standpoint, it is now next to impossible to know the original meaning of Sheela-na-gigs for certain. But that won't stop us from pretending not to notice them as we walk past on our way to worship.

Studland Smutfest

The Isle of Purbeck in Dorset isn't actually an island (it's a peninsula linked to the mainland at its western point) but if you're going to get there from Bournemouth or parts farther east, you might as well take a ferry from Poole and save yourself an hour's drive. That's what we did when we went to scope out the grotesque corbels at St Nicholas's Church in Studland. This is a tiny old chapel dating from 1050, and it has some of the strangest church carvings we've ever seen. It's hardly surprising that this place is only a few miles from a nudist beach – the images here are as licentious as anything we've seen on any public building.

Just beneath the roofline, spaced out every yard or so, there are little corbel carvings with long-tongued monsters, creatures holding their mouths open with their hands, and at least one woman flashing her privates. Some of the statues are worn but could once have been male flashers, and one or two carvings seem to have been chipped off, so goodness knows what they used to portray. There's even a pair of copulating demons tucked away to the right of the main entrance, and that's something you don't often see on the way to morning worship. – *Tiago and Matt*

No photographs, please!

For some reason I spent a long time looking for the Sheela-na-gig at the Church of St Peter in Croft-on-Tees (in North Yorkshire, south of Darlington), despite the fact it is about two feet high and one-and-a-half feet wide, and right next to the main door at head height. If my friend hadn't pointed it out, I would have walked right past it.

The carving is quite crude and differs considerably from the rest of the carving in the church, hence the local legends that suggest it was moved here from somewhere else. John Leech contacted us with the following information on the figure:

In the late 1960s, Revd Littleton used to show the children of the school around the church and tell us loads of things about it. An interesting church with its two family pews, thought to have sprung up as a place of worship for the ford across the Tees of yesteryear. We were told that the carving was an ancient water god that people consulted before braving the water. Well, we were all kids.

The book *Twilight of the Celtic Gods* relates a local tradition that the figure originally resided on a bridge. This may well tie in with the water-god explanation.

There is a tradition that this sheela is very hard to photograph, leaving people with no usable prints. I was completely unaware of this at the time and happily snapped away, coming away with some nice images. Nevertheless, I've since been contacted by an Irish bloke who blamed his inability to photo an Irish sheela on the sheela itself. He ended up asking the sheela if he could take some photos and, voilà, he stopped having problems. These 'you can't photograph it' stories are definitely a bit of folklore in the making. – *John Harding, www.sheelanagig.org*

The Green Man

He's a mystery, a cult and the curious work of surreal folk-art all rolled into one. He rears his leafy head in medieval cathedrals and churches, on Victorian gateways and on 'nouveau pagan' pottery in more or less equal measure. Although he's often associated with some pagan fertility deity whose name is lost to antiquity, nobody's really sure what on earth he's all about. But if you ever do a head count in Exeter Cathedral, you'll discover that images of a man's head with leaves and branches growing out of it outnumber images of Jesus Christ by a factor of about five to one. And that's got to be significant.

The Green Man is a name that first appeared in the inter-war years to refer to an image that had been kicking around for 600 years or more, and which can be found not only in British and northern European churches, but as far afield as the Indian subcontinent. Sometimes foliage sprouts out of his eyes or mouth in what looks like a profoundly painful way; sometimes he is a smiling figure with a face swathed in leaves; but the common ground between all these images is that each Green Man is a strange hybrid of plant and human, and in the absence of any written records, you can read into that anything you want.

Some see the Green Man as a symbol of the rebirth of life, in which dead humans make the ground fertile for plant life. Some see it as a nightmare vision of the tortures that await sinners. Others associate him with legends of Robin Goodfellow, the mischief-maker William Shakespeare had in mind when he wrote Puck into *A Midsummer Night's Dream*. To others, he's obviously Jack in the Green, a character dressed in Lincoln green who dances ahead of the May Queen in traditional May Day parades and obviously symbolises fertility. Yet another of his identities is the character Robin Hood – not the arch-nemesis of the Sheriff of Nottingham, of course, but a pagan woodland god whose name Robin of Locksley assumed as an alias for his Sir Guy of Gisborne-baiting activities. Whatever the Green Man is all about, he's there for all to see on churches, civic buildings, and private houses and gardens right across the country.

Roads Less Travelled

*Two roads diverged in a wood, and I -
I took the one less traveled by,
And that has made all the difference.*
Robert Frost, The Road Not Taken

Ever since the Romans built Watling Street, more than two thousand years ago, England has been on a paving spree. The goal is to transport large volumes of people as efficiently as possible. The route from point A to point B may not always be straightforward, but when you're armed with Ordnance Survey maps, satellite navigation technology and Internet route mapping, the chances are that you will be able to find your way.

However, the most obvious routes are not always the best routes. In the Weird world, we're less interested in A-roads and motorways than those other roads: The ones that wind their way across moors and mountains, or cross rivers by bridges that wail at night. Roads without streetlights. Roads that carry only a few cars, or none at all, to disturb a good night drive. Roads where pale phantom pedestrians flag down the traffic. The kind of road that makes you realise it's the journey that counts, not the destination.

So, hop in and buckle up. With one eye on the speed traps and the other on the translucent pedestrian who's floating across the road, we're about to take a trip down the roads less travelled.

The Belle of Blue Bell Hill

Early in the autumn of 1992, the Maidstone–Rochester Road over Blue Bell Hill in Kent earned its place in the canon of the strangest roads in the country. The place already had something of a reputation for being otherworldly – there's an old Roman temple nearby, and the place is rife with tales of epic battles in a bygone era. There are also a number of prehistoric monuments, including the burial chamber known as Kit's Coty House, in the vicinity. With such a history, the terrible accident that befell a poor man on the night of 10 November is all the more disturbing. Most sources refer to the man in question as Mr S, and, given the jarring realities of the case, we see no reason to reveal his identity any further.

That night, as Mr S drove down the A229 approaching the Aylesford turn-off, a girl dashed out in front of his car. She was staring him full in the face, and she maintained eye contact with him as she was dragged beneath his vehicle. He skidded to a halt in a state of horror and panic, and jumped out of his car to see what he could do for the youngster. He searched frantically but the girl was nowhere to be found. The image of her staring eyes haunted him so badly that he drove straight to Maidstone police station to report the accident. An extensive search of the area showed no evidence that the incident had ever taken place. But for the man involved, nothing could shake the image of those wide staring eyes disappearing beneath the car.

Less than a month later, the same thing happened to a different driver.

At this point in the narrative, the popular press and paranormal groups jumped all over the site. In an attempt to explain what was going on, local newspapers pointed to the fact that the events happened around the anniversary of a terrible collision on the old road in 1965 between a Jaguar and a Ford Cortina full of women on their way to a pub the night before a wedding. Three of the four women died in the accident, and one of the victims was the bride-to-be.

The tale was so poignant that it captured the popular imagination. Yet people who treated the story as more than a quick read in the newspaper poked plenty of holes in the notion that this explained the strange apparition. For one thing, the road phantom was a young girl and not a member of a hen party. For another thing, there had been sightings of all kinds of figures in the area, many of them equally un-bride-like. Only a few months after the November incidents, an entire family driving along the Old Chatham Road that runs close to the A229 encountered an equally scary figure that walked right in front of their car as they rounded a bend just before 1 a.m. on 8 January 1993. This was apparently a much older woman, with black eyes and a gaping mouth that all but hissed at the carload of people. The family's talk of a wizened hag with tiny beady eyes, dressed in a tartan shawl and bonnet, would have been almost ludicrous, but for the fact that they were all clearly scared out of their wits.

Old mentions of a ghost on Blue Bell Hill had been kicking around throughout the late 1960s and 1970s. One incident from 13 July 1974 involved Maurice Goodenough, a 35-year-old bricklayer from Rochester who was driving home late on a Saturday morning. He actually knocked down a girl of about ten, and heard 'a hell of a bang' as he did it. The bruised and weeping girl began crying for her mother, and so the man did what anyone in a pre-mobile-phone world would do: He tried to flag down cars for help. Nobody stopped, and he didn't think it was safe to move her, so he fetched a car blanket to wrap her in and dashed off to the police station. Thirty minutes later, when they arrived at the

scene of the accident, the blanket was all that remained. A search party with tracker dogs scoured the area at first light, but nothing was ever found, and nobody came forward to shed more light on what had happened.

Despite all the stories we've read about Blue Bell Hill in local newspapers, such as the *Kent Messenger* and *Kent*

Today, and in paranormal publications such as the *Fortean Times* and *Anomaly*, we have actually no idea what might be going on. But there's clearly enough activity there to propel the A229, the Old Chatham Road and the smaller roads in the locality to the forefront of Britain's bizarre byways. So if you must go there, go at your own risk.

Dark Forms on the Devil's Elbow

Want a truly awe-inspiringly desolate landscape for a road trip? You can't go far wrong driving from Sheffield to Manchester Airport before a pre-dawn flight across the peaks along the delightfully eerie-sounding Snake Road. Like its namesake, this road sidewinds its way through the windy and desolate hills, screaming at every turn that it could be your last.

At least, that's how it felt to the *Weird England* research team. That's why on the way back from the airport, we headed east from Glossop along the A628 instead. But even that didn't staunch our sense of tingling dread: We were bound for an even more eerie stretch of road known as the Devil's Elbow (or the B6105 to its friends), primed to the limit with strange tales dating back centuries.

Something dark and slithering crosses the road at the Devil's Elbow, and although many people say they have seen it, nobody seems to get a decent look at it.

Something dark and slithering crosses the road at the Devil's Elbow, and although many people say they have seen it, nobody seems to get a decent look at it. It could be a creature of some kind. It could be an animated shadow, or perhaps something cast by headlights. Or, of course, it could just be an overactive imagination heightened by the isolation and fear that moorland and peaks rightly spawn in people. Whatever the cause, if you drive along Devil's Elbow in the right frame of mind, you can probably see it.

Perhaps on our visit we were in too much of a hurry to get to Hunters Bar (or any bar, for that matter), but we didn't see the dark presence. But it was a thrilling ride anyway, in part because of the old Derbyshire folklore attached to the area. They say the place was the site of an abduction by Auld Nick himself: he is said to have waylaid a pair of star-crossed lovers who had been set up by the woman's disdainful father.

(Beware, you dads, of saying 'I'd rather she go to the Devil than marry that boy!') Twisting and wriggling to get out of the Devil's grasp, the young lover snapped Old Nick's arm clean off, and when it fell to the ground it formed the winding pass. It's hard to tell quite what the connection to the shadowy presence that crosses the road might be, but we'd rather not sully a nice atmospheric tale with an explanation that fits together too tidily. How about you?

Hill Devil, a horned creature that supposedly roams the local hills.

One such tale is the cautionary account of a prank the butcher's boy at Rodhuish played on a visiting ploughman's lad he met at the blacksmith's one day. The smith was regaling the visitor with tales of the Croydon Hill Devil, and the butcher's lad decided to dress up in a cowhide and horns and ambush the ploughman's lad. The fatal flaw in this plan was that the ploughman's boy was carrying freshly sharpened tools, one of which he plunged into his attacker before dashing off to safety. By the time the townsfolk had pieced together what had happened, the butcher's boy had vanished, leaving only the slashed animal skin behind. To a town primed with tales of the Devil, it was clear who had claimed the boy's body. And the same Horned One is responsible for the noises you hear on the roads there. – *Hemel*

Dark Figures in Daylight

Befordshire may sound harmless (it is, after all, the home of Milton Keynes), but between two villages just outside of Bedford, there's a haunted road where locals often see a malicious-looking character dressed in black. This is no latter-day fan of goth bands such as Bauhaus or The Birthday Party. This is a strange and supernatural creature. Quite a lot of our friends and their families talk about this person, but we only saw her once. We pulled the car over to the side of the road to try for a close encounter, but in the time it took for us to stop and get out, she'd disappeared. I won't say she vanished into thin air, because she could have just legged it, but we didn't lose visual contact with her for more than ten or fifteen seconds. Perhaps it's just as well we did miss her, because the legend mill has it that she's got a nasty temper and a malicious nature. The road she frequents is a minor track off the road between Ravensden and Wilden. But don't say we didn't warn you about her evil temper. – *Marco*

Exmoor's Ex-Devil

Dark stories surround many of the roads that climb Croydon Hill between Rodhuish and Timberscombe in Exmoor National Park. The place has a natural advantage in the creepy story stakes because it's a hill in the middle of a moor, and the noises that come off it are often taken for wailing or screaming. Perhaps that's why Whitswood Steep, Rodhuish Hill Lane, Stout's Way Lane and the footpaths and lanes around them have attracted such a cult following of thrill seekers. Then again, it could be because of the tales of the Croydon

The Whins Woman of Nether Haugh

South Yorkshire's contribution to phantom pedestrian folklore can be traced to a stretch of road that runs between Greasbrough and Nether Haugh, north of Rotherham. The road changes name to The Whins as it approaches Nether Haugh, and it's at this point that a phantom pedestrian makes her appearance from time to time. There's nothing unusual or deformed about the woman, but she has found a simple way to terrify drivers along the road: She simply walks out into the path of traffic and stays there.

Drivers slam on the brakes, even though they know that they haven't a prayer of stopping in time, and, to their horror, they see the car making impact with the old woman. But they can't find the victim when they get out of the car. Those who think in terms of the paranormal may realise at that point that they

didn't actually feel the contact or hear the thud of body against sheet metal while it was happening. But some refuse to believe in the supernatural, so they whip out their mobile phones and call the police. And, according to stories that have been circulating since the 1980s, when the police show up, they never find evidence of an accident beyond the skid marks. There's no injured or dead body, no blood and no damage to the front of the vehicles involved.

Who the Whins Woman might once have been (if she is indeed a ghost of some kind), nobody knows. But whoever she was, she must have had a cruel sense of humour. Nobody's come to any harm on that stretch of road after seeing her, but enough people have been scared witless for her to qualify as an unfriendly presence.

Taking Stock of Stocksbridge Bypass

A *short haul* from the Whins is another stretch of haunted highway – the A616 Stocksbridge bypass. Around Underbank Lane and on the nearby Pearoyd Lane Bridge, people have reported being distracted by a monk-like apparition who seems to be intent on causing accidents. Drivers speak of a figure that appears out of nowhere and comes so close to the car that they have to swerve to avoid him. Others have reported that they feel someone grabbing their legs. One or two other people have also seen wraith-like children in the area. The bypass may well be an expedient way of avoiding Stocksbridge traffic, but it seems to have been located in just the wrong place to avoid paranormal activity.

Paradoxically, some of the most-travelled roads have the creepiest tales attached to them. In the dead of night when there's no traffic around, the biggest highways can be every bit as eerie as those single-track roads in the middle of the moors. Perhaps the very fact that thousands of vehicles drive along a road by day makes it more susceptible to supernatural traffic by night. Or perhaps there's just something about driving at night that prepares a mind for the paranormal. Either way, strap in for a seventy-mile per hour romp down some major carriageways. And keep your eyes peeled for anything out of the ordinary – you're likely to see it.

Britain's Most Boring Haunted Road

It's a paradox worth noting that the road that's consistently voted the most boring road in the whole of Great Britain has also been called the most haunted. Yes, the M6, that epicentre of congestion between Carlisle and Rugby, has topped the paranormal charts as well as many people's Tedium Top Twenty over the past few years.

On the downside, the M6 routinely plays host to 100,000 more vehicles than it was designed for, so it's the scene of much hamstring-wrenching footwork as people nudge along a few feet, brake and change gears. But on the plus side, this motorway is in the middle of a country where road ghosts are a way of life (or perhaps, afterlife). And any 230-mile stretch of road is bound to attract a strange tale or two.

And sure enough, the M6 has done just that. History buffs get their kicks from reports of legions of soldiers in Roman army kit passing along the road, especially in the M6 Toll area in the Midlands. (Too bad the witnesses had to pay for the show!) It's worth noting that one of the respondents to a tarmac company's poll about paranormal carriageways observed the shadowy forms of about twenty Roman soldiers wading through the M6 Toll as if it were a river – and of course, in Roman times, the road level was a good metre below where it is today. So the millennia-old rerun of army manoeuvres seems to have been at the right elevation at least.

But it's the phantom traffic that we find most interesting. A number of people, including one man who went on to become a leading light in the reporting of strange phenomena, have seen vehicles on that stretch of asphalt that weren't actually there. More than two decades ago, the author and *Fortean Times* contributor Paul Devereux spotted a mini-pickup truck on the M6 approach to Birmingham, and realised almost immediately that it wasn't actually there. The road was almost deserted, and as he passed the truck, he glanced sideways to see the driver. He didn't see one, so when he pulled into the inside lane again, he looked into his rear-view mirror. The road behind him was deserted.

Devereux isn't the only person to have noticed phantom traffic on the M6, but it started him thinking in ways that most people don't. For one thing, he asked the odd but logical question: Does the presence of phantom vehicles mean that machines have eternal souls? The answer is clearly no, and if people see ghostly machines it clearly suggests that ghosts are not necessarily the disturbed spirits of the dead that most people assume they are.

So what *are* they? Well, frankly, we have no idea. But that's not going to stop us from zooming along the M6 in the wee hours, watching for driverless vehicles we can overtake or ancient Romans waist-deep in asphalt for us to run over.

London to Brighton, Ghost-style

Never mind your country lanes: For my money the creepiest road in England runs for about fifty miles from south London to Brighton. It's the A23, and since the 1960s it's been full of reports of transparent spectres. Right after The Beatles' *Sgt Pepper's Lonely Hearts Club Band* came out, I remember hearing about a couple who saw what they called 'a chick in a long white Carnaby Street coat' run across the road and evaporate into thin air. Then, later on, when the Sex Pistols' first singles were coming out (and this was before Sid Vicious got in on the act), a couple was driving north in the rain one night and saw a girl in one of those light Bay City Rollers raincoats that were big back then, only she didn't have any hands or feet. She dashed right in front of the car, but it went straight through her. Then there was the bloke in shirtsleeves who lurched in front of another car, and vanished before impact. There were also two people in light clothes who vanished as soon as the driver undipped his headlights. And my personal favourite is the phantom cricket player (or at least some ghost in cream flannels and a V-necked Fair Isle jumper) who's been seen strutting around there. I don't know who called him out, but it probably wasn't the girl with no hands.
– *Sonny*

Taunting in Taunton

Of course, avoiding the M6 is no guarantee of avoiding strange encounters. Between Appledore and Taunton, the A38 runs parallel to another great motorway, the M5, and it's been the site of several peculiar encounters over the past few decades. A bedraggled figure in a long grey overcoat has frequented the middle of that road for at least fifty years. Most people who see him swerve to avoid him, but they aren't always successful. At least one lorry driver was unable to move his rig in time, and called in that he'd run down a man but couldn't find his body. And there are tales of at least one motorcyclist bringing his bike down in order to avoid a collision.

According to a few ghost-story collectors, one person claims actually to have met the man in grey. Back in 1958, a long-distance lorry driver named Harold Unsworth encountered him on three separate occasions at three in the morning. On the first two occasions, he actually gave the man a lift. Unlike most drivers in phantom hitch-hiker stories, Unsworth claimed to have held conversations with the man, who described to him some of the accidents that had taken place along that stretch of road. On the third occasion he stopped to pick up the man, the figure asked Unsworth to wait while

he picked up his cases, and walked off. Twenty minutes later, he was still gone, so Unsworth started off without him. Three miles down the road, he saw a man in grey in the middle of the road, whom he recognised as his hitch-hiker. The man was clearly angry and shaking his fist; he was obviously not in the kind of mood Unsworth felt like dealing with in the middle of the night. As he made to drive past, the figure leaped in front of the lorry. Unsworth stopped, expecting the worst, which he found. The man was not injured, rather he was still standing, shaking his fist and railing against the driver for leaving him behind. When he'd had enough of shouting, he turned his back on Unsworth and simply vanished.

Where Gravity is Optional

In a country where laws are enforced by ever-present speed cameras, it's nice to know that there are still some laws you can break without fear of fines or endorsements on your licence. The law of gravity is one such example; but there are only a few places where you can fly in the face of Sir Isaac Newton and get away with it. A little town near Aylesbury, Buckinghamshire is one of them, the isles of Wight and Man are others and the hill near Yetminster in Dorset is yet another.

Gravity hills (or more properly, anti-gravity hills) are a worldwide phenomenon, and they work the same way no matter where they happen to be. You drive to them, stop your car on the slope facing upward, and put your car into neutral; then take your foot off the brake, release the handbrake and wait for the car to roll. When it does, don't worry too much about the rear-view mirror, because you'll be rolling uphill. It's a disorienting feeling when it happens but, rest assured, it does happen.

Of course, any apparent attack on the validity of Newton's laws makes people uneasy, so they have to come up with an explanation. Our favourite comes from the hill between Ballabeg and the Round Table on the Isle of Man, where they say that the 'Little People' sneak up behind cars to

push them upwards. A much more common explanation is plastered all over the names people give to these places: The Isle of Man gravity road is called Magnetic Hill, as is one on the A3055 between Shanklin and Ventnor on the Isle of Wight. It's as if the top of the hill is so powerfully attractive to the iron and steel in your car, it can drag it upwards. However, this is frankly even less realistic than the idea of it being pushed by 'Little People', because a magnet powerful enough to drag several tons of passenger vehicle uphill would mess with anything electronic – from watches and pacemakers to car stereos and satellite navigation – and you don't see that happening on these hills. Also, if you slap a builder's level on the road or hold a plumb bob over it, those will point uphill too.

There's actually not much mystery to these places. Most people agree that the eye is so easy to trick that gravity-hill roads are simply an optical illusion. You're actually on a downhill slope, but visual cues all around the area trick the eye into thinking you're uphill. And the strange feeling of disorientation you get when your car appears to roll the wrong way is compounded by the fact that the balance detectors in your inner ear know that you're rolling downhill and are disagreeing with your eyes.

Tring Hill Bucks Gravity

The hill between Aston Clinton, Tring and Drayton Beauchamp in Buckinghamshire plays fast and loose with gravity. It's easy to get to: Take the Tring Road out of Aylesbury (it's designated as the A41) and keep going straight instead of taking the Aston Clinton bypass. The road changes name a couple of times, but just as you leave town there's an intersection on the right with Upper Icknield Way and a small slip road called Dancers End Lane. That little road is the gravity hill, but it's a pretty treacherous road to mess around on because it's so small and the intersection is busy. If you're going to put your car in neutral and roll, make sure there's no traffic around and that you're facing the direction you're going to roll (that is, uphill). – *BoyRacer*

What's in a Name?

English is a peculiar language. It's basically a cocktail of Anglo-Saxon and French with a pinch of Viking, thrown into a Moulinex and blended for several hundred years. Because of this, we as a nation tend to be fascinated by words, and delight in double entendres, puns and wordplay of all kinds. And no wordplay delights more than strange place names, especially the rude-sounding ones.

Cause for a Titter

As a case in point, we get gobs of fun out of the simple town name Spital in the Street, even though we're pretty sure it got its name from a hospital that once stood there. *Spital* or *spitel* is Middle English for hospital, and *stroet* is Old English for a Roman road, so after that information is out in the open, things should calm down a bit. But, of course, they won't – not when England is

littered with other absurd road and place names.

You have to wonder what kind of low self-esteem plagued the town fathers of Great Snoring (Norfolk), Crapstone (Devon), Germoe and Mousehole (Cornwall); or who would choose to name their home street Old Sodom Lane or Crapple Lane (except, perhaps, the town planners in Dauntsey, Wiltshire, and Scotton, Lincolnshire); or why anyone would willingly spend time in a place called Deepsick Lane (even if it is in the delightful Calow, Derbyshire).

One has to wonder, too, why Thong near Gravesend in Kent is so far from Upper-thong outside of Huddersfield, and why neither of them is

anywhere near the Dorset coastal feature known as Scratchy Bottom or the town of Lower Swell in Gloucestershire, or Fanny Avenue in the Derbyshire town of Killamarsh or Crotch Crescent in Oxford.

Even the hills are alive with the sound of silly names. One of the great delights of visiting the Lake District is the knowledge that slightly north of Derwent Water is a hill called Great Cockup. And nearby, there's the only slightly less disastrous Little Cockup.

Another random thought: Is it possible to get anything other than a single entendre out of the names Titty Ho in Northamptonshire, Titley in Herefordshire, Fockerby in Lincolnshire and Fingringhoe in Essex? We don't think so.

It's Near the Ring Road

Sometimes it's hard to get past the point of inane snickering. If you want proof of that, consider a widely reprinted Reuters article from 2004 that reported on a South Yorkshire family who moved from their £150,000 bungalow on a street in Conisbrough because they were embarrassed by its name. For the record, it was called Butt Hole Road, and no matter how hard you try to brazen it out, people just don't take that address seriously. Pizza delivery folk and taxi dispatchers would hang up on them, thinking they were making a crude joke. But there are several streets with similar names, including Butthole Lane near Loughborough. And while we're on the topic, there's a road called Happy Bottom in Corfe Mullen in Dorset, a Pratt's Bottom in Orpington, Kent, a Wham Bottom Lane in Rochdale, Greater Manchester and, in Scunthorpe, the delightful-sounding Scotter Bottom.

But none of these names should raise a blush among the residents. Whenever you see the word 'butt' in an English place name, you should think of archery. Why? Because, in times past, archers used to practice by shooting at targets which were placed on mounds or structures known as butts. So, guess what? All these places with 'butt' in their name were once archery ranges. And whenever you see 'hole' (or, for that matter, 'bottom') in a place name, think back to your geography lessons: It's the lower bit of a hollow, nothing more than a shallow valley. So quit snickering and move on to the next absurd place name.

It's Enough to Drive You Mad

Residents of the North Yorkshire town of Bedlam have no connection whatsoever to a madhouse, well, not semantically anyway. The original Bedlam asylum was a medieval hospital in London called Bethlehem, but over the centuries all the syllables ran together and its original spelling followed suit.

(The same thing happened to Magdalen College in Oxford, which is pronounced 'maudlin', but the scholars there were a bit better about keeping the original spelling.) The North Yorkshire town name actually originates from the Anglo-Saxon words *bodle lum*, innocently meaning 'at the buildings'.

Respect (just a little bit)

Blushing grannies should be able to mention the towns of North Bitchburn in County Durham and Bitchfield in Derbyshire without thinking of derogatory terms for women or biological terms for lady dogs. Both places used to have lots of beech trees and, as with any English term that's used a lot, the vowel sound has been shortened over time. In conversation, you could probably pronounce it Beechfield and Beechburn as the namers intended and get away with it.

On the same note, there's nothing derogatory to the good women of Scunthorpe in the street name Basic Slag Road or those of Haydock, Merseyside in Slag Lane. Both places were once heavy-industry sites with heaps of slag (singular), not heaps of slags (plural); though post-industrial clean-up has improved the look of both places considerably.

However, some names are just too hard to handle. Case in point: The women of Ugley in Essex were apparently so irritated at being members of the Ugley Women's Institute that they changed their name to The Women's Institute (Ugley Branch).

It doesn't take much thought to conclude that in England, ghosts are not weird at all. They are about as mainstream as any paranormal phenomenon can be. Do you doubt it? Think about the traditional Christmas entertainment: Watching a Dickensian miser being haunted by his deceased partner and three other disembodied spirits. Channel-hop on your remote control until you catch sight of scared people in night-vision reality TV, jumping out of their skins. Or pay a visit to any stately home and hear the tour guide cheerfully recount tales of some lady in white who glides across the ramparts by night.

But popular television shows, tour guides and Charles Dickens aren't the only proponents of ghost lore in the country. Intellectuals and investigators have been trying to apply science to these ethereal experiences since the 1880s, when the Society for Psychical Research (SPR) was formed. This group of university professors and other earnest seekers of the truth have mounted investigations, interviewed witnesses, weighed the evidence and theorised over what it all means for well over a century, and they have come up with lots of theories along the way. Some haunting events are intelligent entities interacting with humans, they say; some are simply going through the motions, as in an ethereal re-run.

This Spectred Isle

And some are not visible at all, but unaccountably go bump in the night. According to the SPR's researches, somewhere between 9 and 17 per cent of people have personal experience of some kind of haunting. (Sadly, that leaves those of us who haven't still in the majority.)

And when somebody reports they've seen a ghost, heard mysterious noises in the dark or felt a clammy presence, in come the investigators with their electromagnetic field detectors, optical equipment and even a psychic or two to fill in the backstory. Most of the time they find it hard to arrive at a definite conclusion. If you believe in ghosts, continue believing and see what you think of this collection of reports. If not, just sit back and be entertained.

Phantom Drummer of Tidworth

Forget everything you've heard about poltergeists and try to imagine how you would feel if your house spontaneously began to resound with noise, relentlessly, unpredictably, day and night. And we're not talking about powerful subwoofers from a neighbour's stereo here. What we're talking about occurred in the pre-electronics era, the age of reason, wit and optimistic enlightenment that followed the superstitious and ruthless rule of the Puritans. King Charles II had reclaimed the throne, and things were getting better.

Except in John Mompesson's house in Tidworth, Wiltshire, that is, where everything was terrible. Loud noises wracked the house, objects flew around of their own accord, the bed elevated off the ground, phantom smells wafted around and the sounds of scratching and panting could be heard. In short, everything we now associate with poltergeists happened — but this phenomenon was as yet unknown.

The case found its way a few decades later into a classic work of demonology, Joseph Glanvil's bestseller of 1681, *Saducismus Triumphatus*. But by that time the story had been written and repeated by people whose world view was so overpopulated by demons and witches that it is now difficult to disentangle the actual events from their interpretations. Fortunately,

some contemporary accounts do survive, including Mompesson's letters to his family and to a confidant named William Creed. Briefly, this is what seems to have happened.

John Mompesson, a well-off magistrate, would often go to London on business, and one night when he was away, his wife heard loud noises that she took to be thieves. The intruders seemed to have been frightened away, however. When Mompesson returned, he too was awoken one night by 'a strange noise and hollow sound', so he armed himself and searched the house, but found nothing. Over the next few nights, the same

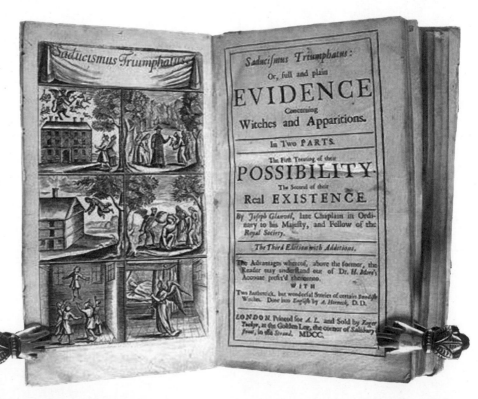

thing happened; a noise like the beating of a drum was heard, seeming to rise from a point near the ground, and gradually getting fainter. It carried on for five days, then went silent for three days, then took up again. This continued for a month, until it finally seemed to settle in Mompesson's mother's room.

Visitors to the house also heard the sound, and agreed it was very much like a drummer practising a common beat of the time — a refrain called 'Roundheads and Cuckolds' — but the noisemaker would also mimic any beat that it heard in the room. The stairs would resound with the sounds of bowls falling down them, or chains being dragged down them. Chairs, tables, trunks and anything that could move would move around the room at will. And a foul smell would sometimes waft around.

After more than seven months of disturbances, Mompesson's letters show that the family had become desperate. They do not bear the mark of an attention seeker or of a frivolous man; rather he appears to be genuinely distressed and at pains to discover what caused the noises. Mompesson brought in ministers of the church and intellectuals, all of whom seemed to think witchcraft was involved. The question remained, who was the witch? They interviewed Mompesson about events leading up to the drumming, and he hit upon a trial he had presided over the previous year. A wandering confidence trickster had attempted to use fake papers to get a handout from the public coffers at Tidworth, and Mompesson punished him by confiscating the only thing of value he had: His old army drum. In a monumentally bad impulse, Mompesson took it home for his children to play with, and stored it in his mother's room to encourage them to visit their grandmother more often.

One visitor to the house challenged whatever made the noise (to be safe, he addressed it as Satan) to knock five times if the drummer had set him about this business, and sure enough, it knocked five times. In his letters, Mompesson wrote that he doubted Satan's word, but that he didn't see any harm in taking out the drum and reducing it to ashes in one of his fields. When this failed to stop the noises, he tracked down the drummer, who was in jail in Gloucester for stealing hogs. He discovered that he had been a drummer in the Parliamentary army, had returned to his trade as a tailor after the war, but quit to take up a trade Mompesson described as 'going up and down the country to show hocus pocus feats of activity, dancing through hoops and such-like activities.' This discovery didn't particularly help matters, and into the eighth month of paranormal activity, a noise like snapping pincers could still be heard; his daughter was disturbed at night by a dog-like panting noise in her room; and hats had taken to flying off visitors' heads in the house. On one occasion, Mompesson believed he heard a voice saying 'A witch! A witch!', but after all those nights of being disturbed, perhaps his mind was playing tricks on him.

It's hard to say how the story actually ends. Some accounts say that the drummer stood trial for witchcraft and was imprisoned, at which point the noises stopped. But this seems too tidy an ending, and isn't supported by historical sources. People who have studied poltergeist activity more recently wonder whether the drum and drummer were nothing but red herrings that threw researchers off the real trail. Experts now tend to think that poltergeists fixate on young people in the house, often girls, and Mompesson had two young daughters at home at the time. Their bedroom and their grandmother's room, where the drum was stored, were both epicentres of the strange events. In the rush to tie things up neatly, perhaps Mompesson and the writer Joseph Glanvil, who popularised the story, missed the point altogether.

The Cock Lane Affair

Although it sounds more like a saucy music-hall song, Scratching Fanny of Cock Lane was a paranormal event that once had London society struggling to come to terms with the supernatural. This strange case took place in the early 1760s, when such intellectuals as Samuel Johnson and the then resident American polymath Benjamin Franklin were setting the tone for the city. But along a narrow street near Smithfield Market and St Bartholomew's Hospital, something that distinctly defied reason was taking place.

It began when a young couple expecting a baby moved to Cock Lane and lodged with Richard Parsons and his young daughter. William and Fanny Kent got on well with the Parsons family, so much so that William even lent his landlord money. And when William went out of town one night, Richard's eleven-year-old daughter Elizabeth stayed in Fanny's room to keep the young woman company. But odd things went on that night: A strange mix of rapping, bumping and scratching noises with no apparent source. This went on for two nights, and when William returned the friendly relations between tenant and landlord fell apart quickly. William sued Richard Parsons for the money he was owed, and Parsons betrayed a confidence by broadcasting that the Kents were not actually married. The Kents moved out, and in her terrified and heavily pregnant state, Fanny fell ill and died soon afterwards. The cause of death was listed as smallpox.

A year later, scratching and thumping noises began again in Cock Lane. Now thirteen, Elizabeth Parsons began to suffer ill health and seizures, compounding her grief over the death of her friend Fanny. Her father tore the panelling from the walls to uncover the source of the noises, but found nothing. Elizabeth moved to

another room, but the scratching and thumping followed her. The Reverend John Moore was called in to look for a supernatural cause, and held a series of seances in the young girl's presence. Before long, the Parsons house became the unlikely site of a fashionable society salon. Leading lights of the day, including Dr Johnson, Oliver Goldsmith and Horace Walpole, convened in Elizabeth's bedroom to attend seances. In an attempt to explain the prevailing noise, that of 'cat's claws scratching over a cane chair', people hit upon the idea that it was the ghost of the former tenant, Fanny Kent. Pursuing this line of questioning in his seances, the Reverend Moore concluded that William had murdered his soi-disant wife by lacing her beer with arsenic. When this was reported in the newspapers, the widowed William Kent, now a stockbroker, showed up at one of the seances and shouted down whoever or whatever was rapping out the answers. 'Thou art a lying spirit . . . not my Fanny . . . she would never have said any such thing!' he exclaimed.

Because the case had escalated to accusations of murder, things got serious. The authenticity of the phenomenon became a legal matter, and needed to be tested rigorously. So began a horrible series of tests with the teenage girl as the subject — or victim. To make sure she was not faking the whole thing, they bound her in a hammock to see if the noises still happened, and they insisted she keep her hands in full view during seances. Being an inexact science, the seances held in these strict conditions yielded no scratching or rapping noises. In the end, they told Elizabeth that if there were no noises in a final test, her father would go to jail for fraud. They then kept a watch on her through peepholes, and saw her concealing two pieces of wood beneath her nightgown. They hit upon this as evidence of fraud, and jailed her father anyway. As far as the legal system was concerned, the case was closed, and Richard Parsons was put in the pillory where he would surely be exposed to scorn and pelted with rotten fruit.

However, even at the time, people were not convinced that the whole thing was a fraud. The traumatised Elizabeth could easily have been pressured into faking an event to keep her father out of jail — and how would any grieving thirteen-year-old act after being subjected to the quasi-torture of being bound and stared at by strangers? And so instead of humiliation at the stocks, her father was showered with gifts of money.

To cast further doubt upon the verdict, almost a century later a writer and illustrator decided to revisit the story, and approached the sexton at St John's Church, where Fanny Kent had been buried. They struck a deal and the sexton's son took him to the vault where she had been laid to rest. When they opened the coffin, the face of the long-dead woman was perfectly preserved and showed none of the smallpox that was listed as the cause of death. What could possibly cause such slow bodily decay? One possibility that fits the story is an elevated level of arsenic in her system.

Ghost Writer

England is littered with mawkish local ghost stories polished to a lustrous sheen through overuse. But just because a story has been told and retold since early Victorian times, let nobody say that there can't be a real scalp-tingling haunting at its heart. This certainly seems to have been the case in the little Essex town of Borley, where the inhabitants swapped tales about a phantom nun who had died because of her forbidden love for a monk centuries earlier.

In 1863, a new rectory was built on what locals insisted was the site of the medieval monastery where the love affair had taken place. Servants from the Reverend Henry Bull's household began to circulate tales of strange apparitions peering in at the window and the like, but the bluff rector seems to have found the whole business rather amusing, and this hale attitude prevailed when his son took over the post as Rector of Borley in 1892. It was only in 1927, when Henry Bull the Younger died, that real trepidation seemed to surround the place. Many up-and-coming clergymen turned down the position and the now-dilapidated house that came with it. Finally, the sceptical Reverend Eric Smith and his wife moved in. They changed their tune pretty fast, and left within two years amid such sensational tales that the *Daily Mirror* became interested and ran a story about it in June 1929. The article mentioned a grey lady in a nun's habit passing through the rectory to a gazebo in the garden, and many auditory manifestations, including echoing footsteps, soft moaning and incoherent whispering. The dramatic climax of these manifestations was a low murmur followed by a loud shout of 'Don't, Carlos!' followed by silence.

The article reached a paranormal investigator named

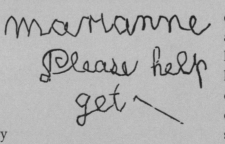

Harry Price, the founder of the National Laboratory of Psychical Research, who kept an eye on the events that followed; he wasn't disappointed. Reverend Smith's replacement was an older man with a young wife and their adopted daughter. The very first day, Reverend Lionel Foyster recorded in his diary that a disembodied voice could be heard calling his wife Marianne's name. Other disturbances came thick and fast. Furniture turned itself upside down in empty rooms. Doors locked themselves. Marianne was bruised by slaps from an unseen hand, and on more than one occasion was thrown from her bed. She had to dodge flying objects both night and day. And then mysterious scrawls began to appear on scraps of paper and walls. The shaky and sometimes rather ornamental handwriting frequently wrote Marianne's name, and if she wrote a response and left the room, it would write a reply. Much of the ghost writing was a mess of scribbling, but among the examples seen in the Harry Price Collection at the University of London, are a couple of chilling pleas for help: 'Marianne Please help get' and, in response to Marianne's 'What do you want?', the stark response 'Rest.'

Price voiced doubts about some of these events — those that centred around Marianne, he reasoned, could have been faked — but over the years, he pieced together a convincing body of evidence that some, at least, were not only genuine, but made some kind of sense. In fact, when the Foysters moved out and the rectory was abandoned, Price leased the place for a year and brought in a team of researchers. At first, they didn't uncover much, but when they started using a planchette (a movable device similar to a Ouija-board pointer but with a pencil), they started to gather

some background to the events. One alleged spirit writer identified herself as Marie Lairre, a French nun who had left her order to marry a wealthy Borley man named Henry Waldegrave, who later strangled her to death and buried her in the cellar of the monastery.

When Price's lease ran out, Borley Rectory, by now almost universally referred to as the Most Haunted House in Britain, fell to a new owner, Captain W.H. Gregson. While the captain was unpacking books he knocked a lamp over and the place burned to the ground. Five years later, Price got permission to dig around in the burned-out shell of the house for evidence to support the story that there was a dead nun in the basement. After several days of excavation, his crew dug up some remains. Forensic study showed the skeleton was female, and apart from some signs of abscess, there were no obvious indications of ill health. The remains were given a Christian burial and four years later the burned-out building was demolished. There has been no sign of a haunting since then, and after more than seventy years of fuss and bother, the locals are in no mood to talk about it.

The classic ghost is not merely a noise in the night. It's a visible creature, at least partly human in form. The temptation to explain away these apparitions is too great for some people. If they can't dismiss the appearance as an illusion, they feel they must discover who the spirit once was, so they can 'understand' it. Sometimes, of course, the apparition defies definition, and, as with anything that is unknowable, these ghosts can be truly scary.

Hexham's Haunted Heads

Houses are not the only things that get haunted. Sometimes, something as insignificant as a carved stone the size of a tangerine can be haunted. That's certainly the case in a curious series of events that began in the Northumberland town of Hexham in 1972. These events have been discussed and written about for more than thirty years, and yet remain as mysterious now as they did the day two boys unearthed a couple of crudely carved stones from their back garden.

The carvings turned out to be Celtic sculptures representing heads, one of a woman and one of a man. The male head was gaunt, with a vaguely skull-like appearance and faint lines etched into the surface to represent hair; the green-grey stone glistened with tiny quartz crystals. The female head was rounder, with comic Marty Feldman eyes, a beaky nose and hair drawn back into a bun and tinted with a pigment. After being examined by the archaeology faculty at two universities, the stones found their way to the home of Dr Anne Ross, a Celtic specialist at the University of Southampton. Shortly after they arrived on Dr Ross's desk, strange things began to happen to her and her family.

One morning Dr Ross woke at two o'clock in a state of great fear with a chill all over her. In the doorway to her room she saw a black figure, at least six feet tall, lurking in silhouette against the white door. But this was not an ordinary intruder, nor was it a regular ghost. 'The upper part,' Dr Ross recalled, 'was a wolf and the lower part was human, and I would have again said that it was covered with a kind of black, very dark fur.' She heard it moving down the stairs and along the corridor towards the kitchen and made to follow it until fear suddenly got the better of her and she ran back to wake up her husband Richard.

The two of them checked first on the safety of their children, who were still sleeping peacefully, then searched the house for evidence of intruders. Nothing had been disturbed and there was no sign of any forced entry. They concluded that Anne must have had a particularly vivid nightmare.

Nothing at this stage connected the vivid apparition with the heads Ross was studying. In her account in the Reader's Digest book *Folklore, Myths and Legends of Britain* (1973), she noted only that she didn't particularly like the look of the stones and left it at that. She would eventually come to dislike them intensely.

A few days later, Anne and Richard came home to find their teenage daughter in a state of terrible distress. She told them that when she had got back from school at 4 p.m. she had opened the front door to see a dark and inhuman form tear down the stairs, then vault over the banister and land with a thud on the floor. The sounds and the appearance of the creature were consistent with the wolf-man figure that Anne had persuaded herself she had dreamed up. And neither parent had told their daughter about their scare a few nights earlier.

Anne and Richard had no idea what had brought this monster into their home, but as Anne did more research on the heads, she began to realise that it was no mere coincidence that the stones and the apparition had arrived on her doorstep at about the same time. Strange things had also begun to happen in Hexham as soon as the two lads had dug them up.

In their council house, the boys would set the heads down and find them turned round when they returned to the room. Objects in the house were smashed for no apparent reason. The boys' sister found her bed covered with shards of glass. And the family next-door experienced a visit from a familiar-sounding apparition: While the mother was keeping a night vigil with her daughter, who was suffering from toothache, something they called 'half man, half beast' came into the daughter's room. They both screamed and the creature exited and was heard 'padding down the stairs as if on its hind legs'. The front door was wide open, but nothing else remained. The incidents appear to have stopped as soon as the heads left the neighbourhood.

It was when she learned this that Dr Ross decided to part ways with the Hexham heads. In fact, she got rid of all her Celtic head carvings, just to be safe, and it's anybody's guess where they are now.

But as the story gained traction, other snippets of

information have come to the surface. One claims that the previous occupant of the house in Hexham had carved the stones himself for his children to play with. So, instead of being more than 1,500 years old, they allegedly date back to 1956. That's not the conclusion scholars at Newcastle and Southampton had drawn, but their test results have since gone missing. So all we're left with is the kernel of the story, a vague sense of foreboding and a whole lot of questions. And in my case, a resolution not to acquire any carved heads without a detailed provenance and a money-back guarantee.

The Haunted Crossroads of Tom Otter's Lane

By Martin Stevens

Just outside the village of Saxilby near Lincoln, two narrow country lanes meet at an unremarkable junction. The roads to Doddington and Harby cross near untidy verges and ill-tended hedgerows, but if you linger here for just a few minutes, even on a bright summer's day, something makes you want to get back in your car, lock the doors and put distance between you and this place. Quickly.

It was here that the decaying corpse of Tom Otter hung on public view for more than four decades and to here that an unholy pilgrimage took place annually for six years after his death. But let's not get ahead of ourselves.

In 1805, at the age of twenty-eight, itinerant labourer Tom Otter was working around the city of Lincoln. Tom was a bit of a philanderer and before long a twenty-four-year-old girl called Mary Kirkham petitioned magistrates for support, having become pregnant by him. Under the poor laws of the time, Tom was obliged to support Mary and her baby. But the magistrates added a twist of their own: Do the decent thing and marry the girl or go straight to gaol. It wasn't much of a choice, so on 3 November the pair was duly hitched. The newlyweds made their way on foot along the turnpike (now the A57) to Saxilby, where they were seen drinking at the Sun Inn before making their way after dark toward Harby.

Somewhat unsurprisingly, Tom had neglected to mention that he already had a wife and child. The magistrates had unwittingly turned a philanderer into a bigamist, and by the end of the day, he turned himself into something much worse. Tom's escape plan was brutally simple: Where the road to Harby crosses the road to Doddington he drew a hedge post from the ground and stove-in Mary's skull.

The body was discovered the following day by two labourers, and on 6 November Tom was arrested in Lincoln. He stood trial at Lincoln assizes on 12 March 1806, with Justice Robert Graham presiding. Moved by Mary's death Justice Graham decided that hanging alone was too good for Tom Otter. He took the unusual step of adding that he was to be gibbeted: The body would be taken from the gallows, encased in an iron cage and hung from a post some thirty feet in the air. The body would be dipped in pitch to slow its rate of decomposition.

Tom Otter was publicly hanged at midday, two days after his trial. His body was taken to the crossroads, near what is now called Gibbet Wood, on 20 March. From the start things didn't go well. The blacksmith dragooned into making the cage had no opportunity to measure his client and made it too small, so that the body had to be badly contorted to get it in. The workmen tasked with erecting the cage struggled in the high winds sweeping across the fens, and it took three attempts to get the thing up. On the second try one of them was badly hurt when the cage and its grisly contents fell on him, and he died of his injuries the following day.

The locals soon came to treat the place as a Sunday picnic spot and tourist attraction. Girls would squeal as young men tried to shin up the post and snatch part of the body as a souvenir. After some time a pair of blue tits made a nest in Tom's lower jaw and successfully raised a brood, inspiring a rhyme chanted by local schoolchildren:

> *Ten tongues in one head*
> *Nine living and one dead*
> *One flew forth to fetch some bread*
> *To feed the living in the dead.*

The gibbet stood until 1850, when what little remained of Tom Otter was buried beside the road now called Tom Otter's Lane. The gibbet post and cage were broken up for souvenirs and only the headpiece now remains, on show at Doddington Hall, a reminder of the grim brutality of the law in an age not so distant from our own.

But it's not time to put this tale to bed yet. After the trial, the murder weapon was acquired by the landlord of the Sun Inn. On the anniversary of the murder in 1807, it was discovered under the gibbet, covered in what appeared to be fresh blood. The same thing happened again the following year and the year after that. Many saw it as a cheap publicity stunt to drum up business for the Sun, but even after the landlord offloaded the wretched thing to the Peeweet Inn at Drinsey Nook, it again disappeared on 3 November, and turned up under the gibbet. The following year the stake was fixed in place with iron staples, but somehow it still made its way back. The next year, guards holding a vigil to protect the post succumbed to sleep, and I'll give you three guesses where it turned up. Prank or not, the Bishop of Lincoln decided that enough was enough and the stake was burned to ash in the yard of Lincoln Minster.

Even that didn't quite bring the story to an end. A few years later a priest was summoned to the deathbed of John Dunberly, a Lincoln labourer who confessed that he had witnessed the murder of Mary Kirkham, but failed to come forward. He recounted how Otter told Mary to sit and rest, then drew the hedge stake and, with the words 'This will end my knobstick wedding!', swung it at her head. Dunberly described the sound of the blow as being 'like smashing a turnip'. His guilt and horror was bad enough, but every year on 3 November, he would be woken from sleep by a ghostly Tom Otter, who would lead him to wherever the stake was and remove it. The ghost of Mary would then join a horrific little procession to the crossroads, where

Dunberly would witness the terrible slaying exactly as it had first happened. Dunberly lived in torment waiting for the annual re-enactment until the stake was finally destroyed, and only as he lay close to death could he overcome his fear to tell the story. Having unburdened himself to the priest, he died.

Local tradition has it that the ghost of Tom Otter still haunts the crossroads and the Sun Inn. Total nonsense, most likely, but even so, I haven't taken a drink at the Sun Inn for years. Let's just say I don't like the atmosphere.

The much-published American ghost hunter, archaeologist and polymath Jefferson Davis once wrote 'Very few ghost stories are published about bathroom encounters. This is unreasonable, since we all spend a good deal of our lives there.' This statement raised a smile and made a lot of sense at first, but it turns out that toilet hauntings are not quite as rare as we might think. Here are two cases in point, one of which happened to Jeff himself.

Feet Under the Bathroom Door

By Jefferson Davis

I went to university in Sheffield, and every year or so, I try to go back to visit. One year my wife Janine and I stayed with our friends, Heather and Sean. They made us a comfortable bedroom in the converted third-floor attic. A few days into our visit, Heather and Sean went away and we stayed in their flat alone. We came in late and I paused to use the bathroom on the second floor. I heard Janine walk up the rickety stairs to our bedroom.

I had been in the bathroom for a few seconds when I heard the cowbells Heather had put on her laundry basket clang as if someone had brushed against them. The light in the outside hallway was turned on, and I saw the shadow of a pair of feet standing outside. I waited a minute, expecting to hear Janine knock on the door. Finally, I called out, 'Janine?'

There was no answer, but the shadow of the feet retreated from the door. The cowbells clanged again and I heard footsteps walking away. I thought that was strange, but did not investigate, intent on the original reason I was in the bathroom. A few seconds later, I heard the cowbells again, and looked at the door to see the shadowy feet under the bathroom door. It finally occurred to me that something strange was going on. I remembered how creaky the stairs were, and there was no way Janine could have walked down them without making any sound, and I had not heard anyone walk up the stairs to the second floor either. As quietly as I could, I walked to the bathroom door.

As I approached, the feet retreated and, again, I heard the sounds of the bells. I hesitated for a minute. I am not afraid of ghosts, but I was in my apartment once

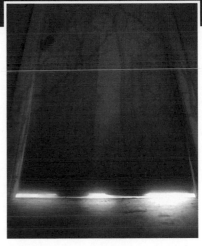

when burglars forced their way in. I would always rather face a ghost than a burglar, but if it was a burglar, Janine was still upstairs. I opened the door, and found the second-floor landing empty. The bedroom door was open, and the room was empty. I went upstairs, and found Janine safe and already asleep. After checking the first floor I went to bed, but did not sleep well that night.

The next day, Heather and Sean returned home. I asked Heather, 'By any chance, is your flat haunted?'

She smiled a bit and replied, 'I didn't want to tell you, just in case, but yes it is. We got the place already furnished. The previous tenant was an elderly lady, who died in her bed, on the second floor. Her son left all the furniture, including the bed we sleep in.'

Heather always was matter-of-fact about the oddest things. I told her about my experiences. She nodded. 'I sometimes feel her about the flat, particularly the bedroom. I guess that she knew we were gone, and wanted to check up on you.'

The Lady in the Loo

By Donna Mucha

If you want to stir up paranormal activity, one of the best ways is to begin renovations on an old building. Something about having the builders in seems to wake up any ghosts you may have in residence. This certainly seemed to be the case in the Low Valley Arms pub near Barnsley, Yorkshire.

On 24 April 2006, during a bout of redecorating, the pub's landlord noticed a lady in white on his premises. Normally, this wouldn't be unusual, but this lady had only half a face, and the sight of her constricted the landlord's throat so much he could neither speak nor scream. His wife, seeing her terrified, choking husband and believing there to be an intruder, called the police. In the meantime, the toilet began to flush repeatedly. It continued for more than four hours. The police arrived, and although they did not see any ghost, they did observe the handle of the toilet move up and down. A police spokesperson later made the statement: 'Officers saw the toilet flushing, but could not explain it.'

While the pub's water usage continued to rise in huge increments, further occurrences suggest that our lady had other interests as well, such as defrosting the refrigerator without unplugging it, turning the television sets on and off, and causing a rapid drop in the gas pressure. The landlord called in a local paranormal specialist, Darren Johnson-Smith, who found inspiration in the ladies' loo and came out with a tale of a nineteenth-century traveller named Mary Quantrill, who had been murdered with

a hoe by an unknown individual. No historical records supported his statement, and however evocative it might be, knowing the story didn't stop the activity. So, on 1 May 2006, the landlord brought in an exorcist to flush the house of all unwanted paranormal activity. Apparently, sprinkling the place with holy water and holy words did the trick, and the staff can now wash their hands of the whole affair.

Phantoms of the Tube

The London Underground can be very scary at night, with its echoing tunnels and the sudden gusts of wind you feel as trains push the air around. And, as with many century-old structures, the stations and platforms have acquired tales of the supernatural over the years. Many commuters have looked into the curved windows of their trains to see reflections of themselves and the people sitting next to them, and then noticed that one or more of the seats next to them is vacant. True, travelling on the tube is an exercise in avoiding any kind of contact, so it's entirely possible that fellow passengers may slip away without being noticed, but it still makes you wonder. For some reason, the Bakerloo line seems to attract more of these tales than other lines.

And they are not all ghost stories — there's a perennial myth that a motley clan of Dickensian characters colonised the tube in the late nineteenth century and never returned to the surface. Their descendants strangely mutated and have lived off rodents, discarded food and the occasional late-night passenger ever since. The London Subterraneans are a classic example of a local scare story, but there's a bit more substance to some of the ghost tales that are told. It's hard to say whether tales of wailing spectres are any more realistic than tales of cannibalistic mutants in the tube, but they have certainly seemed real enough to their witnesses over the years.

Two Stops Past Barking

To a Londoner, Barking means two things: half of a borough conjoined with Dagenham, and a jokey euphemism for madness. The expression 'barking mad' is so well known that to make a wittier allusion to someone's craziness, you call them Becontree, which District line travellers will know is two stops beyond Barking. But Becontree's overland station seems to have spawned something a little more disturbing than a jokey euphemism. Since the early 1990s, when station employees first spoke out about it, people have been swapping stories of a strange female apparition inhabiting the premises. Regulars at the station claim that doors to the station office rattle without apparent cause and, every so often, a woman with long hair, sometimes described as blonde, can be seen nearby. But she's no ordinary woman: The face that's framed by her long tresses has no features — it's nothing but a smooth expanse of skin.

MIND THE GHOST

Wailing Women

No matter how scary an apparition may be, the sounds of human suffering or anguish are much scarier. And that's the most common type of haunting in the Underground, where any sound whooshing through those tiled tunnels can take on an eerie wail. Whatever the cause, people love trying to match the sound of a soul in suffering to a verifiable historical happening. And in many cases they find a plausible explanation without too much effort.

Take the odd keening you 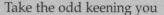 can sometimes hear at Farringdon station on the Underground's oldest line, the Metropolitan. People insist that this is the ghost of a trainee milliner named Anne Naylor, who was murdered there by her mistress and mistress's daughter. Anne died at the age of thirteen, back in the mid-eighteenth century, long before the station was built, which raises the question: Why would a ghost haunt an area beneath where she was murdered? Most people think ghosts who replay parts of their lives do so exactly where they happened, right down to the elevation. (There are many tales of Roman soldiers marching in York and the Midlands who are visible only from the waist up because the roads have been elevated above their first-century levels.) But none of this undermines the story of poor young Anne, who locals call the Screaming Spectre.

There are more moaners on the Piccadilly line between Knightsbridge and Green Park. The original Hyde Park Corner station building is now used for commercial purposes and can only be accessed by the public as an emergency exit, but its corridors echo at night with the sound of girls crying. The source of the sound remains a mystery, but the Underground staff are apparently reluctant to go there alone.

Early in the last century, there was a station between Holborn and Tottenham Court Road that led directly to the British Museum above it. The station closed in 1933, but not before it had spawned a ghost tale that somehow managed to incorporate a cursed exhibit from the museum above. The phenomenon was a screaming noise that echoed through the tunnels, and the cause (when it wasn't attributed to the Subterraneans) was supposedly a ghost that haunted an Egyptian artefact in the museum vaults. People attributed the keening to an Egyptian princess, and sometimes a voice could be heard calling her by name, Amen-Ra. After the station closed, people began to hear faint echoes of the crying at Holborn station. If you listen closely at night, you may still hear a high-pitched noise in the tunnels; I always thought it was squealing brakes myself, but I'm no expert.

The Bethnal Green Disaster

The most chilling tale of subterranean weeping is also attached to one of the most chilling tales of accidental death in London. In the early 1980s, the area around Bethnal Green station wasn't a particularly safe place to be at night, and it was also around then that people started to hear odd noises — the muted sounds of weeping, punctuated by the odd scream — that seemed to be coming from below ground. At the time there was no clue as to what might be going on. However, in the early 1990s, a plaque was erected on the wall above the staircase commemorating the victims of an incident in March 1943 that killed the largest number of English civilians in World War Two.

The event this discreet plaque commemorates began just like so many nights during the war: The air-raid sirens went off and the locals made their way to the tube station to take refuge, *Mrs Miniver*-style, in the tunnels. About 1,500 people had made it to the platforms when the anti-aircraft barrages began. A panic ensued among the 300-odd people still above ground, particularly when shouts of 'It's a bomb!' were heard.

At first, the surge carried people forward quickly, but the conditions were ripe for disaster: The steps were wet, there was no handrail, and the blackout lighting underground consisted of a twenty-five-watt bulb. Soon, the inevitable happened, and as people slipped and stumbled on the stairwell they were crushed by waves of panicked citizens trying to get underground. In less than twenty seconds, 173 people had been crushed and suffocated to death. Some remains were so badly mangled that they had to be identified by their clothing.

At the time, newspapers reported the incident as a direct hit by the Luftwaffe — a way of turning the senseless tragedy into resolve against the enemy. It took three years and the end of the war for the true story to come out. By then, the fifteen funerals per day the community had experienced in the weeks that followed the disaster were a bitter memory. Perhaps the panic and confusion and frustration and anger and pain of that night was so great, those who suffered it then are now playing it back in a kind of paranormal rerun. Who knows? But at least the surviving community has started to consider a proper memorial to the victims. Shortly after the sixtieth anniversary of the disaster, two architects began pitching the idea of a fitting memorial — a statue of the stairs with 173 lights on it — to the local council. If the funds can be raised for the sculpture, perhaps the suffering of the victims will finally come to an end.

A Hint of a Haunting

Not all ghosts appear in a form you can recognise. Sometimes, you catch an odd whiff of a smell that doesn't fit the surroundings. Other times, strange smoky images or odd flashes of light appear on photographs for no apparent reason. And then there are sudden drops in temperature or bizarre changes to the atmosphere. To sensitive people — that is, people who are sensitive to paranormal activity — these are signs that something unusual is going on. It's easy for blustering insensitive people (such as this author) to miss these things and their significance. But to others, they loom as large as life. Or perhaps that should read as large as the afterlife.

A Peep at Pepys?

There are numerous large and small ghost-tour operators serving London. One of the largest is The Original London Walks, with five historic ghost walks around London day and night. On the West End tour, we stopped for a brief time at 12 Buckingham Street, the house of Samuel Pepys from 1679 to 1688. In 1660, this civil servant began a detailed diary of his and British society's doings. On several occasions since his death, he has been seen standing on the second-floor stairs or the first-floor landing looking up the stairs. People described him as a solid-looking, grey figure who smiled softly at them before disappearing. At the time when Pepys' house was built, it was fashionable to erect gargoyle-like figures over windows to scare away evil spirits. I was taking a picture of these figures when I got this interesting print. I took this photograph around 7.30 p.m. in late May. The street lights had just been turned on, but this could not account for the light you see in the centre of this photograph. You can also see strong shadows in nearby window sills indicating the light source is above and behind the building. So what are these globes and vaporous streams of light? – *Jefferson Davis*

Load of Jorrocks?

Barmen are notoriously unpredictable when you start talking to them about ghosts on their premises. When you get them started, they'll often slip into storyteller mode for the crowd, and repeat the old stories with the occasional embellishment for added colour. Yet when I visited the famous George Inn on Iron Gate in Derby, I felt the barman was hiding something as he joked about the whole ghost business for the lunchtime crowd. To me it sounded as though that was how he wanted to feel about it rather than how he actually felt.

The George, which has undergone plenty of name changes in recent years, including Jorrocks, and is currently known as D. Lafferty & Son, has been around almost 400 years, and used to be one of the most famous coaching inns in the Midlands. Although it's a perfectly pleasant old pub to visit (notwithstanding the human skull that sits behind the bar), the place has its dark side. In today's pedestrianised and gentrified city centre, it's hard to imagine the brutality that used to hang over the place. There have been several documented murders nearby, even quite recently. And in the late eighteenth century, the large pub sign that hung outside fell on a horse-and-chaise, killing the horse. A mere accident? Or the work of something more dangerous, perhaps?

The most repeated stories mention a long-haired man in a blue coat who walks along the landing and down the stairs into the bar when the place is all closed up. Something also likes to displace the crockery in the kitchen, though it never actually breaks anything. And recognisably human groaning can be heard at night when the place is empty.

But the barman's slightly nervous joking on the subject made me wonder if there wasn't something more behind these tales than a bit of fun for the punters. After working the conversation for a while, he finally confessed to experiencing an event that had really spooked him. A group of ghost hunters were meeting in the basement while he was in the bar, when he experienced a moment in which all the goodwill and warmth seemed to be sucked out of the place — rather like when the Dementors are circling overhead in the Harry Potter books. He found out shortly afterwards that just when the atmosphere turned bleak, they were having a seance downstairs. He hadn't asked what the ghost group had been up to, and he didn't want to know. But whatever they had done below ground had had marked repercussions upstairs.

Tombstone Tourism

The bone orchard. The people plantation. The dead centre of town. Cold storage. No matter what you call cemeteries, if you happen to like visiting them, there's a word for you. No, it's not gruesome, mentally ill or, worse, a genealogist. It's *taphophilia* — the Greek term for an attraction to cemeteries. But, before you start to wrinkle your nose too much, remember that this is not a morbid complaint.

Graveyards are fascinating places to visit, if you look at them through the right pair of eyes. It's interesting, funny and touching to see how people choose to be remembered. Some people choose a pithy epitaph; others can afford to build a crazy structure that speaks volumes about how they lived their life; and there are even those who aren't buried at all, but who are stuffed and put on display for their friends.

It's a weird world out there, and it just gets weirder when you die. So get a good pair of hiking boots, strap yourselves in and come with us for a whirlwind tour of the tombs in the churchyards, crypts, municipal cemeteries and beyond of this sceptr'd isle.

Richard Burton's Sheik Rattle and Roll

A century before the name Richard Burton became a byword for a hard-living, gravel-voiced Welsh actor with a penchant for marrying Elizabeth Taylor, it carried much darker and more scandalous overtones. The Victorian Richard Burton – Sir Richard Francis Burton – was a man whose colleagues at the Foreign Office used to shun, fear and whisper about behind his back. After his death, the memorial he had erected cocked a further snook at their sensibilities.

Although he was never a practising Catholic, Burton was nevertheless buried in the Catholic Church of St Mary Magdalene in Mortlake, Surrey. Here, his stone sarcophagus rests in a mausoleum shaped like a sheik's tent, in contrast to many other fancy Victorian graves which instead often drew on classical or Egyptian themes and Christian symbols.

This strange memorial was just the last instalment of a fascinating life. Burton was a brilliant translator, explorer and not-very-diplomatic diplomat. From his early army career onwards, he wrote extensively about the sexual mores of the peoples he encountered, including the trips some British soldiers made to male brothels. The fact that he and his wife never had children during decades of marriage led to a whispering campaign about his sexual orientation. And if murmurs of homosexuality weren't enough to raise Victorian eyebrows, he was widely believed to have committed murder.

During an early journalistic project, he disguised himself as a Muslim making his haj to the holy city of Mecca so that he could write about it for a Christian audience. The rumour was that a fellow pilgrim (some say he was just a boy) discovered he was a European infidel, and Burton killed him to prevent exposure. Even those who did not believe he had actually committed the crime believed that he was eminently capable of it – and of much worse.

Burton did nothing to dispel the rumours. When a priest tried to get him to talk about the allegations, he blithely claimed, 'I have committed every sin in the Decalogue'. And when a doctor pressed him to say how he felt about killing people, Burton archly replied 'Quite jolly. How about you?'

Despite his outlandish side, Burton performed many services for the nation, including explorations of Somalia and the central African lakes, army service in the Crimea, and diplomatic posts in Guinea, Brazil and Damascus. These services earned him a knighthood in 1886 (even though he skirted legal boundaries in publishing translations of erotic verse such as *Kama Sutra, Arabian*

Nights and *The Perfumed Garden*.)

When, in 1890, he died of a heart attack in Trieste, his wife Isabel added to the controversies surrounding his life. She convinced a Catholic priest to administer the last rites, even though her husband had never adopted her faith. After his death, she unconvincingly recast him as a good Catholic, and ensured he was given a good Catholic burial. She also destroyed many of his papers, including a new translation of *The Perfumed Garden*, and generally tried to give his reputation a new spin. But at least she honoured the memory of Sir Richard's more outlandish

side with the tent-shaped mausoleum.

From Mortlake railway station, stroll along North Worple Way to St Mary Magdalene's to see the spectacle. Just make sure you walk round the back before you leave. The tomb has a cast-iron stepladder leading up to a window in the roof, through which you can see the sarcophagi of Sir Richard and Lady Isabel, as well as several religious paintings and a little altar. Just don't expect any sign of some dodgy bedside reading or murder weapons – his widow did too good a job of trying to rewrite that part of his history.

Bend it Like Bentham

When it comes to the disposal of one's mortal remains, great minds do not think alike. Some great men wish to be buried in Westminster Abbey; others want to be cremated and have their ashes scattered in a place they loved; while yet others want nothing more than to lie near their loved ones in a family plot.

Very few people of any stripe wish to be disemboweled, decapitated, fitted with a wax head, dressed up and stuck in a display case. In fact, as of this point in our research, we've found only one such man: The philosopher Jeremy Bentham.

While Bentham was still alive, he was a hugely influential thinker; and after his death, his writings went on to influence the entire social and political climate of Victorian England. Born in 1748 and trained as a barrister, he quickly decided that writing about social and economic theory was better than actually practising law. By his early forties, he was an avid proponent of a school of philosophy called Utilitarianism, which basically held that people's behaviour and a nation's laws should be governed by a central principle: To ensure 'the greatest happiness of the greatest number' of people.

A noble cause indeed, and one Bentham took very seriously. He decided early in his life that when he died, his body should be donated to medical science – a rare gesture in the late eighteenth century, when most anatomists had to pay shady characters to bring them cadavers with no questions asked. Nevertheless, Bentham wrote this provision into his first will at the age of twenty-one, and more than sixty years and several wills later, he held true to his theme. However, by the time of his last will, he had tacked on some curious additions.

Nobody could express Bentham's wishes more clearly than himself, so in this series of extracts from his last will, we'll leave him to explain exactly what he intended.

My body I give to my dear friend Doctor Southwood Smith to be disposed of in manner hereinafter mentioned . . .

The Head is to be prepared according to the specimen which Mr Bentham has seen and approved of.

The Body is to be used as the means of illustrating a series of lectures to which scientific & literary men are to be invited. These lectures are to expound the situation structure & functions of the different organs the arrangement & distribution of vessels & whatever may illustrate the mechanism by which the actions of the animal economy are performed.

The object of these lectures being twofold: First to communicate curious interesting and highly important knowledge and secondly to show that the primitive horror at dissection originates in ignorance & is kept up by misconception and that the human body when dissected instead of being an object of disgust is as much more beautiful than any other piece of mechanism as it is more curious and wonderful.

After such lectures have been given those organs which are capable of being preserved for example the heart the kidney &c &c to be prepared in whatever manner may be conceived to render their preservation the most perfect and durable . . .

The skeleton he will cause to be put together in such manner as that the whole figure may be seated in a Chair usually occupied by me when living in the attitude in which I am sitting when engaged in thought in the course of the time employed in writing. I direct that the body thus prepared shall be transferred to my executor. He will cause the skeleton to be clad in one of the suits of black occasionally worn by me.

And that's pretty much how it happened. Once Dr Southwood Smith was finished with Bentham's preserved body, it was padded out with straw, fitted into one of his suits and delivered to the University

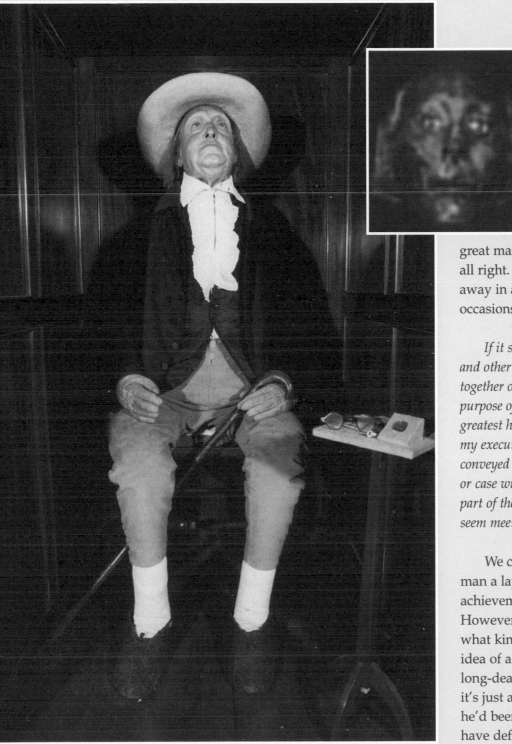

of London (now University College London). Topped off with a very lifelike wax bust of Bentham, the philosopher's bones are still on display in a wooden cabinet at the end of the South Cloisters of University College London's main building. All you can see of the great man are his clothes, but he's under there all right. And his mummified head is tucked away in a box and only trotted out on special occasions, as requested by Bentham himself:

If it should so happen that my personal friends and other Disciples should be disposed to meet together on some day or days of the year for the purpose of commemorating the Founder of the greatest happiness system of morals and legislation, my executor will from time to time cause to be conveyed to the room in which they meet the said Box or case with the contents there to be stationed in such part of the room as to the assembled company shall seem meet.

We can forgive an eighty-four-year-old man a lapse of modesty in describing his achievements – they were considerable after all. However, try as we might, we just can't imagine what kind of party he was envisioning. If his idea of a fun evening was to stand around with a long-dead philosopher with a wax head, perhaps it's just as well he specialised in philosophy; if he'd been an event planner, his career would have definitely flopped.

Ghastly, Grim and Great

A few centuries back, Londoners really knew how to build a church, and I'm not talking about any of the obvious ones. The most compelling one, in my opinion, is St Olave's on the corner of Hart Street and Seething Lane in London's EC3. You can almost hear the architect's voice echoing down the ages . . . 'Forget the vaulted arches, corbels, flying buttresses and rose windows. Bring on the skulls, man. We'll have three of them over the middle of the gate and two on either side, impaled on spikes. It will be timeless.'

If the architect of St Olave's ever did say that, he was absolutely right. The grim gate of this little parish church has borne its five eyeless sentinels since 1658, with a Latin inscription that I'd freely translate as 'Death is cool'.

The church itself is much older, dating back to 1450. It was old when Queen Elizabeth I went there; it was venerable when it survived the Great Fire in 1666; and was approaching ancient when the Blitz knocked holes in it, but failed to bring it down. This is a church that even managed to weather weekly visits from the raucous Samuel Pepys, who had a pew there during his diary

years. And the church, which is just round the corner from Tower Hill Underground station, is still going strong today.

The macabre entrance is not the only strange thing about this graveyard (even though it's instantly recognisable). The swollen graveyard contained within the gruesome gateway is, quite disturbingly, elevated as a result of the cumulative effect of thousands of burials, especially mass burials during the plague years before the Great Fire. One of the unmarked graves on record is that of Mary Ramsay, who legend says was responsible for bringing the Plague to London.

Apparently, although we've had difficulty tracking it down in the burial register, the church records claim that Mother Goose is buried there – seriously. It is said that this eccentric Elizabethan woman got her nickname because she corralled her geese to market wearing little boots to keep their feet warm. The name must have stuck fast, because it is said to appear in the records as her given name.

The final word on this churchyard goes to Charles Dickens, because, well, he tends to get the last word on everything. In his book *The Uncommercial Traveller*, he describes a visit to St Olave's one night during a storm:

I repaired to the Saint in a hackney cab, and found the skulls most effective, having the air of a public execution, and seeming, as the lightning flashed, to wink and grin with the pain of the spikes. Having no other person to whom to impart my satisfaction, I communicated it to the driver. So far from being responsive, he surveyed me – he was naturally a bottled-nosed, red-faced man – with a blanched countenance. And as he drove me back, he ever and again glanced in over his shoulder through the little front window of his carriage, as mistrusting that I was a fare originally from a grave in the churchyard of Saint Ghastly Grim, who might have flitted home again without paying.

When gravestones passed from being simple markers to a way of summing up someone's life, the epitaph came to be viewed as an art form, The real joy of burial became the noble art of putting something on your grave that would leave people smiling, weeping or guessing for centuries to come. A few people truly succeeded.

Spike Milligan

Brilliant humorists like to write witty epitaphs for a laugh (who can forget Dorothy Parker's 'Excuse my dust'?), but almost none of these gags make it to an actual grave. This, however, was not the case with Spike Milligan. The famously eccentric writer of memoirs, poems, novels and The Goons shows wanted his headstone to bear the words 'I told you I was ill'. And, after his death in 2002, his fans waited for more than two years to see his will carried out. The Chichester diocese where he was buried was reluctant to allow jokes on their graves, and while his family was locked in discussion about the wording on his memorial, things looked bleak for fun-loving Spike fans. Eventually, though, the former Goon, formally known as Terence Alan Milligan, got the last laugh – sort of. In the churchyard of St Thomas's in Winchelsea, East Sussex, you can find Spike's grave bearing an epitaph translated into Gaelic (he was, after all, an Irish citizen). Fortunately, Spike's fans don't need to be a Gaelic scholar to know what *Dúirt mé leat go raibh mé breoite* means.

John Peel

It's hard to sum up the contribution that one radio disc jockey's forty-year career made to the British music scene. John Peel's late-night Radio One show, road shows and recording sessions brought all kinds of music to the public's attention, and launched the careers of such diverse artists as Rod Stewart and The Fall. Peel himself is commemorated on his gravestone in a Bury St Edmunds churchyard by the opening line of his favourite song, Teenage Kicks by The Undertones. It's hard not to wonder what future generations will make of it. Why, after all, would a grown man want to be remembered with the words *Teenage Dreams So Hard to Beat*? The answer's clear to all those who tuned in religiously to the Festive Fifty countdown every Christmas, even when they were almost as far from being teenagers as Peelie was.

John and Margaret Whiting

John and Margaret Whiting did something that few people manage to do these days, and almost none managed in the short lifespan years of the seventeenth century: They stayed married for forty years. And judging from the epitaph, the death of the wife pretty much took away the husband's will to live. Beneath the details of their lives is a moving couplet which (in modern spelling) reads:

She first deceased; he for a little tried
To live without her, liked it not, and died

Murder-Mystery Grave

When people walked past the grave of Sarah Smith nearly two-and-a-half centuries ago, they must have known exactly who had murdered her. From our vantage point in the twenty-first century, it's a little harder to figure out. The poor young thing died in 1763 at the age of twenty-one, and was buried in St Margaret's churchyard in Wolstanton, near Newcastle-under-Lyme in Staffordshire. If we can believe her gravestone, she was poisoned by a mysterious man identified only by a few letters in his name.

The slab that covers Sarah's grave is old, cracked and covered in lichen, but its message is clearly visible: 'It was C__s B__w that brought me to my end . . . with half a Pint of Poyson He came to visit me'. Those lines between the letters hint that the man in question was too important to name, but beyond that, there's almost nothing to go on. There are no contemporary accounts of a murder trial and no anecdotal record has survived. In fact, until a few years ago, all we had to go on was what Sarah's parents had had inscribed on the stone.

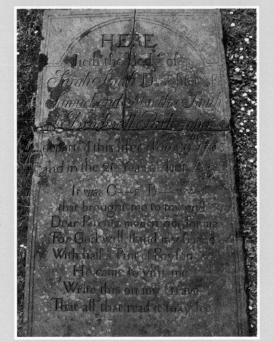

That was until Jeremy Crick entered the picture. Jeremy's flat overlooked the graveyard and he spent two years investigating the story before making his findings public in 2004 in a story in *The Times*. His researches uncovered a motive for C__s B__w's actions: the mystery man had most likely fathered Sarah's child and was anxious to brush the liaison under the carpet. Sarah's baby girl was baptised on the same day that Sarah herself was buried, and the parish register listed the child as 'base born' (born out of wedlock) and without a father's name. Within days, the baby also died (though in an age where infant mortality was high, the quick death of a motherless child is not necessarily suspicious).

As for the identity of the mysterious C___s B___w, Jeremy Crick believed that he was a well-to-do farmer named Charles Barlow, the wealthiest man in the district. It's certainly a plausible scenario: Rich farmer gets young girl pregnant, and does whatever he can to avoid scandal. But this is not the only explanation. Even if Charles Barlow is the mystery man, it doesn't necessarily mean that he actually committed murder. The grieving parents/grandparents may have blamed Barlow for their daughter's death, which could just as plausibly have been a complication from childbirth, or Sarah might have died by her own hand in a fit of post-natal depression. Her distraught parents could make any accusation against Sarah's estranged lover on a gravestone (it wasn't until later that parishes began to regulate what was written on grave markers).

Now that so many years have passed, it's unlikely that we'll ever know for sure the truth about Sarah's demise. We have some tantalising clues and some solid historical research, but the rest is just guesswork. The one thing we can be certain of is that three years after Sarah died, Charles Barlow was married with a legitimate daughter. We can only speculate what his wife and child thought if they ever walked past Sarah's grave.

In years gone by, if you wanted to hear a good creepy story about the dead, there was only one person in the parish to talk to: the sexton. This man was the caretaker of the graveyard, the digger of graves and the repository of all the local lore about the dearly departed, their families and their all-too-frequent exhumations.

Sexton's tales are an old tradition that, like their subjects, are dying out, and that's a trend we want to reverse. So here is a small sample of sexton's tales from around the country.

Pre-Raphaelite Hair

Of all the faces you've ever seen in Victorian paintings, the most recognisable must be that of Elizabeth Eleanor Siddal, who modelled for the Pre-Raphaelite Brotherhood and ended up marrying Dante Gabriel Rossetti. Elizabeth's long auburn hair graced dozens of Pre-Raphaelite works, including Rossetti's *Proserpina*, Holman Hunt's *Valentine Rescuing Sylvia from Proteus* and Sir John Everett Millais' *Ophelia*. In fact, it was modelling for *Ophelia* that ultimately led to her death and to one of the most macabre graveyard tales of the Victorian era.

In 1852, Millais hit upon the drowning of Hamlet's girlfriend as a suitable image for public consumption, and thought the copper-coloured tresses of his pal Rossetti's wife would look great floating in water. So, he procured a bath, filled it with hot water, flowers and Elizabeth, and started painting. Naturally, the water was going to get cold long before he was finished, so he arranged to have a fire burning on a low flame under the bath to keep his model warm. That was a nice thought, but the fire ran out of fuel long before Millais was done, and he was too involved in his work to look under the bath. Elizabeth was a diligent model and didn't like to complain. She did, however, catch a severe chill that weakened her system, and after a couple of years of chronic lung complaints, she became heavily dependent upon the opiate laudanum. In the end, she overdosed on the drug and died.

Rossetti grieved extravagantly at his wife's death (probably out of guilt for his many infidelities), and ostentatiously placed a notebook of his poems in her

In 1852, Millais hit upon the drowning of Hamlet's girlfriend as a suitable image for public consumption, and thought the copper-coloured tresses of his pal Rossetti's wife would look great floating in water.

casket before she was buried in Highgate Cemetery. Seven years later, Rossetti's career had nose-dived. He wasn't producing any new work, he was using whisky and sedatives heavily, and he was strapped for cash. His manager, Charles Augustus Howell, was clamouring for some new work, but the only thing of merit Rossetti had produced that hadn't been published was the poetry he had buried with his wife. Howell smelled a great publicity campaign, and asked for the poems. Rossetti told him that there were no copies, only the originals in the coffin. Howell wheedled Rossetti's consent for an exhumation order. He played up the drama of the moment by insisting that it took place after dark, lit by a large open bonfire, and timed it to coincide with the chiming of midnight. Rossetti stayed away, but when Howell returned from the exhumation, he came back with more than a stained notebook: He had a tale of great wonder to tell. When they lifted the lid on Elizabeth's coffin, she looked as if she had been buried only yesterday, with her waist-length copper hair now grown to enormous length, practically filling the coffin.

Despite Howell's best efforts, Rossetti's new book of love poems was not a financial or literary success, and the poet was haunted by the fact that he had desecrated his wife's grave to get them. So much so, that when he died, he couldn't bear to be buried next to her.

Of course, Howell's ghoulish story was probably a convenient fiction dreamed up by him to promote sales of the book. The Victorians may have believed that hair grows after death, but modern science knows better. However, the idea that a body in Highgate Cemetery had remained intact for seven years stuck around for another century and helped fuel tales of the Highgate Vampire that would excite later generations. And for that alone, this sexton's tale deserves to be repeated.

The Bleeding Tombstone of Hinckley

One of the more colourful ways we have of describing something as impossibly difficult to attain is to say 'It's like squeezing blood from a stone'. If a Leicestershire legend with origins in a graveyard in Hinckley is anything to go by, this feat is not only possible, it also happens every year, and aptly enough, shortly after the Inland Revenue's tax deadline.

The story began on 12 April, 1727, with a saddler named Richard Smith and his armed assailant, whose name was never known. That day, the army was in town on a recruiting mission, and, by all accounts, the recruiting sergeant was doing a poor job of raising troops. Apparently seriously the worse for drink, he soon began railing against the passers-by in the town's Regent Street. Eventually, he got into a shouting match with Richard Smith, calling him a coward from a cowardly town. Smith argued that he had a good trade and that his town always rallied round the colours in time of war, but that this was not such a time. There was no reasoning with the sergeant, however, and before long the argument came to blows.

This is where Richard Smith made his fatal tactical error: He was a tradesman and the sergeant was an armed fighter. The sergeant drew his bayonet and stabbed his opponent in the chest. The wound proved fatal, and some people say that as he lay dying, Richard Smith swore the town would always remember this infamous attack.

As proclaimed, on the first anniversary of his death, Smith's grave marker in St Mary's churchyard was mysteriously covered with blood. On subsequent anniversaries, the same thing happened. Perhaps this began as a staged event, some mourner's way of keeping the memory of this vicious assault alive. Or perhaps it was a natural phenomenon, some combination of April showers and red lichen. Or perhaps it's something more supernatural. No-one can say. Yet the story persists to this day. And we find it a peculiar irony that just a week after the government attempts to squeeze the tax-paying public that blood should literally come from a stone.

Molly Haunts Burslem

Before our visit to the grave of Molly Leigh, her story was flagged for our Reject pile. The story of an eighteenth-century witch who haunted the Staffordshire pottery town of Burslem with her pet raven . . . Well, it reeked of a tale that Victorian vicars would slip into a volume of folklore for a little local colour. Unconvinced, we nonetheless asked three workmen in the town square where we could find St John's Church so that we could do our research. 'Take a left here and go down to the bottom of the hill. Oh, and did you know that's the place where Molly Leigh's buried?'

The story took on a whole new complexion. If the first person you meet in Burslem volunteers information about Molly Leigh, you know it's a bone fide local legend. She died in 1748, but from her birth sixty-three years earlier, she was the most ill-favoured person in town. Not only was she strange looking, she probably also had wall-eyes or a squint because one look from her was supposed to give you the Evil Eye. The townsfolk blamed her for all kinds of problems, from outbreaks of illness to crop failure, and she ended up as a recluse living on the edge of town. For company she kept a pet raven – one of the darkest and most evil-looking creatures you could imagine, which everyone naturally identified as a witch's familiar. But as nobody had gone to the trouble of actually accusing her of witchcraft formally, when she died the local clergy had no cause to banish her from the hallowed ground. So she was duly buried in St John's churchyard.

But the story does not end with Molly's death. They say that the priest who buried her went out

to her house to bless it after the funeral, and came tearing back to town in a state of terror, gibbering about having seen her ghost inside the house. Clearly, her grave needed prayers to be said over it, so he enlisted the help of three other priests to exhume the body and bless it. Naturally, they did this at night. When the coffin was opened, Molly's pet raven swooped down over the vicars' heads and attacked them. The three visiting clerics beat a hasty retreat, but the local man grabbed the bird, stuffed it into the coffin, and slammed the lid shut. With the bird sealed in Molly's coffin, the terrifying ordeal was over.

When you visit St John's, it's very clear which grave is Molly's, even though its inscription has long since weathered away. It's a table-high sarcophagus standing at the back of the church. Every other grave runs perpendicular to it: After Molly had been taken from the hallowed ground, she was placed in a sarcophagus in a north-to-south orientation, rather than with her head facing east towards the Holy Land like everybody else.

Doing the Molly Run

There's an old custom in Burslem that's supposed to be able to raise a witch from the dead. When we were in school, the older kids would dare us to run round Molly's grave three times, anti-clockwise, chanting 'Molly Lee, Molly Lee, Follow Me, Follow Me'. They called us chicken when we didn't, but I never noticed any of them doing it either. Of course, when we got older, we made the same dare to the little 'uns. You'll still see some nipper tearing through that graveyard on the way back from school, looking terrified. Even after 300 years, she's still terrorising Burslem. – H. Hancock

Jay's Dartmoor Grave

Back in the days before city cemeteries and crematoria, you had only one honourable method of burial: In a churchyard or in the crypt of a church. Unrepentant sinners were buried at crossroads – partly because this was unsanctified ground and partly because it was hoped that the cross of the crossroads would prevent the evil of their sins from spreading after their death. Crossroad burials date back at least as far as the sixteenth century, and probably much further. And this was the fate handed down to Kitty Jay in the early nineteenth century.

The burial mound universally known as Jay's Grave stands at the intersection of a dirt track and a minor road through Dartmoor and, to this day, it is regularly marked with fresh flowers and other offerings, including coins and candles. 'Jay' was an old term for a prostitute, so many assume that's why the young girl was buried by the roadside. However, if you dig a little deeper a more heart-rending tale of woe rises to the surface.

In the late eighteenth century, an orphaned baby girl turned up at the Newton Abbot poorhouse and was raised there until she was old enough to work. The girl's name was Mary Jay, though she went by the nickname of Kitty. Kitty was eventually sent to a farm, where life was

very hard with little or no hope of advancement.

Before long, Kitty fell pregnant, and her hopes of staying on at the farm were scotched. When called upon to name the father of the unborn child, she pointed the finger at the farmer's son. True as this undoubtedly was, the farmer laid the blame on Kitty Jay and threw her out. With a child on the way and with no hope of supporting herself, she ended up taking her own life. And this desperate but criminal act earned her a roadside grave.

Soon after the event, people began speaking of a dark and heavily cloaked figure kneeling at the grave in the moonlight. Naturally, people say it is Kitty, grieving for her lost innocence or her lost child, or that it is the farmer or his son, doomed to stand vigil for driving the poor girl to her death. For as long as anyone can remember, fresh flowers and other offerings (including money and candles) have appeared on the burial mound. The more fanciful among us suggest that fairy folk of one sort or another are responsible.

The facts behind the grave are sparse: It was unearthed by a farmer more than 200 years ago, and found to contain the bones of a young woman. The remains were re-interred in the same spot, with her grave marked by a mound and a headstone. Many people believe that the custom of offering floral tributes was started by a Dartmoor eccentric named Beatrice Chase in the early twentieth century, but now, more than fifty years after Ms Chase herself died, the flowers are still fresh.

To find the grave, drive along the B3344 from Bovey Tracey onto Dartmoor; a couple of miles past Manaton, you'll reach a big crossroads. Take a left and after about half a mile keep your eyes peeled on the right-hand side of the road. The two dirt tracks at which Kitty was buried are now the main road and a bridle-path.

Exploding Sarcophagi

When Highgate Cemetery opened in 1839, its rural hillside location above the grime of the smoky city made it instantly attractive as a place to bury beloved relatives. To make the place even more attractive to the wealthy middle classes of the capital, the London Cemetery Company that managed the property built a gorgeous avenue in the Egyptian style, with chambers designed to make its customers think they could be buried like pharaohs. However, the damp English climate, strict burial legislation, and lack of embalming had an unfortunate side-effect that never plagued Tutankhamun or his kin.

The 840 sarcophagi that the London Cemetery Company had set aside for above-ground burials had to be lined with lead for sanitary reasons. The trouble was that, as the bodies decayed in the damp London air, the caskets were put under immense pressure from the noxious gases that built up during the decaying process. In some cases, the pressure was so great that the caskets blew open to release the pressure. The company came up with a novel solution: They would drill a small hole in the coffin, break off the stem of a clay pipe, and jam it into the hole. After a few days, a sexton would put a match to the pipe stem. When the gases caught fire, they lost their noxious properties, and would continue to burn for several weeks until the decaying process was finished. In their delightfully verbose Victorian way, they described this process as 'dispersing the deleterious effluvium hygienically and with maximum efficiency'.

Strange Slabs

'Show me first the graveyards of a country and I will tell you the true character of the people.' With respect to America's favourite quotation mill Benjamin Franklin (who wrote those words) and archaeologists throughout time (who live by them), we think the saying could be improved upon. For, if you want to know how *weird* a society was, look at the strangest grave markers you can find, and wonder 'What kind of a society would let that thing commemorate the dead?' So, go on . . . look at them and ask questions. There are plenty of examples in the next few pages.

Bowled Out

If you were a famous Victorian sporting-goods manufacturer, you'd probably choose a grave ornament just like Alfred Edward Prosser's. When he was laid to rest in Highgate Cemetery, Prosser had enough tennis racquets and balls engraved on his headstone for a set of mixed doubles, along with a cricket bat, stumps and a cricket ball. And there's a nice touch you don't see at first glance: The cricket ball has just sent one bail flying. There's only a couple of things missing: A record of who or what bowled Prosser out and the good man's batting average.

Piano Man

No prizes for guessing what Frank Thornton did in life. The half-sized grand piano that marks his grave in Highgate Cemetery also marks his career as a renowned concert pianist. We put the maudlin inscription on the side of the piano down to his artistic bent: 'Sweet thou art sleeping, cradled on my heart, safe in God's keeping while I must weep apart.' It doesn't hurt that the words are translated from an aria by Puccini.

For the Lack of a Backspace

We feel rather sorry for Thomas Grieve. When the poor bloke died (just before Christmas in 1851) the event clearly occasioned an argument between his two sons, William and James. And this argument played itself out all over the dear departed's gravestone. James put up a gravestone in the small town of Wooler in Northumbria that opened with the line, 'Erected by James Grieve in memory of his father, Thomas Grieve'. William clearly didn't like being left out one little bit, and insisted that his own name should also appear on the stone. But neither of them would pay for a new stone. Instead, the brothers reached a compromise. William's name was added in a bit of free space on the top right of the stone (throwing out the symmetry of the text), and the stonesmith hacked out the word 'his' to leave a rectangular recess where he could just cram in the word 'their'. The stone rests in the churchyard in Wooler as a reminder that once something's written in stone, it's not at all easy to rewrite it.

Fancy Caskets of Darley Dale

As you stroll past St Helen's Church after a pint or two in the Church Inn in Darley Dale, Derbyshire, it's hard not to do a double-take as you see the ornaments on one of the stone sarcophagi next to the church. We've seen a lot of symbols in churchyards over the years, but this is the first time we've seen an ornate pentagram poking out from between the tombstones. And any five-pointed magic symbol in a graveyard warrants a closer inspection. Like many of its neighbours, the sarcophagus with the pentagram on it has four carved panels topped off by a plain stone slab. The name of the deceased has long since worn off, and judging by how loosely the slab fits the stone casket, the deceased himself has long since gone, too: You can see through the gaps in the stone and there's nothing inside.

But who needs to see inside when you have all this decoration on the outside? On one side there's a Celtic pattern, on the other is the peculiar machine that gives the grave its common name – The Weaver's Tomb – and at the foot-end of the casket is another symbol that seems out of place in a Church of England graveyard: A Star of David. So, here's the breakdown from the top: We've got a Protestant church burial and symbols associated with Judaism, paganism and Devil worship. If you can make any sense of this, let us know. We're still scratching our heads.

The Great Pyramid of Mad Jack Fuller

Eccentrics come in all shapes and sizes, and in the case of Mad Jack Fuller, that would be pear-shaped and enormous. This might have had something to do with a steady supply of sweet stuff from his family's sugar plantation, but it was more likely because he knew how to live large. He got a solid start by being born into a wealthy Sussex family with a lucrative military contract to supply cannons to the Royal Navy; and he inherited the family estate at the young age of twenty. He served four terms as the Member of Parliament for his home town of Brightling, and whenever there was a shortage of work for the local labour force, he would dream up eccentric public works projects to keep them employed.

As a result, the area around Brightling is dotted with follies, including an obelisk, a tower and a strange structure called the Sugar Loaf after the cones of sugar that his family's plantations shipped out.

They say this last structure was created to win a bet about the number of church steeples you could see from his estate. The figure he bet was one short of the actual number, so he cheated by erecting a building that looked like a steeple.

Fuller also used his money for some serious purposes, including a £10,000 donation to establish the Royal Institution in London. And in this age of pay-for-peerage, it's encouraging to know that he refused honours when they were offered to him.

Fuller's final bold architectural statement was his decision to be buried beneath a pyramid. He secured permission to erect a twenty-foot-high tomb in Brightling's St Thomas à Becket churchyard by putting up the cash for a new wall and gates for the church. After he died, he was laid to rest in it

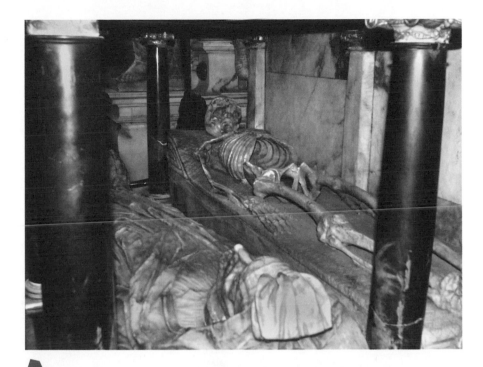

pharaoh-style. Or at least, that's how one of the stories goes. Another is that he was propped up at a table dressed in a top hat, with a bottle of port in front of him.

The tales, unfortunately, are as tall as the pyramid itself. When the structure needed some repair work in the 1980s, the restorers entered the tomb, and found nothing more extraordinary in it than some lines from Thomas Gray's *Elegy Written in a Country Churchyard* written on an inside wall. But you have to ask yourself this question: Just how much more eccentric did Mad Jack need to be? He got buried inside a pyramid in Sussex . . . isn't that weird enough?

Mad Jack's Run

Around East Sussex, there's a legend about Mad Jack's Pyramid. If you run round it anti-clockwise three times, it is said that the Devil will appear. I don't know how many people have tried it in the nearly 200 years since the thing was put up, but I'm not about to add to their number. If I want the Devil to appear, I'll do it the old fashioned way: Live a life of reckless abandon.
– Mad Bob Fuller-Vitte

Accurate Description of Contents

You've just got to love a family that goes to great lengths to depict their dearly departed in startlingly accurate terms. That's exactly what the Cavendish family did when the first Duke of Devonshire, their most honoured member, passed on. They devoted an entire wall to the Duke's memory in a chapel above the right transept in St Peter's Church in Edensor. There are large statues of armour, a massive marble canopy and huge framed slabs of marble. And on top of the stone casket is a beautifully carved marble statue of the Duke . . . as a skeleton. True taphophiles describe this type of memorial as a cadaver sculpture, and there are several such examples dotted throughout England. It may not be how most of us would want to remember our beloved, but there's no denying the fact that it is an accurate representation of the contents of the box.

Tea, Toast and Tombstones

The parish church of St Martin-in-the-Fields seems like an incredible misnomer these days. It should be called something like St Martin-Opposite-the-National-Gallery or St Martin-Near-Trafalgar-Square. In fact, it's hard to imagine a less rural church than St Martin's. Heck, you can walk to Oxford Street from it in no time at all. It's best known to music lovers for playing host to Neville Mariner's baroque ensemble, but to more or less everybody else, it's best known for having a great subterranean teashop.

The Café in the Crypt at St Martin's has won awards for its atmosphere, food and prices. Les Routiers named it the London Café of the Year in 2003. We can only assume that the reviewers were concentrating on the vaulted ceilings and the food when they issued the awards (because respectively they look and taste great). But if there's one thing everybody knows about church crypts, it's that they were designed to house the dead. And if you look down at the floor in the café, you'll see plenty of evidence of this – it's paved with tombstones.

Like most sixteenth-century churches, St Martin's used to have a graveyard around it, but as the local fields were replaced by the ever-expanding city of London, the contents of the graves were relocated underneath the church. From that point on, all new coffins were slid down the stone stairs for storage. Where people now chow down on their bangers and mash, the dead were once stacked in lead coffins. Among the dead filed away here were Charles II's favourite greengrocer, Nell Gwyn, and the dressmaker Anne Turner, who was hanged in 1615 for her part in poisoning Sir Thomas Overbury.

The murder of Sir Thomas was a great and sordid tale from the court of King James I. It began with the marriage of society belle Frances Howard to the Earl of Essex. Essex was a gloomy man many years her senior (she was just thirteen at the time), and she successfully shunned his advances for years. This was hardly girlish

about what a 'filthy base woman' Frances was, and how unsuitable for marriage to an important courtier. Frances retaliated by using family connections to accuse Overbury of publicly insulting the king, a crime that got him thrown into the Tower.

Although free to marry, Frances's position was precarious as long as Overbury was around to spread the truth about her checkered past. So, she enlisted Anne Turner and some of her cronies to mix arsenic and sublimate of mercury into Overbury's prison food. This slow poisoning had the added advantage for Frances of making it appear that Overbury had syphilis, which severely undermined his moral stance against her. After a period of slow poisoning, a massive dose of mercury was administered to finish him off. Ten days later, Frances married Carr.

Of course, she didn't get away with it. A year later, the apothecary who prepared the fatal dose of mercury confessed all on his deathbed, and the wheels of justice began turning. But they didn't turn full circle. Anne Turner and her three colleagues were hanged, but Frances and her husband were pardoned and lived out their lives far away from court in Oxford.

So it was Anne Turner, madam, dressmaker and accessory to murder, who ended up in some dark chamber of St Martin's crypt. Her burial marker, if there ever was one, has not survived, although her story has.

In 2003, John Walsh of *The Independent* newspaper declared, 'If the idea of conviviality, inexpensive food and olde-worlde atmosphere appeals, arrange to meet at the buffet bar in the gothic style crypt of St Martin-in-the-Fields.' We agree, but we'd have to add that tales of marital humiliation, murder and mercury poisoning, consumed over a pavement of grave markers, adds a certain something extra to the experience.

modesty, since she was actively pursuing Robert Carr, a dashing young favourite of King James. In fact, Frances, now Lady Essex, ended up trysting away furiously with Carr in one of several houses maintained by Anne Turner, whose dressmaking business was little more than a cover for her true trade of madam.

A combination of extreme abstinence in the marital bed and the opposite with another man eventually led to a successful annulment of Essex's marriage. But the earl's friend Sir Thomas Overbury petitioned vigorously to prevent Frances from marrying Carr, talking openly

Abandoned and Underground

in a top ten list of the most evocative words in the English language, two perennial favourites would have to be 'abandoned' and 'underground'. They have their direct and obvious interpretations, of course, but their dictionary definitions are shrouded in layers of suggestion.

'Abandoned' doesn't just mean left alone, it also conjures images of something left to fall apart; it creates an image of desolation, decay and isolation, and brings to mind the lines from Percy Bysshe Shelley's nihilistic poem *Ozymandias*, 'Look on my works, ye Mighty, and despair!' For its part, 'underground' can suggest something much more than just being beneath the earth: It carries undertones of being hidden and shrouded in secrecy.

In short, both terms carry with them a hint of something unnerving. And, in some ways, that's the same feeling you get when visiting some of England's abandoned and underground sites. Nevertheless, there's some fun to be had in running around the Dorset ghost town of Tyneham, or in bird watching at the abandoned military facilities of Suffolk's Orford Ness.

Yet beneath the surface, both literally and figuratively, lurks something undeniably unnerving. Perhaps it's a mild case of claustrophobia getting the better of you or a more profound kind of excitement as you try to imagine what once happened in these places, how they came to be and why they were abandoned. Whatever it is, there's certainly no feeling quite like it.

INLET.

OUTLET.

The Orford Ness Monster

On the face of it, a nature reserve off the Suffolk coast is unlikely to qualify as a weird site. Orford Ness National Nature Reserve boasts three hiking trails cheerfully marked in red, green and blue; provides breeding grounds for Little Terns and Lesser Black-backed gulls and its brackish lagoons and shingle marshes play host to much varied vegetation. It's all very interesting in an anorak-wearing way, but it's not exactly the stuff of weirdness.

But there's another side to this ten-mile shingle spit that makes it well worth a second and third glance. For much of the twentieth century, Orford Ness was a military weapons testing site. It is full of abandoned military buildings, which are always good for a visit. And it also has the Pagodas, two off-limit sites where Britain tested bits of its experimental nuclear arsenal during the Cold War – and that's simply too good to miss.

But visiting this desolate place is hardly a congenial excursion. The ferry that runs between 10 a.m. and 2 p.m. from Orford Quay takes you to a largely bleak and forbidding place where watchtowers and Ministry of Defence signs basically tell you at every turn that you don't belong there. True, the MOD no longer has any presence in the place (it was evacuated in 1985 and later sold to the National Trust), but its presence looms so large that even polite National Trust requests not to stray off the footpaths seem to carry the weight of military menace.

And that degree of menace has a long history. The Ness was taken over by the War Office in 1913, and its swamps were drained to create airfields for testing experimental aircraft and other military hardware. During World War Two and the Cold War, the place was used for a few relatively innocent experiments in radar but mainly for much less innocent lethality and vulnerability trials – a process that involved firing hundreds of rounds of ammunition at things to see what would happen.

Then, in 1956, came the nuclear bomb trials. These were carried out in six laboratories built on the site, including Labs Four and Five, which became known as the infamous 'Pagodas'. The buildings were fitted with ten-tonne cranes for lowering explosives into deep pits. The pit chamber could be sealed and air conditioned, vibrated on a shake table, and occasionally battered with a hydraulic ram to see how the bomb reacted to various environmental conditions. Just to be on the safe side, the Pagodas initially had lightweight aluminium roofs designed to blow off easily in the event of an accident, though later they installed heavy concrete

roofs intended, rather optimistically, to contain a blast. The fact that the MOD believed this to be an effective method of containment underscores their assertion that they never used nuclear material on the Ness: Instead, they were testing the highly explosive initiator that would set off the nuclear component of the bomb.

Apparently all the trials ended without incident, since the Pagodas are still there. And what a threatening and awe-inspiring sight they make, a glorious combination of dereliction and permanence. You have to figure that if they were designed to withstand and contain massive explosions, the elements won't wreak any great havoc. Doors and signs and hinges may have rusted or faded, but the big structures themselves are intact and blast-free.

Oddly enough, the most bizarre tales about Orford Ness don't concern its nuclear weapons testing. They come from the next

phase of testing in the 1960s; a trial with a code name that could just as easily describe a fancy cocktail: Cobra Mist. Declassified papers now identify Cobra Mist as a new kind of radar that could see over the horizon. But the strange eighteen-string antennae that fanned out over a ground net made of aluminium looked so weird that legends began to sprout up, reflecting what was a favourite paranoia of the time: The belief that the rig was designed to track UFOs.

It's a testament to the awesome power of nature that thick concrete floors designed to withstand the most powerful conventional weapons of the last century have since been split open by flowers. It will take quite a while for the transformation back to wildlife haven to complete itself, so you have plenty of time to scope out Orford Ness's decaying bunkers and airfields and Pagodas. Just be sure to dress up warmly and don't miss the last ferry back to the mainland at 5 p.m. You really don't want to be stuck overnight on the Ness.

Ghost Towns

Most people associate ghost towns with America's Wild West, and the image of a lone cowboy riding down a dusty main street to the sound of saloon doors banging in the wind.

Well, there's another kind of ghost town, and it's a lot nearer to the HP-Sauce-pouring, Marmite-spreading, tea-brewing world than anything you've ever seen on the big screen. Many of England's ghost towns were once bona fide communities, complete with churches, pubs and squares; others were purpose-built to house the infirm or insane.

But whatever they once were, these places are now abandoned and contain only memories. Except in a few cases, where they contain only memories, spent artillery and obsolete nuclear equipment. And that makes all the difference.

Imber: Stolen from the People By Stuart Campbell

In the winter of 1943, the War Office informed the inhabitants of the small Wiltshire village of Imber that their home was being requisitioned for the war effort. With the D-Day landings just a few months away, the government needed places to train troops for the sort of house-to-house fighting that they expected in Nazi-occupied Europe, and Imber seemed to be an ideal candidate. The villagers were given a month to evacuate, and told they'd be allowed back when the war was over.

They never returned.

Imber has remained an Army training ground, but for most of August, and on some public holidays, the roads through the village are open to the public. On one day every year (usually the first Saturday in September), the 200-year-old village church, St Giles, holds a service to allow the few surviving villagers and their descendants to visit the graveyard where their relatives are buried.

It's not easy to find the ghost village of Imber as its name doesn't appear on any road signs. You only know you're in the right area when you spot a 'Tank Crossing' sign about a mile south of

West Lavington and glance across to the unassuming little single-track road bearing a notice telling you whether the roads through the village are open or not. ('Not' is nearly always indicated.)

A few dozen yards farther on are the first of countless admonishments not to leave the carriageway for fear of UNEXPLODED MILITARY DEBRIS. This is a serious place. Just *how* serious becomes even clearer as, idly scanning the vast rolling plains, your eyes suddenly pick out a couple of wrecked tanks, their rusting brown hulks blending in with the low scrub. They seem to multiply the closer you get to the village, increasing the sense of menace.

Still, a mile or so along the lonely track, you catch your first glimpse of the bell tower of St Giles's Church, and then you appreciate what a peaceful place this must once have been. Look past the tank hulks and warning signs, and you could pretty much believe yourself returned to the Middle Ages. No electricity pylons, no overhead cables, no aeroplanes, no petrol-station canopies, no traffic noise, and nobody in sight for at least a mile in any direction. The only thing you'll notice, in fact, is how bloody loud crickets are in their natural habitat.

Arriving in Imber itself abruptly smashes this illusion. Far from being silent and deserted, the village is considerably populated, even when not actually accessible by the public. This fact was brought starkly home when a very polite young soldier explained that even during times of public access, all but the main road are out of bounds, on account of the large presence of weapons and live ammunition and the chance of getting one's head blown off.

A combination of factors gives Imber its eerie, chilling character. The few original buildings not destroyed in all the simulated fighting mingle with purpose-built brick shells with simple corrugated-iron roofs. You have an acute sense of being somewhere nobody really wants you to be, a long way from anywhere, surrounded by armed squaddies eyeing you suspiciously. It's a Slaughtered Lamb kind of experience.

Indeed, given how little of the original village

survives, it's surprising how much character remains. You can't get near the church, but the other traditional centre of the English village community, the pub, is right on the main road. You can even poke your camera through a hole in the wall and use its flash to illuminate the ruins within.

A few feet past the pub, a sign announces BAPTIST CHURCH, with the words OPEN appended below it, though the church itself became so dilapidated that it had to be demolished years ago. The church building must have been pretty tiny; not many Baptists in Imber, evidently. A small number of gravestones can still be seen from the road, and it is within this enclosure that perhaps the most poignant thing in Imber is located. Away from the other

graves, and barely visible above the overgrown grass, is a tiny white marble headstone. Picked out in simple black lettering are the words IN MEMORY OF THE BAPTIST COMMUNITY OF IMBER. There's no further elaboration, but it's the closest thing to a memorial for at least some of the inhabitants of the stolen village.

Beyond the Baptist church, there's very little more (that you're allowed) to see. Having been sternly warned by a fat, toothless policeman for exceeding the 15-mile per hour speed limit, your reporter left the modern-day inhabitants to their war games and drove out onto the plains beyond. After a couple more miles of tank wrecks and warning signs, you come to the military installation proper (including an excellent tank-washing park). Somewhere on this western side, the Army actually constructed a second, purpose-built village, but unsurprisingly there's no public access to that. So, at this point, it's off to find the road back into the real world.

Tyneham   By Stuart Campbell

Imber isn't the only place in Britain that was stolen from its inhabitants and never returned. Dorset too has a ghost village, but unlike the bleak and forbidding Imber, this one is a bucolic, idyllic and welcoming place. In fact, it may be the single most perfect pocket of beauty in England. It's called Tyneham.

In 1943, the 250-odd inhabitants of the Tyneham valley in Wiltshire were given one month to vacate their homes and compensated only to the value of the vegetables in their gardens. And, just like the people of Imber, they too were never allowed back. For many years Tyneham looked as if it would suffer the same fate as its Wiltshire cousin, but their paths diverged in 1975, when a fairly liberal amount of public access was restored to the village. You can now visit Tyneham most weekends of the year, as well as certain other special times. And you should.

The village is quite easy to find, being helpfully signposted from the main Lulworth–Wareham road.

You approach along a long and winding country lane, and when you reach the village, you spot the first of Tyneham's new user-friendly features: a car park capable of holding maybe a hundred vehicles at the suggested donation of a pound for the day.

In a further marked contrast to Imber, when Tyneham's open to public access, it's fully open. You can go anywhere you like, including right inside the buildings (most of which are roofless shells), and look as closely as you like at what remains. When your reporter arrived, a small group of young children were running around playing hide-and-seek in the row of cottages nearest the car park, and there were no distrustful wardens or rope barriers or CCTV cameras to discourage them. It feels, if you'll forgive the momentary flight of fancy, that the village is just happy to be hosting some kind of life again.

And even aside from the restored church and school, there's a lot of fascinating stuff to see amid the ruins, including quite a few original features. One cottage even has a curious, very deep copper basin for washing clothes in. What you can't help noticing is how small most of

them its original one. Primarily it's a museum full of charts and displays, recording both the broad history and the minutiae of village life – there are documents, artefacts, timelines, old photographs and everything else you'd expect to find in a small town museum. The second function of the church is to act as a shrine to the way of life that the former inhabitants had so unfairly taken away from them. The names of those villagers now line the church's interior walls in a restrained but unmistakable protest against the authorities who betrayed them, and it's quietly moving.

the houses are, which is slightly odd given that space was hardly at a premium. But then again the village does date back to the thirteenth century, when building was far more labour-intensive and you couldn't just turn the thermostat up to heat large rooms.

Still, for all the interesting things to be found in the various cottages, the majority of the noteworthy content in Tyneham is held in the church and school. Tyneham's church now serves two separate purposes, neither of

Tyneham itself is very tranquil, but the church is an epically still and silent place, in which you find yourself shushing your own heartbeat. Time seems to stand still when you're inside it, and I discovered that forty minutes had passed by the time I eventually emerged into the blinding sunshine of the church's graveyard. And a brief glance at the dates on the gravestones brought home just how long humans had been living in this place. With seven hundred years of history and heritage all around them, who could ever have imagined the consequences for their own tiny village of Hitler sending his tanks across the Polish border in 1939?

Abandoned Mental Hospitals

There is nothing quite as unnerving as an abandoned mental hospital whose rooms and corridors were designed partly for treatment of the darker side of people's minds and partly to restrain that darker side when it lashed out. For twenty years, ever since a new ideology in mental-health care called for these institutions to close down, the old asylums have lain empty. The only way you can legally see Severalls Hospital in Colchester, Rauceby Asylum near Sleaford in Lincolnshire or Netherne Hospital in Surrey, and the many other crumbling structures that exist, is through the chain-link fence with the 'No Trespassing' signs on it.

This lack of access has spawned a new class of day trippers called 'urban explorers' who visit attractions without admission fees, or entrances or even permission to enter. Our advice is not to join their ranks; few thrills are worth getting arrested for, especially when you can read about these places and see pictures of them at urban explorer websites such as www.abandonedpast.co.uk or www.simoncornwell.com/urbex. Or, for that matter, right here.

Cane Hill Asylum.

Cane Hill Asylum

Cane Hill in Surrey is a pretty typical example of England's abandoned asylums. An imposing and beautiful building, it's been unoccupied since it closed in 1991, and has the same desolate look of any large abandoned workplace. It's a listed historic building, so at least it won't be replaced by executive housing or a shopping centre, but, at the same time it's unlikely to be used for anything else much either. And that makes it a sad monument to the noble intentions of its creators.

Cane Hill was a showcase of humanitarian design when it opened in the 1880s. It was built on a hill with a lovely view of Coulsdon, the Farthing Downs and, in the distance, the City of London. It was built with wards radiating out from a central hub so that it could treat 2,000

patients while keeping
the genders separate and
preventing the more disturbing cases
from frightening the higher-functioning patients.

Like most Victorian mental institutions, it was built because
the County Asylums Act of 1845 charged local councils with the
care of the mentally ill. Surrey County Council brought in the best
man they could to design and build this institution. Charles Henry
Howell was the nation's most celebrated asylum architect and
architectural advisor to the Lunacy Commission, and Cane Hill was
his magnum opus. It included every amenity a small town needed,

Inmate Tales

In its century and more of operations, Cane Hill treated the relatives of several celebrities. In the early days, Charlie Chaplin's mother Hannah, herself a retired vaudeville performer, spent some grim times there. Charlie and his brother Sydney visited her in 1912, and were thoroughly depressed by the experience. 'She had just got over an obstreperous phase of singing hymns, and had been confined to a padded room,' Charlie would later write. 'Sydney saw her, but I had not the courage, so I waited. He came back upset, and said that she had been given shock treatment of icy cold showers and that her face was quite blue.'

In more recent times the half-brother of David Bowie, who inspired such songs as *Aladdin Sane*, *All the Madmen* and *Jump They Say*, lived here for more than a decade. And in 2002 Michael Caine revealed in an interview with Michael Parkinson that he had had a half-brother in Cane Hill that nobody in his family knew about. His mother had given birth to him before meeting Caine's father, and the boy had sustained brain damage during an epileptic fit. She had visited him at Cane Hill every Monday for fifty years, taking cakes and sweets and pictures of his half-brother. She had sworn all the staff to secrecy, but a newspaper reporter visiting the hospital had learned the story from another patient. When the story came out – after his mother's death – it was news to Caine, too. In the Parkinson interview, he explained 'I wanted to go and see him immediately . . . I went and saw him and had long conversations with him through the nurse because I couldn't understand what he was saying.

'I felt absolute amazement, how she'd fooled us all for years, every Monday. She used to come to the country every Sunday and my driver would drive her home the next day in the Rolls-Royce. One day the driver said, "she always gets out at the bus stop on Streatham High Road" and the penny never dropped.'

from accommodation and feeding areas to recreation buildings, a chapel and a huge brick water tower. The semi-rural setting was calming to the patients, and provided plenty of land for the patients to farm and for sporting activities such as cricket and tennis.

Of course, this wasn't exactly a country club and rest home. It cared for some seriously disturbed and incapacitated people for more than a century. By the early 1980s, improved antipsychotic medication and a lack of political will to maintain large-scale mental institutions changed the landscape for ever. The policy of Care in the Community brought higher-functioning patients into halfway houses and emptied the old asylums, and so in 1991 Cane Hill was finally closed.

Thanks to its Grade II listing as a historic monument and the slow wheels of planning departments, Cane Hill has lain empty ever since. Who knows what the future holds for this glorious building? We only hope it remains as awe-inspiring as it is now.

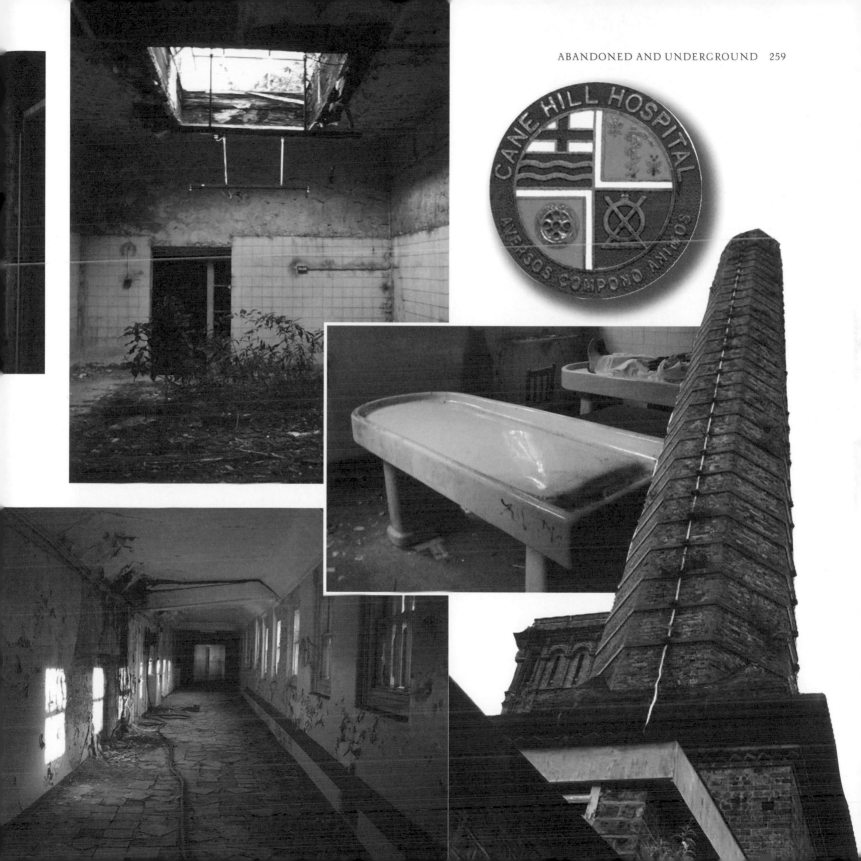

What Lies Beneath

Deep beneath the surface of our green and pleasant land there's a completely different England. It's one that is darker than midwinter, and yet strangely temperate and cosy. It's the great English Underground, and it's located in a few scattered pockets all over the country. We are not talking about the most obvious subterranean sites, of course, such as massive civil engineering projects as London's tube system or the Channel Tunnel, or even the subterranean city of Burlington beneath Corsham in Wiltshire, which was built to keep the country running in the event that the Cold War took a turn for the worse.

All of these are worth a visit, of course. But we're more interested in a different kind of English Underground, one that's less practical than the sort that provides an efficient urban transport system or protection from nuclear fallout. The weird subterranean projects that attract us were often the brainchild of a single inspired person . And we're grateful for their inspiration, for reasons that will become clear over the next few pages.

Doncaster's Sandstone Catacombs

It takes a peculiar kind of genius to sell tickets for a self-guided tour of a sewage system. It takes something even more sublime to tout fungus sprouting from blocks of wood as a tourist destination. Yet, around 150 years ago, that's exactly what a Doncaster entrepreneur did. William Senior's Sand House and Catacombs near Green Dyke Lane were a huge attraction in their day, and truly a sight to behold.

When Doncaster's rail works opened, quarryman William Senior was poised to expand his commercial empire to help house the influx of workers to the area. But the increased population brought a side effect that would have dismayed a lesser man: The town corporation decided that it needed to run a huge drainage tunnel right through Senior's quarry to carry sewage out of town. They paid him a pittance for access rights, and with the law of eminent domain on their side, they were free to do their dirty work.

William Senior never missed a trick, though. He began selling tickets for a walking tour of the tunnel, and had his own vaulted catacomb-style tunnel dug right next to it. The Catacombs were full of interesting architectural details, with thick columns sweeping into vaulted roofs, and huge arched doorways twice a man's height. Senior commissioned a series of large-scale carvings and statues to be set high on the walls. His foreman picked the ideal sculptor for the job: A man who had restored the gargoyles on the nearby parish church, and the figures ranged from rather dour-looking

medieval-style saints to winged cherubs.

A few postcards survive from the Catacombs' Victorian heyday, and they show a space strangely evocative of a Norman cathedral, with daylight filtering through the darkened passageways to cast huge shadows in the vaulted chambers. The scale of the project becomes clear only when a person features in the picture, dwarfed by the gaping doorways and huge sculpted heads around him.

As if these attractions weren't enough, William Senior found a way to expand his visitor base from engineering fans and lovers of art to include botanists. Some of the oak used to hold up the roof began to sprout a fungus known as Jove's Beard, a white hair-like growth that expanded into a massive thirteen-foot web of white filaments. By 1858, *The Illustrated London News* was running pictures of the fungal phenomenon.

Eventually, William's son Henry expanded the Catacombs another thirty feet farther beneath Victoria Street. But that was decades after William had hit upon another eccentric architectural plan that Henry saw to fruition. The corporation's drainage scheme had left a massive block of sandstone in the quarry near the Catacombs. With his strange knack for envisioning what others could not, William looked at this block and thought it would make a good house. And that's exactly what it became.

Unlike most stone buildings, the Sand House wasn't built of stone blocks piled on top of each other. It was a chunk of stone carved into a house. It expanded under Henry's care to include a ballroom for swanky charity events, and a sunken garden that was open to the public on Good Fridays, Easter Mondays and Thursdays during the summer months, and people happily parted with sixpence for the privilege.

Unfortunately, the glory days of the place ended when Henry died in 1900. Before long, the Sand House and grotto fell under the control of the local government and were being used for storage by the city sanitary and cleansing department. Dances were still held in the ballroom, but with horse-drawn refuse carts at the rear of the house, it wasn't quite the attractive venue it had been. By the mid-1930s, damp and structural weakness forced the corporation to board up the house and tunnels. In the

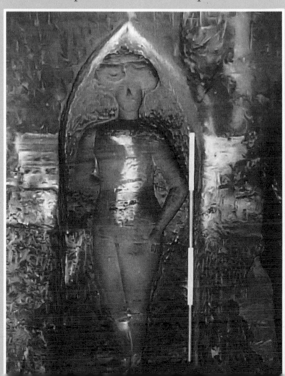

1960s a seventeen-storey tower block called Silverwood House was built on the site.

The best way to experience the place now is to track down a copy of *The Sand House* by Richard Bell, a member of the Senior clan who tapped the family vault for facts and photographs of the place. And we're grateful that he did, because without it, this subterranean strangeness might be forever lost to the world. And that would never do.

Mole Man of Hackney

There's a reason most of history's mole men are rich or titled, as Hackney's William Lyttle found out to his detriment. In the summer of 2006, this retired electrical engineer's forty-year compulsion to dig beneath his Victorian home in east London came to a sudden screeching halt when Hackney Borough Council evicted him in the interests of public safety. Apparently, the council had an issue with anything that makes roads collapse. They're weird that way.

In his mid-thirties, William Lyttle began a series of unusual home improvements to the four-storey property he inherited at 121 Mortimer Road. As the twenty-room house fell to rack and ruin, he dug a wine cellar and kept on digging. Almost four decades later, in 1999, a fire destroyed the roof. He patched the hole with corrugated iron and went back to digging. Finally in 2001, he opened his underground work to public view. Actually, he didn't intend to open it, but gravity had other ideas. The pavement collapsed outside his house and revealed his handiwork to anyone who cared to stick their head down the hole.

What they could see was pretty shadowy, but if the council's ultrasound scanners can be trusted, Lyttle's burrowing ways had created a network of caverns and tunnels up to twenty-six feet below the surface, spreading up to fifty feet in every direction from his house. It took five years

for Hackney Borough Council to get the courts to grant permission to evict Lyttle from his house so they could make the road safe for the public.

The odd thing is that Lyttle denied the extent of his underground network, saying they were only shadows. But when he agreed to appear on a television documentary filmed soon after the pavement first collapsed he rather undermined this claim. The premise of the show, great DIY disasters, pretty much summed up the whole debacle. He showed the cameras his excavation techniques using merely a shovel and a pulley system straight out of *The Great Escape*, and pointed out his vision for the cavernous expanse beneath his house: 'This is going to be the leisure centre,' he said, 'And this in here will be the sauna.'

When the council workforce went in, they found the foundations shored up with makeshift scaffolding poles and pit props, and the derelict house and garden above were littered with more than twenty tonnes of soil and other rubbish. The bill for rendering the area around the house safe could run to £100,000, which Lyttle himself will have to pay.

This is where the sizeable fortune or powerful family connections that history's other mole men possessed would come in handy. Too bad such a bill had to fall to a retired electrical engineer whose greatest assets seem to be a derelict house, a network of clandestine chambers (soon to be filled in) and a powerful will to dig.

The City of Caves

This may sound a bit fanciful, but there are bits of Nottingham that look more like an alien landscape than a Midlands city. The hill that serves as a display stand for Nottingham Castle is honeycombed with strange holes that once served as homes, workplaces and walk-in larders. Vast boarded-up cave openings pepper the ridge along Canal Street; they loom over Brewhouse Yard; in fact, in the area surrounded by Parliament Street, Maid Marian Way, Canal Street, Bellar Gate and Cranbrook Street, there are more than 200 caves – and possibly another hundred that have been filled in over the centuries.

Geological forces had nothing to do with any of these caverns and tunnels: At some point before 800 AD, people began to take pickaxes to the bunter sandstone and hollow out rooms for themselves. The trend caught on and from that point onward the place was known as the City of Caves (or 'Tigguo Cobauc' as it was known in the local parlance).

Nottingham's subterranean chambers had huge benefits. For one thing, they provided affordable housing. They were also surprisingly dry, because bunter sandstone doesn't drip water like most rock. And the manmade caves maintained a constant temperature, which made them ideal for storing food and brewing beer. It's no surprise that drink is a central theme to

at least two of the city's most obvious dug-outs – the Brewhouse Yard and the ancient pub called Ye Olde Trip to Jerusalem, which is half-built alongside and half-burrowed out of the hillside.

The caves were an integral part of Nottingham for a thousand years, but now, except for a few tourist

At some point before 800 AD, people began to take pickaxes to the bunter sandstone and hollow out rooms for themselves.

areas, they're largely off limits. The best place to get a quick look at some caves is the Brewhouse Yard, but the most exhaustive exploration of what these places once meant to the citizens of Nottingham is the City of Caves attraction in the unlikely setting of the Broadmarsh Shopping Centre. After you pay your entrance fee in the temple of commerce up above, you climb down into the depths to an old tannery, where processes too smelly and vile for the above-ground world took place. The raw material of the tannery was animal skin; the end

result was leather. In between, lots of malodorous stuff happened, including long periods of immersion in vats of urine.

The people who run the City of Caves attraction use a salty old character actor who pretends to be recruiting for an apprentice tanner and doing a poor job of making the job sound like a good prospect – which is a bit twee but doesn't detract from the fact that three minutes ago, you were brushing past Top Shop princesses in a sanitised twenty-first-century shopping centre and now you're in a thirteenth-century sweatshop. A short walk later, and you're in a Victorian slum basement so cramped and vile that you can see why the humanitarian politicians of the time banned the renting of caves as dwelling places. This isn't a re-creation of a slum cave, of course, but the actual remains of Drury Hill, a run-down district that was cleared in 1968 to build the shopping centre. And, finally, there's the most recent use of this underground space – as a bomb shelter during World War Two. And then you're back out into the current century, wondering what on earth just happened.

I found it so disorientating to be back in the world of fluorescent light that the only antidote was to take a quick trip back to 1189, when the country's oldest pub, Ye Olde Trip to Jerusalem, was first hacked out of the hillside of good old Tigguo Cobauc. Being a suggestible soul, I ordered a pint of the eponymous Olde Trip and retreated upstairs.

There, in a sandstone chamber hewn from the hillside, a light dusting of sand had fallen from the wall. It coated the table beneath it, where pint pots ground a pattern of shallow scratches into the surface of the wood, as they had been doing for a reassuring 800 years. And somehow, even as the mobile phones bleeped out the latest downloadable ring tones all around me, everything felt as though it was in its right place again.

INDEX

Page numbers in **bold** refer to photos and illustrations.

A

A23, ghosts on, 199
A38, ghosts on, 200
abandoned and underground places, 246–265
    Cane Hill Asylum, 256–258, **256–257, 258, 259**
    Doncaster Catacombs, 260–261, **260, 261**
    Hackney tunnels, 262, **262**
    Imber, 251–253, **251, 252, 253**
    Orford Ness, **248,** 249–250, **249, 250**
    Tyneham, 254–255, **254, 255**
Agglestone, 28, **28**
Alien Big Cats
    Beast of Bodmin, 94–96, **95**
    Beast of Exmoor, 98–99
    Surrey Puma, 97–98, **97,** 99
aliens. See UFOs and aliens
Alleyne, Tony, 152–153, **153**
ancient mysteries, 32–55
    Avebury circle, 42–45, **42–43, 44–45**
    cups and rings, 37–38, **37, 38**
    floating island, 53–54, **54**
    hermit's cave, 52, **52**
    labyrinths, 34–36, **35, 36**
    leys, 55
    Mên-an-Tol, 46–47, **46, 47**
    Stonehenge, 40–41, **40, 41**
    whispering corner, 53, **53**
Angel's Runway, 140
anti-gravity hills, 201
Armstrong, Colin, 146
Arnold, Larry E., 79
Arthurian legend
    Dozmary Pool in, 70
    Glastonbury Tor in, 71, **71**
    London Stone in, 13, **13**
Avebury circle, 42–45, **42–43, 44–45**

B

Bailey, Robert, 79–81, **80**
Bamford, Joseph Cyril, 168
Barlow, Charles, 233
Bates, Roy, 120–122, **120**
bathroom ghosts, 217–218, **218**
beasts, bizarre, 92–111
    Beast of Exmoor, 98–99
    Bigfoot, **104,** 105–107, **107**
    Black Dogs, 100–103, **100**
    Bodmin Moor Beast, 94–96, **95**
    Duergar, 108
    mermaid of Zennor, 111, **111**
    Morgawr, 109–110, **109, 110**

Surrey Puma, 97–98, **97,** 99
wild man of Orford, 111
wolf-men, 212–213, **213**
Becontree station ghost, 219, **219**
Bedlam, 203, **203**
Bentham, Jeremy, 228–229, **229**
Bethnal Green disaster, 221, **221**
Bigfoot, **104,** 105–107, **107**
Big Hairy Monsters, **104,** 105–107, **107**
Billings, Bill, 172
Birchover hermit, 52
Black Cat of Gloucestershire, 99
Black Dogs, 100–103, **100**
Black Shuck, 100–102, **100**
bleeding tombstone of Hinckley, 236
Blue Bell Hill ghost, 192–193, **193**
Bodmin Moor, Beast of, 94–96, **95**
Bolam, Beast of, 106–107, **107**
Boombastic, Mr, 130
Booth, Richard, 123
Borley Rectory ghosts, 210–211, **211**
Bower, Doug, 85
Bowie, David, 258
Brighton, eccentrics in, 130, **130**
British Psychic and Occult Society, 64, 65
Brutus, Stone of, 12
Burl, Aubrey, 37, 55
Burslem ghosts, 236–237, **237**
Burton, Richard, 226–227, **226, 227**
Butthole Lane, 203, **203**

C

Caine, Michael, 258
Cane Hill Asylum, 256–258, **256–257, 258, 259**
canine heroes, 129, **129**
Cannock Chase Bigfoot, 105
Carew, Richard, 70
Carlisle reiver's curse stone, 173, **173**
Carn Euny fogou, 51, **51**
Carr, Robert, 244–245
Castlerigg, 48
Catacombs, Doncaster, 260–261, **260, 261**
cats, big. See Alien Big Cats
Cavendish family tombs, 243, **243**
caves, 52, **52**
    Hackney, 262, **262**
    Nottingham, 263, **263, 264–265,** 265
Cement Menagerie, 136, **137**
cemeteries and tombstones, 224–245
    Bentham's body in, 228–229, **229**
    bleeding tombstone of Hinckley, 236
    Burslem grave of Molly Leigh, 236–237, **237**

Burton mausoleum, 226–227, **226, 227**
Cavendish family, 243, **243**
cricket tombstone, 240, **240**
Darley Dale, 241, **241**
exploding sarcophagi in, 238
Grieve tombstone, 241, **241**
Highgate, 235, 239
Jay Dartmoor grave, 238
Milligan epitaph, 232
piano tombstone, 240, **240**
pyramid of Mad Jack Fuller, 242–243, **242**
Siddal's death and, **234,** 235
St Martin-in-the-Fields, 244–245, **244, 245**
St Olave's, 230, **230, 231**
Cerne Abbas Rude Man, 21, **21, 22,** 23
Chalice Well, 71, **71**
Chaplin, Charlie, 258
Chesterfield, twisted spire of, 26, **26**
Chorley, Dave, 85
churches. See also cemeteries and tombstones
    Druid's Temple, 144, **144–145**
    gargoyles and grotesques on, 184–185, **184, 185**
    labyrinths and, 34–36, **35, 36**
    Old Operating Theatre, 160–161, **160, 161**
    Sheela-na-gigs in, 186–187, **186, 187**
    St Martin-in-the-Fields, 244–245, **244, 245**
    St Olave's graveyard, 230, **230, 231**
    twisted spire of Chesterfield, 26, **26**
    Tyneham, 254–255, **254, 255**
Churchill Square Dancer, 130
City of Caves, 263, **263, 264–265,** 265
Clearbury Ring, 55
Cobra Mist, 250
codes, Shugborough Hall Shepherd's Monument, 182–183, **183**
Crick, Jeremy, 233
Crooked House pub, 175–177, **175, 176–177**
crop circles, **84,** 85–87, **85, 87**
cups and rings, 37–38, **37, 38**
Curse Stone, 173, **173**

D

darkness, sudden, 77
Darley Dale sarcophagi, 241, **241**
Davis, Jefferson, 217
de la Hey, Serena, 164–165
Derwent Water floating island, 53–54, **54**
Devil's Arrows, 27
Devil's Bonfires, 82
Devil's Elbow, 194–195, **194–195**
Devil's Eye, 46–47, **46, 47**
Devil's Stone, 28
Dickens, Charles, 78, 204, 230
digger statue, 168, **168**
dinosaur sculptures, 166–167, **166–167,** 172, **172**

Doncaster Catacombs, 260–261, **260, 261**
Dorset Ooser, 19, **19**
Doyle, Arthur Conan, 101
Dozmary Pool, 70, **70**
Drekly Stone, 143
Druids, 39, 48
    Ilton temple, 144, **144–145**
    Isle of the Dead and, 72, **73**
drummer, phantom, 206–207
Duergar, 108
Dunbar, Gavin, 173
Dutt, W.A., 103

E–F

electric cars, 116–117
epitaphs, 232–233
Exmoor, Beast of, 98–99
fabled people and places, 56–73
    Chalice Well, 71, **71**
    Dozmary Pool, 70, **70**
    Highgate Vampire, 64–66
    Isle of the Dead, 72, **73**
    Kinder Scout, 68–69, **68, 69**
    Lantern Man, 61
    Owlman, **62,** 63
    Pig Woman, 60–61, **60**
    Spring-Heeled Jack, 58–59, **59**
    vampires, 64–67
Fairnington, John, 136
fairy haunts, 82
Falmouth Bay sea serpent, 109–110, **109, 110**
Farrant, David, 64, 66
Farringdon station ghosts, 220
fertility rites
    Rude Man of Cerne Abbas and, 23
    Sheela-na-gigs and, 186–187, **186, 187**
Fleming, Abraham, 101
floating island, 53–54, **54**
fogous, 51, **51**
Forbidden Corner, 146, **146, 147,** 148, **148, 149**
Fort, Charles, 76–77, **76,** 104
Fosser, the, 168, **168**
Fountain House, 136, **137**
Franklin, Benjamin, 240
frogs, raining, 77
Fuller, Mad Jack, 242–243, **242**

G

gargoyles and grotesques, 184–185, **184, 185**
geometric properties
    Pack o' Cards, 156, **156**
    Round House, 157, **157**
    Tresham's lodge, 154–155, **154, 155**
Geordie Yeti, 106–107, **107**
ghosts, 204–223
    A23, 199

A38, 200
    bathroom, 217–218, **218**
    Bethnal Green disaster, 221, **221**
    Blue Bell Hill, 192–193, **193**
    Borley Rectory, 210–211, **211**
    George Inn, 223, **223**
    Hexham's heads, 212–213, **213**
    London Underground, 219–221, **219, 220, 221**
    M6, 198
    Pepys, 222
    phantom drummer of Tidworth, 206–207
    Scratching Fanny of Cock Lane, 208–209
    Stocksbridge bypass, 197
    Tom Otter's Lane, 214–216, **214, 215, 216**
    Whins Woman of Nether Haugh, 196
ghost towns, 251–255
giants, 14–15, **14**
Gladden, John, 152
Glanvil, Joseph, 206, 207
Glastonbury Tor, 71, **71**
Gog and Magog, 14–15, **14**
Gog Magog Hills, 15
Goodfellow, Robin, 188
graveyards. *See* cemeteries and tombstones
gravity hills, 201
Green, Stanley, **114,** 115
green children of Woolpit, 82–83, **83**
Green Man sculptures, 188, **188, 189**
Grieve, Thomas, 241, **241**
Gwyn, Nell, 244

H

Hackney, underground tunnels in, 262, **262**
Haddon Hall, 52
hagstones, 50
Happy the Bus Man, 130
Harding, John, 186
Hardy, Thomas, 19
Harman, Martin Coles, 119, **119**
Harris, Elsie, 102
Harrison, J.H., 102
Harrison, Lucy, 48–49
Hastings, Sean, 121
Hayes, Paul, 81
Hay-on-Wye, secession of, 123
Heaven, William Hudson, 119
Heine, Bill, 150–151
henges, 39–50
    Avebury, 42–45, **42–43, 44–45**
    'Fauxhenge,' 140–143, **140, 141, 142, 143**
    Stonehenge, 40–41, **40, 41**
hermit's cave, 52, **52**
Herne the Hunter, 17, 18
heroes and villains, 112–133
    Barltrop, Mabel, 133, **133**
    in Brighton, 130, **130**

    Hay-on-Wye secession and, 123
    Kennedy, Hew, 118, **118**
    London Monster, 128
    Lundy Island kings, 119
    Ostrich killer, 126
    Protein Man, **114,** 115
    Richard, King of Hay, 123
    Roy, Prince of Sealand, 120–122, **120**
    Shipton, Ursula, 131–132, **131, 132**
    Station Jim, 129, **129**
    Sutch, David, 124–125, **124, 125**
    trebuchet builder, 118, **118**
    Ward, John, 116–117, **116, 117**
Hexham's heads, 212–213, **213**
Highgate Cemetery, 239
    cricket tombstone in, 240, **240**
    piano tombstone in, 240, **240**
    Siddal and, **234,** 235
    vampire of, 64–66
hill figures
    Cerne Abbas Rude Man, 21, **21, 22,** 23
    Long Man of Wilmington, 24, **24**
    White Horse, 25, **25**
Holborn station ghosts, 220
horned creatures
    Dorset Ooser, 19, **19**
    Herne the Hunter, 17, 18
Howard, Frances, 244–245
Howden Moor incident, 90–91, **90–91**
Howell, Charles Augustus, 235
Howell, Charles Henry, 257–258
Humphrey the camel statue, 167
Hyde Park Corner station ghosts, 220

I–K

Ilton Druid Temple, 144, **144–145**
Imber, ghost village of, 251–253, **251, 252, 253**
inventors, 116–117, **116, 117**
island, floating, 53–54, **54**
Isle of the Dead, 72, **73**
Jarman, Ostrich Inn killer, 126
jelly rain, 76
Julian's Bower, 34, 36
Kennedy, Hew, 118
Kent, Fanny, 208–209
Kinder Scout, 68–69, **68, 69**
Kirby, Alice Ann and Amy, 79
Kirkham, Mary, 214–215, 216
Kirklees vampire, 66–67

L

labyrinths, 34–36, **35, 36**
lakes and pools
    Chalice Well, 71, **71**

Dozmary Pool, 70, **70**
Kinder Scout, 68–69, **68, 69**
Lantern Man, 61
Last Post, 138–139, **138, 139**
Laud Manuscript, 17
legend, definition of, 10
legends, local, 10–31
Agglestone, 28, **28**
Cerne Abbas Rude Man, 21, **21, 22,** 23
Devil's Arrows, 27
Devil's Stone, 28
Dorset Ooser, 19, **19**
Gog and Magog, 14–15, **14**
Herne the Hunter, 17, 18
London Stone, 12–13, **12, 13**
Long Man of Wilmington, 24, **24**
Long Meg and her Daughters, 29–30, **29**
rabbits, 20
Rollright Stones, 30, **31**
twisted spire of Chesterfield, 26, **26**
White Horse, 25, **25**
Wild Hunt, **16,** 17
witch marks, 19
Leigh, Molly, 236–237, **237**
Lethbridge, T.C., 15
Ley, George, 156
Leyh, Liz, 170
ley lines, 55
lights, mysterious, 77, 82
UFOs and, 88–91, **88, 90–91**
London
London Stone, 12–13, **12, 13**
Monster of, 128
Old Operating Theatre, 160–161, **160, 161**
Protein Man, **114,** 115
Scratching Fanny of Cock Lane, 208–209
St Martin-in-the-Fields, 244–245, **244, 245**
St Olave's graveyard, 230, **230, 231**
Traffic Light Tree, 174, **174**
Underground ghosts, 219–221, **219, 220, 221**
London Stone, 12–13, **12, 13**
Long Compton Rollright Stones, 30, **31**
Long Man of Wilmington, 24, **24**
Long Meg and her Daughters, 29–30, **29**
Lord of the Rings (films), **16,** 17
Lundy Island kings, 119, **119**
Lytchett Matravers whispering corner, 53, **53**
Lyttle, William, 262, **262**

M

M6, phantom traffic on, 198
Magnetic Hill, 201
Magog. *See* Gog and Magog
Manger, The, 25

M5 dinosaur, 166–167, **166–167**
medical museums, 160–161, **160, 161**
Mên-an-Tol, 46–47, **46, 47**
mental hospitals, abandoned, 256–259
mermaid of Zennor, 111, **111**
military installations
Imber, 251–253, **251, 252, 253**
Orford Ness, **248,** 249–250, **249, 250**
Millais, John Everett, **234,** 235
Millennium Subway, 173
Milligan, Spike, epitaph of, 232
Milton, John, 14
Milton Keynes
cow sculptures, 169–170, **169, 170–171**
dinosaur scupture, 172, **172**
Moddey Dhoo, 100
Mompesson, John, 206–207
Morgawr, 109–110, **109, 110**
Moses (Brighton eccentric), 130
Mother Goose, 230
Mowing Devil of Hertfordshire, 85
Mucha, Donna, 103, 218
museums
Old Operating Theatre, 160–161, **160, 161**
Pitt Rivers, 158–159, **158, 159**

N–P

names, humorous town and street, 202–203, **202, 203**
Nether Haugh Whins Woman, 196
Newburgh, William of, 82
Nottingham City of Caves, 263, **263, 264–265,** 265
Official Monster Raving Loony Party, 124
Old Operating Theatre, 160–161, **160, 161**
Ooser, Dorset, 19, **19**
Orford, wild man of, 111
Orford Ness, **248,** 249–250, **249, 250**
Original London Walks, 222
Ostrich Inn killer, 126
Otter, Tom, 214–216, **214, 215, 216**
Overbury, Sir Thomas, 244–245
Owlman of Mawnan, **62,** 63
Oxford
land shark, 150–151, **151**
Pitt Rivers Museum, 158–159, **158, 159**
Pack o' Cards, 156, **156**
Panacea Society, 133, **133**
Park Ghost, 59
Parsons, Richard and Elizabeth, 208–209
Pateley Bridge, Nidderdale, 178, **178**
Peacemaker, 141–142
Peel, John, epitaph of, 232
Pepys, Samuel, 222
Peterborough Chronicle, 17
Petrifying Well, 179, **179, 180–181,** 181

phantom drummer of Tidworth, 206–207
piano tombstone, 240, **240**
Pig Woman, 60–61, **60**
Pitt Rivers Museum, 158–159, **158, 159**
post-boxes, 138–139, **138, 139**
Price, Harry, 210–211
properties, peculiar, 134–161
Druid's Temple, 144, **144–145**
'Fauxhenge,' 140–143, **140, 141, 142, 143**
Forbidden Corner, 146, **146, 147,** 148, **148, 149**
Fountain House, 136, **137**
Last Post, 138–139, **138, 139**
Old Operating Theatre, 160–161, **160, 161**
Pack o' Cards, 156, **156**
Pitt Rivers Museum, 158–159, **158, 159**
Round House, 157, **157**
shark roof, 150–151, **151**
Star Trek starship house, 152–153, **153**
swordfish roof, 152, **152**
Tresham's lodge, 154–155, **154, 155**
prophets
Barltrop, Mabel, 133, **133**
Shipton, 131–132, **131, 132**
Prosser, Alfred Edward, 240
Protein Man, **114,** 115
Prynn, Ed, 140–143, **140, 141, 142, 143**
pubs
Crooked House, 175–177, **175, 176–177**
George Inn/Jorrocks, 223, **223**
Sun Inn, **215,** 216
pyramid of Mad Jack Fuller, 242–243, **242**
Pytel, Walenty, 168

Q–R

Quantrill, Mary, 218
rabbits, fear of, 20
Ramsay, Mary, 230
Reeder, Arthur and Kim, 138–139, **138**
reiver's curse stone, 173, **173**
Reynolds, George, 86–87
Richard, King of Hay, 123
roadside oddities, 162–189
cow sculptures, 169–170, **169, 170–171**
Crooked House pub, 175–177, **175, 176–177**
Curse Stone, 173, **173**
dinosaur scuptures, 166–167, **166–167,** 172, **172**
False Teeth Bridge, 178, **178**
The Fosser, 168, **168**
gargoyles and grotesques, 184–185, **184, 185**
Green Man, 188, **188, 189**
Humphrey the camel, 167
Petrifying Well, 179, **180–181,** 181
Sheela-na-gigs in, 186–187, **186, 187**
Shugborough Hall Shepherd's Monument, 182–183, **183**

Traffic Light Tree, 174, **174**
Willow Man, 164–165, **165**
roads less travelled, 190–203
    A23, 199
    A38, 200
    amusingly named, 202–203, **202, 203**
    Blue Bell Hill, 192–193, **193**
    Devil's Elbow, 194–195, **194–195**
    gravity hills, 201
    M6, 198
    Stocksbridge bypass, 197
    Tom Otter's Lane, 214–216, **214, 215, 216**
    Whins Woman of Nether Haugh, 196
Robin Hood, 66–67
Rollright Stones, 30, **31**
Ronde, A La, 157, **157**
Ross, Anne, 212–213
Rossetti, Dante Gabriel, 235
Roughs Tower, 120, 122
Round House, 157, **157**
Roy, Prince of Sealand, 120–122, **120**
Rude Man of Cerne Abbas, 21, **21, 22,** 23

S

Saffin, Jeannie, 81
Saffron Walden labyrinth, 36, **36**
Sand House, Doncaster, 260–261, **260, 261**
Scott, Michael, 30
Scouring, The, 25
Scratching Fanny of Cock Lane, 208–209
sculpture
    Cavendish family tomb, 243, **243**
    Cement Menagerie, 136, **137**
    cow town, 169–170, **169, 170–171**
    dinosaur, 166–167, **166–167,** 172, **172**
    Forbidden Corner, 146, **146, 147,** 148,
        148, 149
    The Fosser, 168, **168**
    gargoyles and grotesques, 184–185, **184,**
        185
    Green Man, 188, **188, 189**
    Hexham's heads, 212–213, **213**
    Humphrey the camel, 167
    shark roof, 150–151, **151**
    Sheela-na-gigs, 186–187, **186, 187**
    swordfish roof, 152, **152**
    Traffic Light Tree, 174, **174**
    Willow Man, 164–165, **165**
Sealand, 120–122, **120**
sea serpents, 109–110, **109, 110**
Senior, Henry, 260–261
Senior, William, 260–261
Seven Sisters, 142
sexton's tales, **234,** 235–239
Shakespeare, William, 13, 188
shark roof, 150–151, **151**

Sheela-na-gigs in, 186–187, **186, 187**
Shiels, Tony 'Doc,' **62,** 63
Shipton, Ursula 'Mother,' 131–132, **131, 132,**
    179, 181
Shugborough Hall Shepherd's Monument,
    182–183, **183**
Siddal, Elizabeth Eleanor, **234,** 235
Silbury Hill, 34
Simonside, Duergar of, 108
Slaughter Stone, 40
slime-covered house, 77
slingshots, 118, **118**
Smith, Richard, 236
Smith, Sarah, epitaph of, 233, **233**
Society for Psychical Research, 204
Southcott, Joanna, 133
spirals, 34–36, **35, 36**
spontaneous human combustion, 78–81, **80**
Spring-Heeled Jack, 58–59, **59**
St Bartholomew's Pig Woman, 60–61, **60**
Star Trek starship house, 152–153, **153**
Station Jim, 129, **129**
Stocksbridge bypass phantom, 197
St Olave's graveyard, 230, **230, 231**
Stonehenge, 40–41, **40, 41**
stones and rock formations, 32
    Agglestone, 28, **28**
    Avebury circle, 42–45, **42–43, 44–45**
    Devil's Arrows, 27
    Devil's Stone, 28
    Druid's Temple, 144, **144–145**
    'Fauxhenge,' 140–143, **140, 141, 142, 143**
    fogous, 51, **51**
    henges, 39–50
    labyrinths, 34–36, **35, 36**
    London Stone, 12–13, **12, 13**
    Long Meg and her Daughters, 29–30, **29**
    Mên-an-Tol, 46–47, **46, 47**
    reiver's curse stone, 173, **173**
    Rollright Stones, 30, **31**
    standing, 50
    Stonehenge, 40–41, **40, 41**
    Stukeley, William, 32, 48
    secessions, 119–123
Sun Inn, **215,** 216
Surrey Puma, 97–98, **97,** 99
Sutch, David, 124–125, **124, 125**
swordfish roof, 152, **152**
Symons, G.F., 53

T–V

Telly Man, 130
Thornton, Frank, 240, **240**
Tidworth phantom drummer, 206–207
Todd, Sweeney, 126
tombstones. See cemeteries and tombstones

Traffic Light Tree, 174, **174**
trebuchets, 118, **118**
Tresham, Thomas, 154–155
Tresham's lodge, 154–155, **154, 155**
Troy, ancient city of, 12
    Gog and Magog and, 14–15, **14**
    labyrinths and, 34, 36
Turner, Anne, 245
Tyneham, ghost village of, 254–255, **254, 255**
Uffington White Horse, 25, **25**
UFOs and aliens, 88–91, **88, 90–91**
    green children of Woolpit, 82–83, **83**
Underground, ghosts in the London, 219–221, **219,**
    220, 221
unexplained phenomena, 74–91
    crop circles, **84,** 85–87, **87**
    Fort on, 76–77
    ghost lights, 82
    green children of Woolpit, 82–83, **83**
    spontaneous human combustion, 78–81, **80**
    UFOs, 88–91, **88, 90–91**
Unsworth, Harold, 200
urban explorers, 256
vampires, 64–67
Vivant, Pierre, 174

W–Z

Walls of Troy, 34, 36
Ward, John, 116–117, **116, 117**
Watkins, Alfred, 55
Whins Woman of Nether Haugh, 196
whispering corner, 53, **53**
White Horse, 25, **25**
Whiting, John and Margaret, epitaph of, 232, **232**
Wild Hunt, **16,** 17
wild man of Orford, 111
Williams, Rhynwick, 128
Williamson, Cecil, 35
Willow Man, 164–165, **165**
windows, spontaneously shattering, 77
Windsor Great Park, 17, 18
witches
    Burslem grave and, 236–237, **237**
    hagstones and, 50
    phantom drummer and, 206–207
witch marks, 19
wolf-men, 212–213, **213**
Wooler cups and rings, 37, 38
Woolpit, green children of, 82–83, **83**
Wordsworth, William, 29
World War II, Bethnal Green disaster, 221, **221**
Yeti, **104,** 105–107, **107**
Zennor, Mermaid of, 111, **111**
Zeppelins, 88–89, **88**

WEIRD ENGLAND

By
Matt Lake

Executive Editors
Mark Sceurman and Mark Moran

ACKNOWLEDGMENTS

Thanks go out, in no small measure, to Mark Sceurman and Mark Moran and their delightful families for devoting more than a decade to getting the Weird idea right. After all your efforts, it's not that hard to pluck the low-hanging fruit of English weirdness and put it in a book. Richard Berenson: Your design skills are inspiring. Ryan Doan: If my right hand could do what yours can do, I'd never need to type another word. Gina Graham: How did you get to be so creative and so organised at the same time? This is hardly fair. Emily Seese: You are the Fifth Beatle. Chrissie Craig: You are also the Fifth Beatle. Barbara Morgan: How many Fifth Beatles can one planet stand? Julia: Your Scrabble skills and navigational ability save lives. Chris: Which is weirder—where you spent the summer or where I spent the summer? Caroline: I left chocolate for you in the cupboard. Enjoy.

And then there's the cast of thousands (give or take) who provided leads and transportation along the way…

Ministers of Information

Stuart Campbell
Garth Chouteau
John Lake
Colin May
John and
   Melanie Cockshutt
Margaret Ferreira
John Ward
Iris Lake

Sarah Parker
Lucy Harrison
Karen and
   Tom Nuttgens
Stephen Tunstall
Eleanor Lake
Marcus Durham
Donna Mucha
Richard Lake

Ministers of Transportation

Caroline Craig
Mary-Ann Kilby
Tiago Gambogi
John Lake
Richard Lake
Emma Lake
Nicole Tiedemann
Mary Kelly
Mary Lou Kimble
Marion Krelbourne
Richard Branson

PICTURE CREDITS

All photos by the author or public domain except as listed below:

Page 2 top centre © Getty Images/Hulton Archive, top right © Ryan Doan (www.ryandoan.com), bottom left © Stuart Campbell; **3** © Julia Lake; **7** © Ryan Doan (www.ryandoan.com); **9** © Julia Lake; **11** background © Adam Woolfitt/ CORBIS; **12** © Mary Evans Picture Library/Alamy; **14** top left and bottom right © geogphotos/Alamy, centre courtesy www.arts.gla.ac.uk; **16** © New Line/Saul Zaentz/Wing Nut/The Kobal Collection/Vinet, Pierre; **17** © Bodleian Library; **18** © Geof Slocombe/Alamy; **21** courtesy Simon Garbutt; **22** © Skyscan/CORBIS; **24** © Martin Jones, Ecoscene/CORBIS; **25** © Yann Arthus-Bertrand/CORBIS; **28** © John Farmar, Ecoscene/CORBIS; **29** © David Lyons/Alamy; **31** top left © Paul Felix Photography/Alamy, top right © David Stares/Alamy, bottom © Robert Estall Photo Agency/Alamy; **32–33** top © iStockphoto.com/texasmary; **35** © Adam Woolfitt/Robert Harding World Imagery/CORBIS; **37** © Julia Lake; **40** © Adam Woolfitt/Robert Harding World Imagery/CORBIS; **41** © Reuters/CORBIS; **42–43** © MacDuff Everton/CORBIS; **44–45** © Adam Woolfitt/Robert Harding World Imagery/CORBIS; **54** © Andrew Harris/Alamy; **56** © Steve Atkins/Alamy; **57, 62** © Ryan Doan (www.ryandoan.com); **67** © Barbara Green, Yorkshire Robin Hood Society; **68** © Wideangle Photography/ Alamy; **69** © Peter Wells/Alamy; **71** top © World Religions Photo Library/Alamy; **72** © Steve Atkins/Alamy; **74** © Ryan Doan (www.ryandoan.com); **75** © Lucy Pringle (www.lucypringle.co.uk); **80** © Ryan Doan (www.ryandoan.com); **84, 85, 87** © Lucy Pringle (www.lucypringle.co.uk); **88** © NYPL Digital Library, Humanities and Social Sciences Library/George Arents Collection; **90–91** © Julie Woodhouse/Alamy; **92** © Loren Coleman; **93** © Ryan Doan (www.ryandoan.com); **95** top © Lee Pengelly/Alamy, bottom Tom Brakefield/CORBIS; **97** © W. Perry Conway/CORBIS; **99** © Raymond Gehman/CORBIS; **104** © Brian Quinn; **107** © Mark Moran; **108** © Roger Coulam/Alamy; **110** © Jim Zuckerman/CORBIS; **112** bottom © Mary Evans Picture Library/Alamy; **113** © Hulton-Deutsch Collection/CORBIS; **114** right © Getty Images/Hulton Archive; **118** © Chris Hellier/CORBIS; **120** top right © Getty Images/Hulton Archive, bottom © Sean Hastings; 123 © Kim Gilmour (www. kimgilmour.com) 124 © Hulton-Deutsch Collection/CORBIS; **125** © Julian Calder/CORBIS; **128** © Lebrecht Music and Arts Photo Library/Alamy; **130** © Stapleton Collection/CORBIS; **131** © Michael Nicholson/CORBIS; **132** © Mary Evans Picture Library/Alamy; **133** courtesy www.panacea-society.org; **136, 137** © Julia Lake; **153** still from the ducumentary *Trekkies 2* courtesy of Trekkies Productions (www.trekkies2.com); **181** © Tiago Gambogi; **186** © Steve Sant/Alamy; **190, 193** © Ryan Doan (www.ryandoan.com); **194–195** © Simon Plant/zefa/CORBIS; **197** © iStockphoto.com/Jeremiah Deasey; **199** © JMS/ Alamy; **200** © Phil Wills/Alamy; **201** © Chuck Keeler, Jr./CORBIS; **204–205** © Ryan Doan (www.ryandoan.com); courtesy www.pbagalleries.com; **208** © Mary Evans Picture Library/Alamy; **211** © Robert Estall photo agency/Alamy; **213** © Ryan Doan (www.ryandoan.com); **214–215** © Martin Stevens; **217** © Ryan Doan (www.ryandoan.com); **218** © iStockphoto.com/ Alija; **219** top © iStockphoto.com/Jennifer Conner; **220** © iStockphoto.com/Christian Riedel; **221** © Tower Hamlets Local History Library and Archive; **222** © Jefferson Davis; **226** © Bettmann/CORBIS; **234** © Tate Gallery, London/Art Resource, NY; **242** © Manor Photography/Alamy; **243** © John Lake; **244** © Robert Harding Picture Library Ltd/Alamy; **245–247** © Stuart Campbell; **246** top Collection of Richard Bell; **247** © Mark Russell; **251–255** © Stuart Campbell; **256–259** © Mark Russell (www.abandonedpast,co.uk); **260, 261** Collection of Richard Bell; **262** © Sarah Lee/The Guardian.

SHOW US YOUR WEIRD!

Do you know of a weird site found somewhere in the United Kingdom, or can you tell us about a strange experience you've had? If so, we'd like to hear about it! We believe that every town has at least one great tale to tell, and we're listening. It could be a cursed road, haunted abandoned site, odd local character, or bizarre historic event. In most cases these tales are told only in the towns in which they originated. But why keep them to yourself when you could share them with the world? So come on and fill us in on all the weirdness that's lurking in your backyard!

You can e-mail us at: Editor@WEIRDBRITAIN.com,
or write to us at:
Weird U.S., P.O. Box 1346, Bloomfield, NJ 07003 USA.

www.weirdbritain.com